# Balancing
# Your Life:
### Executive Lessons for
### Work, Family and Self

# Balancing Your Life:
## Executive Lessons for Work, Family and Self

James G S Clawson
University of Virginia, USA

 World Scientific

NEW JERSEY · LONDON · SINGAPORE · BEIJING · SHANGHAI · HONG KONG · TAIPEI · CHENNAI

*Published by*

World Scientific Publishing Co. Pte. Ltd.

5 Toh Tuck Link, Singapore 596224

*USA office:* 27 Warren Street, Suite 401-402, Hackensack, NJ 07601

*UK office:* 57 Shelton Street, Covent Garden, London WC2H 9HE

**British Library Cataloguing-in-Publication Data**
A catalogue record for this book is available from the British Library.

**BALANCING YOUR LIFE**
**Executive Lessons for Work, Family and Self**

Copyright © 2010 by James G. S. Clawson

ISBN-13 978-981-283-906-0 (pbk)
ISBN-10 981-283-906-2 (pbk)

Typeset by Stallion Press
Email: enquiries@stallionpress.com

Printed in Singapore by Mainland Press Pte Ltd.

# DEDICATION

This volume, my 17th book-length manuscript, is dedicated to authentic people. I was 48 before I found some people with whom I could talk with about anything, no taboos. It was a liberating experience. My friends Robert and Dana and I would go to the local watering hole, Sloan's, and they'd have a beer and I'd have a milk or diet cola and we'd talk about money, politics, marriage, parenting, sex, religion, *everything*. My good friend Tanner organized a golf outing, a "Workaholic's Retreat," where these kind of conversations continued. Honest conversation had never been safe before in my life; the people I knew from parents on down were too quick to judge. Through these new conversations, I came to believe that honest, authentic, transparent conversations are like diamonds in life, to be treasured above all the chaff of superficial, tell-it-like-it-*should*-be chit-chat that was a waste of time. I've only had five such people in my life. Robert, Susan, Erick, Tanner and Dana. Dana died of a heart attack at age 51. Now I'm down to four. Erick I pay a hundred dollars an hour to, so does he count? Robert took a new job and disappeared. Tanner lives 10 hours away. So now I'm down to Susan. She's still here. That amazes me in a major way. Wow. I've tattooed the initials of the people who've had a major influence on my life on my wrist. Tony's there. Robert's there. Dana's there. Tanner's there. Susan's there. I hope you have people in your life to whom you can turn to talk about things, anything. Some might say that some things are best left unsaid. In my experience that has always led to more pain and wasted precious "life time" than the shock of learning how things really are. Unresolved and misunderstood realities lead to later pain and bitterness. The light of day on every topic, though, heals and nurtures. May you find and cultivate friendships with people with whom you can be utterly, completely, and authentically you. And may you be the same, non-judgmentally, for them.

# PREFACE

I wrote this book and the stories (cases) out of a desire to show people a more holistic view of executive lifestyles. It's one thing to describe a person's career. You can begin with their resume and then fill in some of the blanks to learn more about how their stepping stones or assignments led to success — or despair. I always found those descriptions deficient. I wanted to know more. I wanted to know how a person organized his or her life to make success possible.

Later, as I began consulting with a variety of people and companies all over the world, I learned that the single most common challenge people everywhere face was balancing work, family and personal life. As new technology came on, the trend intensified. When you can carry your cell phone into the bathroom or the theater or on vacation, when and how does one set boundaries? Where does work end and family life or personal life begin? How do successful people establish those boundaries? How do they create life structures that support the enormous energy and commitment needed to run large organizations? These were some of the questions I've been asking.

Surely a part of my fascination grew out of the fact that I was born into a tiny mountain mining town, population less than 500, in central Idaho. My father had converted a chicken coop into a two room "house" situated on a piece of property covered with four foot high sage brush on the floor of the Big Lost River Valley. I grew up playing in the dirt, learning to shoot rabbits and deer, driving tractors during haying time, picking potatoes, baking in the sun and shoveling snow higher than I stood tall.

When we moved to the big city, Boise, as I entered first grade, I was aware that I was the country bumpkin. Smart, but clearly country. I got good grades in school, my parents divorced, my mom and I survived somehow until she remarried Mr. Clawson, I was adopted (gaining my third last name in life), and I went away to California to college where I saw for the first time, people of privilege and wealth. As my formal and informal educations progressed, (slowly I realize in retrospect) I became more and more curious about how people were able to do so much with their lives. Was it birthright? Was it intelligence? Was it undeviating devotion to something? Was it faith? Was it a good partner? (I couldn't imagine that since marriage was for me by then a very bad thing.) At one point, I applied, and to my surprise got into the Harvard Business School (HBS), and a new life began.

At HBS, a remarkable man took me under his wing. He had been on the cover of *Time* Magazine as one of the country's best professors, so I was at once honored and terrified. He was patient and taught me a lot. One of his lessons delivered while walking down the hall one day, was that socio-economic transitions were the most difficult. I could certainly identify with that. At Harvard, my head was spinning most of the time. My classmate had grown up on Long Island with the *Wall Street Journal* as the source of daily dinner conversation. I'd grown up, on that map of the world that originates with Boston as the hub of the universe and China a tiny speck on the far horizon, somewhere in the distant middle ground, in a nameless, clueless place where we talked about watching the test pattern on the new fangled television and how best to field dress a deer.

My first exploration into the topic of the links between professional and private was an interview with my step-uncle, then the retired CEO of Puget Sound Power and Light. He'd come to Idaho to visit us on occasion, driving up in his baby blue Mercedes 350 SL, which impressed me greatly. "Someday," I thought. When we visited his home in Seattle for family reunions, I discovered that he lived in a beautiful, ecologically advanced house with high earthen berms to manage the heat overlooking Lake Sammamish. His seemed like a charmed life. He and his good wife, Leora, were kind enough to let me document their lifestyle. This first case exploring not just the career of, but the *life* and career of a chief executive officer appears as the last story in this volume.

Over the subsequent 30 years, I've collected more case stories about how people manage the whole of their lives, not just the professional aspects. Sometimes people are nonplussed that anyone would want to know such things. Jackie Woods and Donna Dubinsky, two very successful business women, wondered why anyone would want to read about their life stories.

Even if you interview and inquire about the personal, not private, side of life, people tend to tell you only the positive and laudable things. They seldom talk about how they manage conflicts with their spouses or their kids. They seldom mention how they manage their sex lives. They don't talk much about how they planned their personal finances. Occasionally they will give little snippets into their health — how much they exercise from time to time or how they manage their eating habits, but often not much.

It seems that many executives, or perhaps it's just people in general, draw a big line between what's professional (and therefore public) and what's personal (and therefore private). In my consulting and writing, though, I've tried to extend that continuum to include the "private." So not everything we do is private — we do lots of things that are personal, not professional, but that would be legitimate for students of management success to explore and learn from.

If aspiring managers and leaders cannot learn from the personal side of those who've gone before them, they'll waste a lot of time and energy re-inventing the wheel when it comes to successful life structures. Sure, you say, but there are so many variations, how could anyone be a role model. I agree, and that's why I wanted to assemble a cluster of alternatives so that the reader could pick and choose, learn and incorporate, surprise and suppress, or just add to the richness of their mental maps about how people manage to organize their lives to be productive.

All of the people included in this volume have been very productive — and by some measures successful, even very successful. But what does successful mean? We'll explore that issue in Chapter 3. Most who write and publish about the successful choose the *very* successful, what Gladwell calls the "outliers." The sales of such volumes and magazines suggest that people in general are fascinated by the rich and famous. Yet most of us are not likely to get there.

What about the successful-but-not-celebrity category? What have they learned about effective strategies for building more than a successful career, a successful *life*? This exploration might take us away from executives in the private and public sectors, say into religion or the arts. Here though, and since I've been teaching at graduate schools of business for 30 years, we'll focus on management executives that are closer to home.

I'd like to have included more stories. As I write this, I'm working on the next story/case in this series and wishing it were done and could be included here. Perhaps in the next edition if there is one.

# PREFACE

## THE CASE STORIES

There are 20 stories included here. In business school, we call them "cases." They come from different countries, different professions, include both men and women, and represent different stages in life (see Chapter 2). Some of them have become very wealthy, others have become very powerful, others have become both. Some are single, some are married, some are divorced, some have had life-long spouses. Some have had children, some have not. Some of their stories focus a bit more on the professional side of life (see Chapter 1), while some focus more on the personal side of life. Some are disguised, most are not. Some of them are famous, others you will not likely have heard of — although in their region or professional circles, most are well known. Some are healthy, others have had heart bypass surgery. Some are fit, some are overweight. Some have learned from their past chapters in life, some seem to struggle with the same issues decade after decade. Some have lived traditional lives in the sense of one working person and a supportive spouse and doing what others have asked them to do. Others have carved their own path out of the woods and blazed their own trails. Some are involved in public politics, others in corporate politics. Some are entrepreneurs, some are academicians. In one case, Mr. and Mrs. Tom Curren, we get the benefit of the views of both spouses. Some live traditional lifestyles with one main home and a family structure. Others split their time between summer and winter homes in exotic places. Some travel so frequently, it's hard to know where they are at any given moment.

Some of the stories here are structured around chronological events in their lives, often leading up to some kind of career decision. The decisions are left in the cases with the intent of helping you get more "into" their stories and the challenges they face. In some cases, I'll provide an epilogue, often not. Other stories are structured around a week's time log. The week seems to me to be the basic building block of life. Seldom can one fit every aspect of life into a single day. If you only exercised or spoke to your spouse once a month, clearly that would not be sufficient. So the 168-hour week seems to be the cinder block of time with which we build the structure that will be one day of our lives. These week-long time logs give one a very good, perhaps more detailed picture of what people actually do compared with their sometimes faulty or biased recollections.

Several of the cases are supported by CD-ROMs containing video clips of interviews with the subjects or their work associates and in some cases members of their families. These videos give one a deeper insight into the subjects' minds, style, communication patterns, and personality. These CD-ROMS are available for purchase from Darden Business Publishing. https://store.darden. virginia.edu/ I've designated the cases that have accompanying CD-ROMs with the image to the right for your convenience.

One of the challenges I wrestled with was how to organize the stories. Should it be organized from young to old? By sector (politics, business, academe)? By lifestyle type? In the end, I chose a hybrid of all of these, trying to find stories that seemed to build on one another. That said, please don't feel the necessity to read from front to back. To help you think about different ways to read the stories, I'm providing a dynamic map below so you could chart different paths through the stories if you wanted to.

| Week-Long Time Logs | Government Executives | Corporate Career Paths |
|---|---|---|
| 4. Charles Nelson | 6. Tetsundo Iwakuni | 9. Donna Dubinsky |
| 12. Tom Curren | 10. Ed Norris | 11. Walt Shill |
| **Business Executives** | **Academicians** | 12. Tom Curren |
| 4. Charles Nelson | 8. Erika James | 14. Jackie Woods |
| 5. Hassan Shahrasebi | **Entrepreneurs** | 15. Bob Johnson |
| 6. Tetsundo Iwakuni | 7. Dee Dee Fisher | 16. James Harold Clawson |
| 9. Donna Dubinsky | 9. Donna Dubinsky | |
| 11. Walt Shill | **Chief Executives** | **Women** |
| 12. Tom Curren | 9. Donna Dubinsky | 7. Dee Dee Fisher |
| 14. Jackie Woods | 10. Ed Norris | 8. Erika James |
| 15. Bob Johnson | 14. Jackie Woods | 9. Donna Dubinsky |
| 16. James Harold Clawson | 15. Bob Johnson | 13. Judy Moore Curren |
| | 16. James Harold Clawson | 14. Jackie Woods |

| Service Industry | Manufacturing | Consultants |
|---|---|---|
| 4. Charles Nelson | 7. Dee Dee Fisher | 11. Walt Shill |
| 5. Hassan Shahrasebi | 9. Donna Dubinsky | 12. Tom Curren |
| 6. Tetsundo Iwakuni | 15. Bob Johnson | **Finance** |
| 10. Ed Norris | 16. James Harold Clawson | 4. Charles Nelson |
| 11. Walt Shill | **International/non-USA** | |
| 12. Tom Curren | 5. Hassan Shahrasebi | |
| 14. Jackie Woods | 6. Tetsundo Iwakuni | |

If you find any of these categories of interest, you can read through the book in the sequences suggested to see how different people in the same category have tried to structure their lives.

In the end, though, the value in these stories lies in the subjects' willingness to share with us how they do things. If we can see what people do, think about our own situation, and then pick and choose the parts we want to emulate and the parts we want to leave off, we'll be better armed to create a life structure that will work for us. Life doesn't give us a guarantee of that, of course. As you'll see in Chapter 3, one might just as well end up frustrated and bitter as content and at peace. How you structure your life will have a huge impact on that outcome. Realistically, once you're "there", wherever there is, you can't go back and re-structure the past. Forearmed is forewarned.

My purpose in life is to help people find themselves. I've been working at this, beginning with my own confusions for most of my life. I wasn't able to articulate that perhaps until I was about 35, but once that focus came clear, I was able to do and enjoy so much more. My hope is that you'll be able to see parts of yourself in the mirrors provided by our subjects here.

## ACKNOWLEDGEMENTS

First of all, I'm grateful to the individuals who were willing to have me come and record and write up their life stories. And to get behind the scenes a little and

# PREFACE

reveal a bit about how they manage their whole lives, not just their professional lives. If there are elements in these stories that surprise you, I hope your first reaction will not be one of judgment and criticism, rather of gratitude to these people for sharing their lives with us, with you, so that we/you can learn from them. What a great blessing.

I am also grateful for the skilled and dedicated co-authors and co-researchers over the years who've contributed their talents to the cases. These include Maki DePalo, Catherine Lloyd, Lindsay Houser, Greg Bevan, Jason Clifton, Christopher Allen and Gerry Yemen.

Thank you, again, posthumously, to my friend and mentor, Anthony G. "Tony" Athos for his support, patience, coaching, and guidance. I remember him fondly.

Thanks to the Harvard Business School and the Darden Graduate School of Business Administration who at various times supported the development of the cases employed herein.

Thanks to my wonderful wife of 31 years, Susan, who puts up with more than I can imagine to allow me to write and be who I am. And she still says, to my complete amazement, that she adores me. I can't figure it out.

Thanks to Max Phua and Shujuan Lim at World Scientific for their interest in a volume of this nature. In fact, I was shocked one day to get an inquiry out of the blue from Max asking if I'd be interested in doing a book on executive lifestyles. Was he reading my mind? Was he another of Charlaine Harris' telepathic "supes"? All along the way, Max and his colleagues have been very supportive and professional and, most of all, pleasant to deal with. He truly understands Pine and Gilmore's notion of an experience economy. Thanks, Max.

James Clawson
Charlottesville, VA 22901

# CONTENTS

# CONTENTS

# CONTENTS

Special thanks to Eric Fletcher, General Counsel for the Darden School, who helped with obtaining the permissions for the following:

## Chapter 4

### Charles Nelson: A Week in the Life of an Investment Banking Intern

This chapter, adapted from a case, UVA-PACS-0094, was prepared by Charles E. Nelson, II and edited by James G. Clawson. Copyright © 1999 by the University of Virginia Darden School Foundation, Charlottesville, VA. All rights reserved. Reprinted with permission.

## Chapter 5

### Hassan Shahrasebi: The Golden Boy

This case was prepared by Amir Massoud Amiri, under the supervision of James G. Clawson. This case was written as a basis for class discussion rather than to illustrate effective or ineffective handling of an administrative situation. Copyright © 1995 by the University of Virginia Darden School Foundation, Charlottesville, VA. All rights reserved. Reprinted with permission.

## Chapter 6

### Tetsundo Iwakuni: The Life and Career of a Japanese Executive

This chapter was adapted from a case, UVA-OB-0627, prepared by Maki DePalo and James G. Clawson. Copyright © 1996 by the University of Virginia Darden School Foundation, Charlottesville, VA. All rights reserved. Reprinted with permission.

## Chapter 7

### Dee Dee Fisher: The Life and Career of a Free Spirit

This chapter was adapted from a case, UVA-OB-0871, prepared by Jason Clifton under the supervision of Professor James G. Clawson. Copyright © 2006 by the

University of Virginia Darden School Foundation, Charlottesville, VA. All rights reserved. Reprinted with permission.


## Chapter 8

### Erika James: The Life and Career of a Tenured Professor

This chapter was adapted from a case, UVA-OB-0957, prepared by Gerry Yemen, Senior Case Writer, and James G. Clawson, Johnson and Higgins Professor of Business Administration. Copyright © 2008 by the University of Virginia Darden School Foundation, Charlottesville, VA. All rights reserved. Reprinted with permission.


## Chapter 9

### Donna Dubinsky: The Life and Career of a High-Tech Entrepreneur

This chapter was adapted from a case, UVA-OB-0843, prepared by Jason Clifton under the supervision of James G. Clawson. Copyright © 2005 by the University of Virginia Darden School Foundation, Charlottesville, VA. All rights reserved. Reprinted with permission.


## Chapter 10

### Ed Norris: The Life and Career of a Police Commissioner

This case was written by Senior Case Writer Gerry Yemen and Johnson & Higgins Professor James G. Clawson. It was written as a basis for class discussion rather than to illustrate effective or ineffective handling of an administrative situation. Copyright © 2007 by the University of Virginia Darden School Foundation, Charlottesville, VA. All rights reserved.


## Chapter 11

### Walt Shill: The Life and Career of a Senior Consultant

This chapter was adapted from a case, UVA-OB-0788, prepared by Greg Bevan and Professor James G. Clawson. Copyright © 2003 by the University of Virginia

## Chapter 12

### Tom Curren: The Life and Career of a Senior Executive Officer

This chapter was adapted from a case, UVA-PACS-0023, prepared by James G. Clawson. The introduction was adapted by Tom Curren from an article entitled "Sometimes You Know — Sometimes You Don't" by Jim Sinclair printed in the *Canadian Alpine Journal*, 1974.

## Chapter 13

### Judy Moore Curren: The Wife of a Senior Executive Officer
This chapter was adapted from a case, UVA-PACS-0023, prepared by James G. Clawson. The introduction was adapted by Tom Curren from an article entitled "Sometimes You Know — Sometimes You Don't" by Jim Sinclair printed in the *Canadian Alpine Journal*, 1974.

## Chapter 14

### Jackie Woods: The Life and Career of a Company President

This chapter was adapted from a case, UVA-BP-0330, prepared by Catherine M. Lloyd, MBA 1993, under the supervision of James G. Clawson.

## Chapter 15

### Bob Johnson: The Life and Career of a Divisional Chief Executive Officer

This chapter was adapted from a case, UVA-OB-0872, prepared by Gerry Yemen, Senior Case Writer, and James Clawson, Professor of business administration.

**Chapter 16**

**James Harold Clawson: The Life and Career of a Chief Executive Officer**

# 1

## The Symphony of Life

*"Most people do not accumulate a body of experience. Most people go through life undergoing a series of happenings which pass through their systems undigested. Happenings become experiences when they are digested, when they are reflected on, related to general patterns, and synthesized."*

Saul Alinsky, Rules for Radicals, quoted by Henry Mintzberg in "The Five Minds of a Manager" Harvard Business Review 11/03

*"All people dream; but not equally. Those who dream by night in the dusty recesses of their minds wake in the day to find that it was vanity. But the dreamers of the day are dangerous people, for they may act their dream with open eyes to make it possible".*

T. E. Lawrence

The most commonly mentioned challenge that business managers worldwide face is "balancing work and family/personal time." I can say this after having asked groups of senior level managers all over the world this question, "What is the biggest problem you face in life?"

I wonder what *your* biggest challenge in life is. Write your biggest challenge in life here:

That might seem like an abrupt introduction, "Hello, how are you? What's your biggest problem in life?"

The basis for the question, though, is this: adult learning theory suggests that adults learn best when they are dealing with issues that are current, immediate, and personal to them. When speakers or educators or consultants begin talking about issues or concerns that are on *their* minds and not the issues that are on the listeners' minds, the listeners tend to tune out and glaze over. Unfortunately, that's often a problem in management education sessions.

Many consultants will conduct "needs assessment" prior to making recommendations to clients. The theory behind this is sound, namely, that one should know what the problems are before trying to solve them. Yet many, if not most, educational experiences presume an agenda and jump right in.

So, asking the question, "What is the biggest problem you're facing in life?" turns out to be a great way to begin a program and ground the discussions in current, immediate, personalized issues. We post these on the walls throughout the seminar so we can refer back to them and ensure that our discussions are on track.

## Problems Occur at Four Levels

1. Societal

2. Organizational

3. Work Group

4. Individual

Problems can occur, obviously at several levels including societal, organizational, immediate work group, and individual.

Balancing work and family/personal life is the most commonly mentioned issue in these discussions regardless of where you ask. It's not just a North American issue. The same issue comes up in London, Rio de Janeiro, Bangkok, Sydney, Cairo, Athens, Istanbul, Mexico City, and San Jose, as well as in the United States.

There is ample reason to suggest why this balancing act is a global phenomenon. Friedman's "flat world" suggests that with the advent of the World Wide Web and advances in telecommunication, we can be in touch instantaneously anywhere in the world. Margins are harder to hide. Deals are easier to make. Partners, vendors, and suppliers are more accessible. The competition is working harder. The answer, it seems, is everyone is trying to do more with less and to keep up in the meantime.

Recently, I was standing in the men's room in a well-known four-star hotel chain on a break between program sessions, and the man standing next to me is on his cell phone discussing business matters. Can I cough? Do I flush? What are the business etiquette rules there? I have a friend who sleeps with his Blackberry. If he awakes during the night, he's answering and sending emails, so that associates get up in the morning with several to-do items in their inboxes. How does one balance work and family/personal life when work follows you wherever you go?

Another friend was a CEO who had a conversation with his wife about retirement. Like me, maybe like you, he's been thinking about slowing down and spending more time with his spouse. It turns out that she has been turning her energies to her interests and developed her own professional activities as the children have left home. Slowing down for retirement for him is counter-cyclical to her ramping up at the point of the empty nest. In his words, he's "resigned to more singular activities."

Many have observed that life seems backwards — when you have enough resources to enjoy it, your body and perhaps your mind are in decline. This is not always the case, though. There's a young 26-year old woman in China reportedly worth $2.5 billion.[1] Another young woman, a teenager from Scotland, has already sailed around the world single-handedly. Of course, Michael Phelps, the Olympic swimmer, will have set records that may not be broken for a long time at the ripe old age of 23. What's next for him?

There are at least two sets of issues here, the immediate and the time-based. Let's explore the immediate set of issues first. That is, how are you doing as of today? Are you where you want to be today? How have you used your time on earth so far? Here's a way of making that assessment relatively quickly. Once you've determined where you are, we can move on to how things unfold over time. Then we'll explore the lifestyles of a variety of executives to see how they have dealt with the challenges of modern executive living.

## THE BALANCE WHEEL

We could compare human life to a symphony. Like a symphony, life has a beginning and an end, and in between different movements, different paces for the different movements, and a multitude of contributors who are all playing different melodies and riffs at once. In a symphony, there are violins, cellos, cornets, tympani, and woodwinds, dozens and dozens of different instruments all playing or resting simultaneously. If each of the pieces

Whether we pay attention to these various "-al aspects of life" or not, they are unfolding day by day. If that simultaneous unfolding is connected and balanced, the overall effect is pleasing, even powerful. If it's not, the result can be cacophonous and jarring, even enervating.

[1] "The Worlds Billionaires," *Forbes*, 3 July 2008.

is in tune, on time and played well, the overall effect is pleasing, even powerful and inspiring.

While we don't have musical instruments in life, we do have various "-al" aspects of life: physical, intellectual, emotional, spiritual, social, parental, marital, political, professional, financial, sexual, and so on. Whether we pay attention to these various "-al aspects of life" or not, they are unfolding day by day. If that simultaneous unfolding is connected and balanced, the overall effect is pleasing, even powerful. If it's not, the result can be cacophonous and jarring, even enervating.

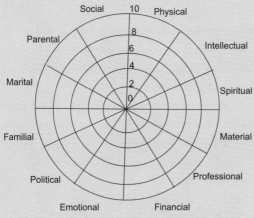

Figure 1.1. A Personal Development Balance Wheel.

Consider the diagram in Figure 1.1. The center or origin of the diagram represents zero development, what we might see in a new-born infant. Each successive, larger circle represents growth or development until we reach the outer circle which represents "world-class development." Note that this is not the maximum potential of the individual, rather the maximum potential of the human race. Each of the circles is numbered from zero at the center to 10 on the outer ring. A 10 on the physical dimension would be a world record holder or an Olympic gold medalist. A 10 on the financial dimension would be, as of 2008, Carlos Slim of Mexico, Warren Buffett or Bill Gates of the United States and Lakshmi Mittal of India, people worth between US$50 and 65 billion. A 10 on the professional level would be a Nobel Prize or the presidency of a large nation.

The definitions for the other dimensions might be more elusive. What is a world-class parent? What is a world-class daughter? What is a world-class citizen? Nevertheless, in society, we recognize these people in their various pursuits and put them forward as examples of some kind of "ideal homo sapiens."

With this simple diagram, we can ask the question, "Given your X years in life, how far have you developed on each of these dimensions?" With an assessment this will give us a picture at a moment in time of the development we've been able to achieve so far. Figure 1.2 shows such an assessment.

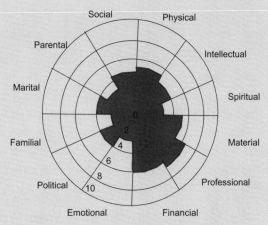

Figure 1.2. An Example of a Development Balance Wheel.

In this example, the individual does not believe he (or she) has developed much on the emotional, spiritual and familial (as a son to his parents) dimensions, but observes significant development on the professional side. He also seems to think he is somewhat underpaid for his professional development.

Where would this kind of assessment come from? It could be self-assessment, simple reflection. Ben Franklin famously rated himself on a variety of dimensions over the course of his life and reported his progress in his autobiography.[2] But self-assessments have the significant risk of benign self-deception. Are we seeing ourselves clearly?

We might get much better data if we could get others who know us well to assess our development as the years go by. Most would not go to that effort, though, so self-assessment is likely the most common way to get such an evaluation.

One could do this annually, say at the beginning of each new year, as a way of charting or seeing one's growth and development over time. This would be comparable to a corporation developing its year-end accounting records into a balance sheet and income statement. These are snapshots of activity to date as of a certain date.

## WHAT DO YOU WANT?

So assume for the moment that we all have such a profile as shown in Figure 1.2 whether we're aware of it or not. Life goes by and we grow in some ways and

---

[2] Franklin, B. (2003). *The Autobiography of Benjamin Franklin*. Touchstone.

perhaps not in other ways. We might have tangible evidence of our development status, like weight or bank account, or perhaps not, like emotional or spiritual.

The overarching issue, though, is whether or not you're developing in the way you'd *like* to develop. Are you building the life you want? Or will you end up one day in a place you don't want to be? I have a shelf of books in my office with titles like *Must Success Cost So Much?; Career Success Personal Failure; The Failure of the American Dream; The Future of Success; Working Ourselves to Death;* and *The Overworked American.* These are filled with stories of people who worked hard, did what they thought they should, and didn't end up with what they wanted.

It's not clear that they knew what they wanted early in life. Perhaps they just did what they thought they were supposed to and then one day woke up and said, "How did I get here?"

So, one of the questions becomes, "What do you want?" Could you write that down at the moment?

As of this moment, this is what I want:

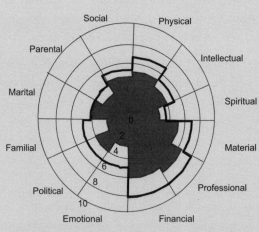

Figure 1.3. An Example of a Personal Development Balance Wheel with Goals Shown.

Some will say that what you want will change from chapter to chapter in life. Perhaps. But beware. If it changes, will you be working toward what you wanted in the last chapter or will you be able to foresee what you're likely to want, given the predictable stages of adult life, in the future?

Be clear that a perfect circle on the diagram in Figure 1.1 is not the ideal. Rather we want to know what *we* want in particular. See Figure 1.3. Here the desires of the individual are represented by a dark black line. You'll see that on some dimensions, the individual is happy with his progress while on others there's a gap. That gap, that "want-got-gap," is a problem. In fact, you could say that the definition of any problem is a "want-got-gap for somebody."

One would expect some satisfaction on the dimensions on which there are no gaps and some dissatisfaction on the dimensions on which there are gaps. With this image, one can begin to think about and/or plan what one wants to do about the gaps. You can consider whether you want to extend the goals on the dimensions on which there are no gaps. This thought process is the essence of development and growth. Without this thought process, you are little more than a leaf floating on the breeze being carried wherever the immediate current takes you.

A simple spreadsheet that will generate a graph like this one is available on my website, http://faculty.darden.virginia.edu/clawsonj/index.htm. With the spreadsheet, *you* simply type in your self-assessment scores and your ideal scores on each "-al" aspect and the diagram will automatically appear. You can change the dimensions if you wish. Then, you can print your profile, thus getting a picture of your "immediate" or current developmental profile. Then, next year, you can do the exercise again, and see if your personal developmental profile is evolving over time in the way that you want it to.

Let's move on now to consider adult development over time, that is, how adults tend to follow predictable patterns as they age. This will give us a foundation for thinking about balancing work and family life in the various chapters of life.

# 2

# ADULT LIFE AND CAREER STAGES

*"I would rather be ashes than dust! I would rather my sparks burn out in a blaze than be stifled in dry rot. I would rather be a superb meteor, every atom of me in a magnificent glow than asleep and permanent as a planet. The proper function of man is to live, not to exist. I shall not waste my days trying to prolong them. I shall use my time."*

Jack London

*"There is more to life than increasing its speed."*

Gandhi

Research conducted over the past half century shows that people's careers tend to follow predictable patterns of development. While we cannot discuss all of the current knowledge about the developmental processes observed in each of life's aspects here, we can consider the most common ones. As we do, keep in mind the developmental "-al" aspects of life introduced in the last chapter and consider how each of them might unfold over time. The image, then, is like a musical score, with each melody line representing an aspect of our lives and each bar representing a developmental stage. The relative strength of each of the melodies (aspects) changes from bar to bar: some are in crescendo, others diminishing. Whether the melodies are all equally salient or not, however, they are there, and together they compose the symphony of one's life.

Although the changes in activity, interest, ability, and tasks that humans experience over a lifetime have been the subject of literary pieces for millennia, modern social scientists have not paid much attention to the topic until relatively recently. As you'll see shortly, there are a variety of data-based views about how human life unfolds. Some might conclude that everyone therefore is unique in that regard. I think that would be a mistake. There are predictable patterns in life. As you read the various perspectives below, you may be surprised at the variations. One way to deal with that would be to declare now, before you read them, what chapter you think you're in now: Whatever your thoughts about adult development might be, what chapter in life do you think you're in now?

My guess is that I'm in the following "chapter" in life:

Let's see what the various researchers have concluded thus far about how adult life unfolds. Maybe you can find your chapter somewhere along the way. As you read the brief summaries of the various adult life development stages that researchers have posited, make notes in the margins about how and where your path has taken you. How did you resolve the issues suggested by each? What elements are still left unresolved for you? Where do you find sudden insights into your life and the things you've been dealing with? Are the issues you see here consistent with issues you see in your culture wherever that might be? How are the issues slanted or managed in your culture?

## ERIKSON'S THEORY

An influential early adult-life-stage theoretician was Erik Erikson. In his book, *Childhood and Society*,[1] published in 1950, he identified stages of human development in terms of several psychological dilemmas that, he said, confronted all individuals. His delineation of the dilemmas common to young people built on the work of Sigmund Freud, the first person to begin to describe human development in terms of predictable stages, but while Freud left off before addressing adult development, Erikson continued to hypothesize. He believed that there were successive dilemmas that humans faced and had to deal with. Unresolved dilemmas would either arrest development or present complications to subsequent issues. Erikson supposed that there were eight such dilemmas. The first five of Erikson's dilemmas related to earlier stages in life while the later ones were central to adult development. The eight stages with their approximate age ranges are:

Trust vs. Mistrust (0–1)

Autonomy vs. Shame/Doubt (1–2)

Initiative vs. Guilt (2–4)

Industry vs. Inferiority (4–11)

Identity vs. Role Confusion (12–17)

Intimacy vs. Isolation (18–30)

[1] Erikson, E. (1950, 1963). *Childhood and Society*. W.W. Norton, New York.

Generativity vs. Stagnation (30–49)

Ego Integrity vs. Despair (50–)

The ages given here are approximations since people grow and develop at different rates. For the newborn, the *experienced*, not thought, learning is whether or not it will be fed when hungry, changed when wet, warmed when cold, and loved when alone and afraid (i.e., when mother leaves will she return?). Children who receive insufficient answers to these basic questions tend to grow up with large holes in their personalities and find it difficult to trust others.[2]

As a child develops control of its muscles and learns to stand and walk, it becomes more aware of its success or failure in the eyes of others and its own. The nature of the coaching and encouragement or lack thereof in this phase may gel into a sense of it's okay to try things or conversely a self-conscious shame about failing that may grow into what Erikson terms a desire to live by the letter of some law rather than the spirit.

If the child has a sense of autonomy, that it is self-conscious and can stand on its own two feet, it may then build on top of that an assertiveness to try new things, to make things happen. If the environment (read to include "parental responses") resists this budding initiative spirit, the child is likely to experience a sense of guilt for not keeping to the laws/rules/guidelines/heuristics for approval. Unresolved, this guilt over what I am, who I want to be, can leave one well into adulthood with a sense of guilt over having inclinations that don't mesh neatly with the expectations of those around.

When the child goes to school, the conditional nature of that social system reinforces the notion that one must perform in order to be accepted or approved of. If one tries and succeeds at this game, patterns of industry and effort begin to form while if one fails at this, a deep, abiding sense of inferiority may settle upon the mind. Some will spend their entire lives trying to deal with that sense.

Identity is a key issue in the teens. Who am I? Who am I to become? Who are my peers and associates? Teens tend to "fall in love", Erikson says, with groups, cliques, heroes, and ideal visions. The central issue here is where do I belong? A sense of belonging is critical to one's sense of peace of mind. In today's highly mobile, technologically inter-connected world, the issues related to identity abound.

[2] Klein, M. (1964). *Love, Hate and Reparation,* Norton.

15

The central issue here is where do I belong? A sense of belonging is critical to one's sense of peace of mind. In today's highly mobile, technologically inter-connected world, the issues related to identity abound.

For example, Ian Buruma's book, *Murder in Amsterdam: Liberal Europe, Islam, and the Limits of Tolerance*,[3] explores in ethnographic detail how issues of identity plague immigrants who move from one society to another.

In my case, for example, I've had three last names in life. My parents were divorced during my early teens, and my mother made a deal with my father, unbeknownst to me, that if it was okay for her to get me to change my name, my dad wouldn't have to pay child support. My father was raised during the Great Depression, so money was a key value for him. My mother hated my father so much she couldn't stand the thought of me bearing his name. So she came to me one day and said, "You need to pick a new last name." I spent several weeks plowing through the encyclopedias, looking at coats of arms, and finally settled on my middle name, Gordon. Throughout high school, I was "James no-middle-name Gordon." Later when I wanted a passport, the government said, "Well, your birth certificate says *Schlafke*, your driver's license says *Gordon*, and you live at the *Clawson* household. When you figure out who you are, let us know and we'll give you a passport." This stage-related change has plagued me my entire life. Who am I? There were and are pros and cons to each of the monikers. I didn't realize them at the time because I didn't know the deal that my mother made. She must have been mortified that I settled on Gordon — my father's first name. How did your identity settle in or not during your teens?

From early adolescence to early middle age, the key psychological task a person faces is one of *intimacy versus isolation*, in which one must learn to care for and be concerned for another person without fear of losing one's self. If one does not learn to do this, life becomes a series of experiences in which the individual feels isolated from the rest of society. Interestingly, Erikson posits that the "utopia of genitality" in this phase should include mutuality of orgasm, with a loved partner, of the other sex, with whom one is able and willing to regulate the cycles of

---

[3] Buruma, I. (2006). *Murder in Amsterdam: Liberal Europe, Islam, and the Limits of Tolerance*, Penguin.

work, procreation, recreation so as to secure to the offspring, too, all the stages of a satisfactory development.[4]

This was a challenging decade for me as well. I'd gone to live in the Orient during the late 1960s on a religious mission, and came home having missed the enormous transitions that occurred in the U.S. during that time. As a freshman at Stanford, I had a part-time job serving meals in a women's dorm. Sounds great, huh? Not exactly. We wore white coats, black bow ties, and carried eight meals on a French tray to serve one whole table at a time. The co-eds were all gussied up, wearing evening dresses and using proper etiquette. When I came back in 1969, the dorm was co-ed and food was served buffet style to male and female residents wearing Levis, shorts, and curlers in their hair. What happened? I didn't know — I'd been isolated with instructions not to read the papers or listen to radio. I finally married at age 30, a virgin, with no clue about "intimacy." What were your twenties like? What did you learn or not learn?

In middle age, the key issue for Erikson is *generativity versus self-absorption*. In this dilemma, the individual has to choose between developing concern for individuals beyond one's own family, including colleagues at work and people in society, and developing the self. Failure to develop a generative approach to life, Erickson said, leaves one feeling stagnant and bitter.

What were your thirties and forties like? Are you there yet? What do you think they *will* be like? I spent my forties working two full-time jobs, one for pay and one not. I learned enormously from both of them, but the decade left me exhausted and out of gas. I thought more about getting the job done (my mother's voice in my head, "Trying doesn't count, you either do the job or you don't.") than about the unsustainable nature of my lifestyle. I lost contact with my children and my spouse. I lost contact with my body and my health. I lost contact with myself. But all in the service of a good cause, I thought. Somehow for me, the forties were about being self-absorbed in generativity. By that I mean, I lost myself by working so hard doing what others wanted me to do. Erikson would probably say I was self-absorbed. What about you? How will you balance your own demands versus the demands that others place on you?

Finally, Erikson saw in old age a battle between integrity and despair. Integrity was defined as the sense that life and all its choices and experiences had

---

[4] *Ibid*, p. 166.

"come together," become whole and integrated. Despair was the feeling that things had not turned out as one would have liked, that one had missed a lot of opportunities, and that it was too late to do anything about it.

At 48, I hit a brick wall. I woke up one day feeling that I was further behind on my charity work, further behind on my school work, further behind with my family, further behind with my health, and worse, I couldn't see a way that this would ever improve. There was never enough time and energy to do all that was being required of me. I was living, in fact, majorly outside-in. Without going through the gory, private details, (Is that in the spirit of this volume?) I will say that I decided that I would have to change the way I was living or I was going to die. I felt enormous despair, a huge, enveloping, dark cloud of despair. This might have been a bit early from Erikson's point of view. But fortunately, it gave me a chance to think more openly about my fifties. Are you there yet? If so, what happened in your fifties and what did you learn from them?

I offer these personal vignettes for two reasons. First, the spirit of this volume is to get behind the professional facades to see more of the personal context from which successful managers spring. It would be disingenuous to ask this of others without modeling one's self. Second, I hope to ground the theory in a story that perhaps will stimulate you to reflect more carefully on your experiences in the various chapters in life. You might have had a similar experience. Or one dramatically different. If we had more space here, we might explore in greater detail how your life story has in fact shaped your ability to lead and manage others. Noel Tichy originated that thought,[5] and I've adapted it and extended it. When I use those materials[6] in executive education and consulting, I'm amazed at the power and depth they bring to the discussion.

Following Erikson's work, not much was done in the field of adult development for many years. Then, in the late 1970s several social scientists began publishing the results of their observations from clinical practices and formal research projects. As you skim through these models, I invite you to make some notes in the margins where you see similarities or dissimilarities to your own experiences so far. This will help you identify and "own" the patterns.

---

[5] Tichy, N. (2002). *The Leadership Engine.*
[6] Clawson, J. (2008). *Level Three Leadership 4th edition:* Workbook Exercise on Life's Story Exercise, Prentice Hall.

## LIFE STAGES

### Gould's Theory

Roger Gould was a psychologist in California who began to notice common patterns in the issues clients of similar age groups brought to him. In his book, *Transformations,*[7] he presented a series of "false" assumptions he noted that people learned in their formative years and that must be reviewed and reconciled in later life, typically at predictable stages in life. He outlined the following adult-life-development themes:

*Age 16–22: Leaving the parents' world.* False Assumption: "I'll always belong to my parents and believe in their world." During this period, young people move from a set of beliefs that revolves around their parents' teachings and support to developing confidence in their own ability to care for themselves and to making decisions that will affect their lives. They feel half-in, half-out of the family. They wrestle with learning about their independence, their own opinions, their own ability to provide, and with relying on people other than family members.

*23–28: I'm nobody's baby now.* False Assumption: "Doing things my parents' way with willpower and perseverance will bring results. But if I become too frustrated, confused, tired or am simply unable to cope, they will step in and show me the right way." Although people in this period are feeling their autonomy, they are still learning what "works" in the world, and they confront the notions that people who play the game by the rules do not always get rewarded, that there is no one best way to do things, that others cannot do for us what we cannot do, and that rationality does not always win. They are also learning about commitment to spouses, to children, to work — and the responsibilities that all of these bear — and in so doing, are learning many new roles that they will play in society.

*29–34: Opening up to what's inside.* False Assumption: "Life is simple and controllable. There are no significant coexisting contradictory forces within me." Having spent nearly a decade establishing oneself in family and work, an individual now begins to look internally and to question whether the commitments and responsibilities assumed during the twenties were really independently chosen or were mere inertial extensions of parental guidance. People in this period typically begin

[7] Gould, R., M.D. (1978). *Transformation: Growth And Change In Adult Life,* Simon & Schuster, New York.

to confront the difference between the intellectual (rational) and the emotional; they realize that, in some ways though they did not want to be, they are like their parents; they learn that others are not so neatly understood as they once thought; and they realize more fully than before that their security depends on them alone. Marriage and career lives are established. Children are growing.

*35–43: Mid-life decade*. False Assumption: "There is no evil or death in the world. The sinister has been destroyed." Gould believed that this period is centered on the question of vulnerability. In this period, he says, people work to come to grips with the reality of their own mortality and with the illusion that safety can last forever. They also work to face the notion that they are not "innocent," but invite others to play complementary roles to the ones they assume. This practice occurs most obviously in marriage, and in this period, people examine these "unhealthy conspiracies" to make their own roles and their relationships more comfortable. Gould notes, "It is always unhealthy to sacrifice our identity for the stability of the relationship."[8]

*44–50: Post-mid-life period*. Realization: "That's the way it is, world. Here I am." In this period, finite time is resigned to as reality; one feels that "the die is cast." People become more actively involved with young-adult children and depend on their spouses for sympathy and affection. People may regret "mistakes" they made in raising their children. Money becomes less important. They attempt to reconcile what is with what might have been. Life settles down, becomes even. Those in the post-mid-life period accept the new ordering of things.

*50+: Meaning making*. The false assumptions of childhood have been encountered, if not all proven false. This period is one of mellowing, of making sense of the things that have happened both within and without. Children are seen as potential sources of comfort and satisfaction. People value spouses more than before. They have greater self-acceptance. There is little concern for past or future; the present is emphasized. People renew their questioning of the meaningfulness of life and as they are concerned about their health, hunger for personal relationships they realize they we cannot do things as well as they once did.

You can see the connections and overlaps with Erikson's eight ages of man. The mid-life realization in Gould's terms of "that's the way it is, world, here I am" links

---

[8] *Ibid*, p. 280.

with Erikson's notion of integrity *versus* despair. If the way I am at 50 is okay, then I'm feeling good about myself and likely to mellow into later stages in life. If the way I am is not self-pleasing, despair about the lost years and the unlikeliness of changing may set in.

## Levinson's Theory

Daniel Levinson, a psychiatrist at Yale University Medical School, and his colleagues studied the lives of 50 men from five different walks of life.[9] His theory concludes that there are a series of transitions and periods of relative stability in the adult male life. Each transition examines the life structure that preceded it and evaluates its appropriateness for the next era. Transitions are often times of turmoil and stress. The stable periods are often ones of renewed commitment and focus. Levinson's cyclical stages are:

*Age 17–22: Early adult transition*. In this critical transition, the young man is half-in and half-out of his parental family. He is faced with the necessity of leaving his family but is not yet sure how to enter the adult world before him. His choices in this transition begin to form his adult self as he and others will see it.

*22–28: Entering the adult world*. In this period, the young man attempts to establish a link between his view of himself and adult society. He often seeks assistance in this endeavor and may become a protégé. He begins to engage in adult relationships and explores what that means to him. He attempts to establish a life structure that is flexible, leaving him options to changes, and sufficiently stable to allow him to get on with his initial choice of means for making something of himself.

*28–33: Age 30 transition*. The young male adult now feels that, if changes are to be made, he had better begin, for time is passing. The life structure initiated in his twenties is reevaluated. Once-fondly-held dreams are reassessed in the light of several years of adult experience. Some people continue on rather smoothly, but, for many, it is a time of stress — of struggle with how to make the changes one desires. These three periods — EDT, EAW, and ATT — together form the early adulthood or novice stage.

*33–40: Settling down*. In this period, the male adult attempts to consolidate his experience and his efforts to build a life structure that will allow him to invest

[9] Levinson, D. J. (1978). *The Seasons of a Man's Life*. New York: Alfred A. Knopf.

heavily in the things most central to him. Becoming an expert and valued member of society are key objectives. He is no longer a novice, but is now a full adult determined to "make it." At the end of this period, he looks for a sense of "becoming his own man" — a male adult with seniority and respect. As he becomes more of his own man, the need for active mentors wanes.

*40–45: Mid-life transition.* Now the reexamination focuses not on where one is going, but on where one has been. The man becomes concerned about his accomplishments — whether they have fulfilled his dreams and ambitions or are less significant diversions. Aspects that have been suppressed during the early adulthood period bubble up for reassessment. He wonders if the path taken thus far is really the one that is right for him. He begins to notice physical declines and a sense of being no longer young. For some, these issues bring reconfirmation; for others, great turmoil and perhaps drastic changes — in career, in relationships, in activities and/or in the attempt to resurrect long-neglected, but valued, parts of the self.

*45–50: Beginning of middle adulthood.* This period is one of consolidating the reassessments conducted during the mid-life transition. Old relationships receive new attention, and new ones are developed, more consciously than before. The man settles into his new or reconfirmed view of himself and savors it. Some sense that a period of decline and constriction has arrived; others begin to find a deep sense of fulfillment in their lives and a mature sense of creative ability. For some, this period is the most satisfying season of life.

*50–55: Age 50 transition.* Levinson did not believe one can escape at least a moderate transition crisis. Therefore, in this period, issues that were brushed over or not fully treated in the previous transitions come forcefully to the fore.

*55–60: Second middle adult structure.* As in the settling down period, this period is one of completion and settling into. The man must prepare for the next transition — from middle adulthood into late adulthood. For some, this is a time of rejuvenation and realization, filling out the structure outlined in the Age 50 Transition.

*60–65: Late adult transition.* This transition anticipates the change in structure from the previous period to late adulthood, in which career changes are likely to have a significant impact on one's self and relationships. This period is often one of deep reflection. For some, this change is particularly painful, and they try to avoid it.

*65–Late: adult era.* The man must now not only decide the meaning of his previous existence, but also begin to establish the structure that was formulated in the late adult transition. Much more needs to be learned about this period.

You can see from Levinson's work that the timing of the stages of adult (male) development are not necessarily neatly aligned with the decades. Do you see elements common in Levinson's subjects beginning to emerge in your own life? Let's turn now from the broader focus on life stages to the narrower one on career stages. These would be the common patterns that observers have seen in the professional side of life. What follows, then, is a more fine-grained look at the professional aspects of life and the phases that are exhibited there.

## CAREER STAGES

While the previous writers on adult development took a broad, holistic approach to life, several researchers have focused on the professional lives of adults. Below we introduce the common views on the stages of working lives and the careers that we all have.

### Miller and Form's Theory

In 1951, two pioneer researchers Miller and Form identified five career stages that they believed delineated career-development patterns throughout a person's lifetime.[10] The ages are again approximate.

*0–15: Preparatory work period.* From the time one is born, one is socialized by our parents, schools, and the experiences to which an individual is exposed in the immediate environment into a set of views about the world of work. These views and values tend to follow the individual into his or her adult working careers. Young people develop their attitudes as they go about their first work (chores and homework) in limited doses. Not only do parents and teachers affect this formation, but also peers and social cliques. One of the main features of this preparatory socialization is the American cultural injunction to "make good."

---

[10] Miller, D. C. and Form, W. H. (1951). *Industrial Sociology.* New York: Harper and Row.

Beware the impact of overemphasizing the four main values of Puritanism. (1) Man's duty is to know how to work and how to work hard. (2) Success in work is evidence of God's favor. (3) The measure of success is money and property. (4) The way to success is through industry and thrift.

Miller and Form note that most young people are socialized into what the authors call the four main values of Puritanism:

1. Man's duty is to know how to work and how to work hard.

2. Success in work is evidence of God's favor.

3. The measure of success is money and property.

4. The way to success is through industry and thrift.

*15–18: Initial work period.* This period is a temporary time of getting one or more first (part-time) jobs until one accepts full-time, year-round employment. One knows that the initial jobs are temporary and, therefore, commitment to each position is low. The common goals are to make "spending money" and to "prepare oneself" for something else. Psychologically, the authors note, common agendas are to manage the transition from school to work, to gain independence, to demonstrate an ability to work hard, to learn how to get along with people, to get money as a symbol of independence, and to establish a good track record. Most of the occupational frustration people in this period feel comes from a conflict with work values held as a result of social class membership, failure to achieve expectations of reward based on educational achievement, a decline in the generally accepted intrinsic value of work (see Puritan value no. 1 above), and expectations of specific monetary rewards for work.

*18–34: Trial work period.* The trial period begins when one takes one's first "permanent" job (the period is often marked by considerable changing of jobs). Finally, after trying several different jobs, one "finds," "steadies," or perhaps just "resigns" to a long-term position. Miller and Form characterize six distinct types of career orientation that begin to form in this period: (1) the ambitious worker who has confidence he can move up; (2) the responsive worker who fulfills the career expected of him by others; (3) the fulfilled worker who has attained his

occupational goal; (4) the confused worker who is uncertain about past and future decisions and whose career pattern is erratic; (5) the frustrated worker who feels thwarted; and (6) the defeated worker, who views himself as a failure. Common to all these types is the cultural imperative the authors call the "American Career Stereotype" of a young, ambitious man who, with average intelligence but high character, unbounded determination, initiative, and hard work, climbs from the "lowliest jobs" to higher income levels that signify "success."

*25–65: Stable work period.* This period is characterized by long-term commitment to "the kind of work that I've always wanted" or to the resignation that one will not find it. Not everyone, Miller and Form state, will continue in one stable work period through-out the rest of their careers, but many reasons cause one to stabilize in one company or job: (1) realization or rationalization of the trial-period goal; (2) advantages gained by seniority; (3) age; (4) higher levels of income; (5) family responsibilities; (6) home ownership; (7) friendship ties; (8) institutional ties; (9) identification with the company and community. The emotional tasks faced in this period relate to redefining occu-pational goals that may have been achieved or will never be achieved, to waiting for promotions in informal seniority systems, to doing work for which one is overqualified and which no longer is stimulating, and to changing personal and family interests that may no longer fit job aspects. The authors note that some people will enter another trial period later, although Miller and Form say little about why.

*65+: Retirement period.* Anthropologists claim that the elderly have four common psychological goals: (1) to live as long as possible until the troubles of old age exceed the benefits of living; (2) to remain active in personal and group affairs; (3) to protect the privileges accumulated over the career; (4) to withdraw from life honorably with high prospects for the next life. According to Form and Miller, some do not accept the withdrawal in the fourth goal and, hence, develop a nega-tive attitude towards retirement.

## Super's Theory

In 1957, six years after Miller and Form, Donald Super and his colleagues pub-lished an expanded career theory that built on the earlier works of Eli Ginzberg, his colleagues, and several other researchers and psychologists.[11] Ginzberg and

---

[11] Super, D., J. Crites, R. Hummd, H. Moser, P. Overstreet and C. Warnath (1957). *Vocational Development: A Framework for Research*. New York: Teachers College Press.

his colleagues had outlined a sequence of occupational choice that they believed was an irreversible process. Each stage in this process is influenced, they said, by four factors:

(1) the reality of the occupational environment,

(2) a person's educational experience,

(3) certain personal emotional characteristics, and

(4) a person's values.

These four factors, especially the trade-offs between the first two factors and the last two factors, shaped the decisions a person would make in the Fantasy, Tentative, and Reality stages of career development. Super expanded Ginzberg's theory as follows:

### 0–14: Growth stage

Fantasy substage (age 4–10) is characterized by fantasy, role-playing.

Interests substage (11–12) emphasizes likes.

Capacity substage (13–14) emphasizes abilities.

### 15–24: Exploration stage

Tentative substage (15–17) is characterized by making tentative choices.

Transaction (18–21) by entering the labor market.

Trial (22–24) by beginning work.

### 25–44: Establishment stage

Trial substage (25–30) may see a change of occupation.

Stabilization substage (31–44), an effort to settle down.

### 45–66: Maintenance stage

Holding on to what one has.

### 65+: Decline stage

Deceleration (65–70) is the beginning of retreat from work.

Retirement (71–), a move out of the career.

Super's theory outlined activities characteristic of periods covering one's entire lifetime, but most of his work and focus was on the Exploration stage.

## Schein's Theory

Ed Schein of the Massachusetts Institute of Technology has written a number of classics in many sub-fields of management including process consulting, career management, leadership, organizational culture, and more. He posited the following frames in his volume on careers.[12]

1. Preentry and entry, in which one prepares for work by exploring possibilities and making a choice.

2. Basic training and initiation, in which one is socialized by the people in the organization into the formal and informal rules and norms of behavior in the organization.

3. First assignment and promotion, in which one establishes one's reputation as probable managerial material or one who will "level off."

4. Second assignment, in which one either continues toward further advancement or continues to level off.

5. Gaining tenure, in which one is admitted to the inner circles of the organization as a permanent member.

6. Termination and exit, during which one withdraws from the organization.

7. Postexit, in which one tries to come to grips with a lifestyle in which the career plays a very reduced or very different role.

Perhaps the most distinctive characteristic of Schein's scheme is the conical view of organization structure that he used to describe the movement of individual careers within organizations. There are, he said, three directions of movement: (1) *Up*, which approximates the conventional notion of promotion up a hierarchical ladder; (2) *In*, which describes the movement of a person from the outer circles at entry to the inner circles later on; and (3) *Around* which follows a person as he or she moves from one functional area to another in job rotation assignments. Each promotion may, of course, involve one, two, or all three of these kinds of movement.

---

[12] Schein, E. (1978). *Career Dynamics*, Addison-Wesley, Reading, MA.

## Dalton, Thompson, and Price's Theory

These three researchers from Brigham Young University studied the careers of thousands of people, many of them engineers, and report the following typical pattern:[13]

*Stage one: Apprentice* — the individual must learn how to make the transition from school to organizational life, how to be an effective subordinate, and how to live within the informal and formal social system of the organization. This stage is critical, because the novice learns values, beliefs, and habits of organizational and interpersonal life that he will use throughout his career.

*Stage two: Independent specialist* — one begins to work without supervision. In order to develop one's abilities to contribute and one's reputation, one works hard to build competence, often by specializing. One of the main tasks of this stage is to take the initiative for one's own work so that one is no longer dependent on supervision for decisions about what needs to be done.

*Stage three: Mentor* — one becomes concerned not only about one's own work but also about the work of those who follow. One of the main tasks here is to move from a frame of mind that focuses on doing to one that focuses on managing the work and development of others — to coaching and directing rather than producing.

*Stage four: Sponsor* — one becomes involved not only with the objectives and activities of face-to-face subordinates but also with the goals and work of large groups of people or systems of groups. Sponsors begin to ask about the goals of the organization or how the organization fits into the rest of society and to take initiative for answering those questions.

One way to summarize the work of Dalton and his colleagues is to note that each stage in their theory describes an increasingly broad perspective of the work that needs to be done and of the people involved in doing it. In stage one, for instance, the apprentice focuses on her or his boss and the demands that person places on the new employee. In stage two, the full-fledged employee is now interested primarily in his or her own work. In stage three, the employee's view expands to include the activities of immediate contacts. In stage four, the

[13] Dalton, G., Thompson, P., Price, R., "The four stages of professional careers: a new look at performance by professionals," *Organizational Dynamics*, Summer 1977.

sponsor is concerned about the work of hundreds, thousands, perhaps hundreds of thousands of people and how to structure their place in society.

These researchers also noted that individuals do not necessarily move through all the stages. Some people (probably Driver's steady-state type (below)) prefer to remain in the independent specialist stage, and others may not move from the mentor to the sponsor stage.

## Driver and Brousseau's Theory

Mike Driver and Ken Brousseau at the University of Southern California discovered what they called four naturally occurring career concepts.[14] These four different but voluntarily chosen career paths were linear, steady-state experts, spirals, and transitories.

Linears in Driver and Brousseau's model were those who sought to rise in the ranks of an organization. Their innate drive was to increase their power and status over time so that those who rose quickly were more successful than those who did not. This linear model of career success is the dominant model one sees in the media and in most organizations.

Steady-state experts are those who are willing and in fact would rather do the same things over and over again in their careers because their sense of satisfaction comes not from managing but from doing a job well done. One sees this pattern highly evident in the professions (law, engineering, medicine, teaching, etc.) and in the skilled trades (carpentry, masonry, electrical, etc.). Most of the participants in management seminars in cities all around the world have seen steady-state experts ruined by promotion into management.

Spirals are those who are willing to *give up* power and status for the sake of learning something new. They crave learning and new experience. Unlike linears when a spiral get 80 percent of the way to the top, they tend to get bored and are willing to sacrifice status and influence for the sake of doing something new and invigorating.

Transitories are not motivated by work, rather work is a means to get enough money to go off and do the things they'd really rather be doing like sail around the

[14] Driver, M. (1979). Career concepts and career management in organizations. In *Behavioral Problems in Organizations*, Cooper, C. (ed.), Prentice Hall, Englewood Cliffs, New Jersey.

world single-handedly, climb Himalayan peaks, or raft down white water. On the negative side, these primary passions might include drugs, alcohol, and gambling.

Each of these career concept types has something to offer the organization. For linears, it's drive and ambition. Steady-state experts bring competence and skill. Spirals bring fresh ideas and innovation. Transitories help manage the business cycles since they are willing to work temporarily so that they can go off and do what they'd really rather be doing with their lives. One problem, though, is that the linears tend to get to the top of most organizations and they tend to make the rules. So if one is a steady-state expert or a spiral or a transitory in a linear organization, one is likely to feel like a second class citizen. This tends to lead to one feeling that one "has" to follow the dominant, designed organizational reward systems which, designed by linears, favors linears. Figure 2.1 summarizes the career concepts developed by Driver and Brousseau.

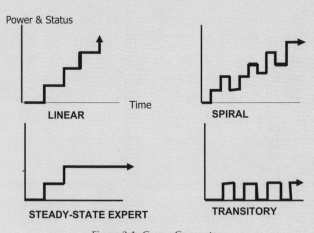

Figure 2.1. Career Concepts.

It's a rare linear type who can see and appreciate the value of the other three types. I was with one client group that included the top 24 people in the organization. As I was explaining the value of the steady-state experts, and asked the group why a person would choose a steady-state career, the first three answers were, and I quote, "retarded," "handi-capped," and "lazy!" The COO of the organization slammed his fist down and said that if the janitor in the company did not want to be the CEO, they should fire him because the desire to move up was central to the "American dream." Wow.

## SUMMARY

This chapter has briefly introduced the main points of several major theories about adult life and career stages. You may have noticed similarities in them, which is to be expected of theories that attempt to describe similar phenomena.

For instance, Erikson's Generativity versus Self-Absorption dilemma may be viewed as a psychological task facing a person near the "end" of Dalton's Independent Specialist stage. The individual who opts for "generativity" is likely to move on to Dalton's Mentor stage, while the person who chooses "self-absorption" is likely to remain an Independent Specialist. Similarly, Levinson's Getting-Into-the-Adult-World stage has many of the same characteristics as Super's Establishment/Trial period.

One relatively common feature of the theories just reviewed is a cyclical pattern. Levinson, for instance, noted that adults experience alternating periods of stability and transition. Miller and Form agreed that many careers are characterized by alternating trial and stable work periods. Thus the theorists believed that a person has a basic internal tension between stability and variety. Although we vary on our personal preferences for a balance between these two psychological interests, we all tend to reexamine our current state (whether it be flux or stability) with an eye towards moving towards the other one. Thus, if our lives and/or careers have been stable and orderly for a while, we begin to get bored and to think about introducing change or variety. If our lives have been filled with change, we may seek stability to consolidate our perspectives and feelings. Perhaps you can identify additional steps in cyclical patterns of adult life and career stages. Consider the chapter in life that you think you're in now as you noted above at the beginning of the chapter. Are you in flux or in a period of stability? Does that feel good to you or not? Why? Which of the dilemmas and challenges identified by these writers seem closest to your experience? Why?

As you read the stories that follow and which describe the lifestyles of a dozen senior executives worldwide, keep the frames introduced above in mind and try to see how our examples model (or don't) the theoretical perspectives. Better yet, review your own life and try to put your current chapter in life in the context of these various theories. What issues are you still working on? Which ones, if any, might be holding you back? How have you resolved those early life issues? Are there any that you need to revisit? Have you been trying to be someone else?

## Living Inside-out or Outside-in

These issues raise for me a fundamental issue in life and that is the degree to which we live inside-out versus outside-in. By inside-out, I mean a person is able

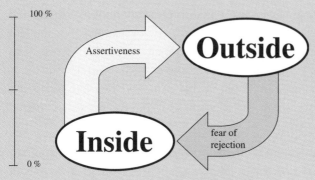

Figure 2.2. How Much of Your Life Do You Live
Inside-out vs. Outside-in?

to express who they are with confidence and high self-esteem. By outside-in, I mean a person tends to hesitate and censor who they are in order to fit in with those around them. Consider the scale of inside-out-ness shown in Figure 2.2. Zero percent inside-out would mean a person is basically a doormat, unwilling and unable to express their own opinions. At the other end of the scale, we would probably describe people who behave 100 percent inside-out as obnoxious, self-centered, selfish and narcissistic.

At whatever chapter you are in life now, how much are you living outside-in? In my experience, people vastly underestimate the degree to which they live outside-in. This is good in part, since we need a willingness to conform to create a viable society. But if we live too much outside-in, we lose our individuality and our capacity not only to lead but to live our own lives and to manage our careers. If you began life with a basic distrust or were unable to develop a sense of initiative, you are probably living largely outside-in — and living with large doses of guilt and self-absorption. If you can resolve those issues and realize that only you can really take control of your life, perhaps you can increase the degree to which you live inside-out and learn to live less in the shadow of issues unsatisfactorily resolved when you were younger.

Mihalyi Csikszentmihalyi offers that this issue raises a fundamental, I will say THE fundamental, question in life: will you ever be anything more than a vessel transmitting the genes and memes of previous generations on to the next?[15] Sadly, he argues, the answer for most people is "no." That is, they spend their entire lives living mostly outside-in recreating the experiences of the past, living as the "mere" riders on the tips of spears thrown by previous generations. To lead one's self, to

---

[15] Csikszentmihalyi, M. (1993). *The Evolving Self: a Psychology for the Third Millennium*, Harper & Collins, New York.

balance one's own life, to be an individual, to be a mature person,[16] requires the ability to live significantly inside-out.

What about you? What chapter are you living in now? What are the major issues that you're facing? What insights have you developed from the concepts introduced here? What's your dominant career concept? How should that awareness affect your career decision-making? How much do you live inside-out? Are you willing, eager, and ready to take control of your life? Or, living outside-in, are you yielding that control to others, living and dead? These questions point us to a consideration of what it means to lead a successful life, the subject of our next chapter.

## REFERENCES

Buruma, I. (2006). *Murder in Amsterdam: Liberal Europe, Islam and the Limits of Tolerance*, Penguin.

Clawson, J. (2008). *Level Three Leadership 4th edition, Workbook Exercise on Life's Story Exercise*, Prentice Hall.

Csikszentmihalyi, M. (1993). *The Evolving Self: a Psychology for the Thrid Millennium*, Harper & Collins, New York.

Davis, J. (1980). "Theories of Adult Life Stages and Their Relevance for the Management of Human Resources." Unpublished subfield examination, Harvard Business School.

Driver, M. (1979). "Career Concepts and Career Management in Organizations. In *Behavioral Problems in Organizations*, Cooper C. (ed.), Prentice Hall, Englewood Cliffs, New Jersey.

Erikson, E. H. (1963). *Childhood and Society*. 2nd Edition, New York: Norton.

Ginzberg, E., J. W. Ginsberg, S. Axelrod, and J. L. Herma (1951). *Occupational Choice*. New York: Columbia University Press.

Gould R., M. D. (1978). *Transformation: Growth and Change in Adult Life*, Simon & Schuiter, New York.

Klein, M. (1964). *Love, Hate and Reparation*, Norton.

---

[16] See Rogers, C. (1961, 1989, 1995). *On Becoming a Person*, Houghton Mifflin, New York.

Levinson, D. J. (1978). *The Seasons of a Man's Life*. New York: Alfred A. Knopf.

Miller, D. C and W. H. (1951). Form, *Industrial Sociology*. New York: Harper and Row.

Osipow, S. H. (1973). *Theories of Career Development*. New York: Appleton-Century-Crofts.

Rogers, C. (1961, 1989, 1995). *On Becoming a Person*, Houghton Mifflin, New York.

Schein, E. (1978). *Career Dynamics*, Addison. Wesley, Reading, MA.

Super, D., J. Crites, R. Hummd, H. Moser, P. Overstreet, and C. Warnath (1957). *Vocational Development: A Framework for Research*. New York: Teachers College Press.

Tichy, Noel. (2002). *The Leadership Engine*, Collins.

# 3

# THE NATURE OF SUCCESS: WHAT DO YOU WANT?

*"There is only one success, to be able to spend your life in your own way."*

*Christopher Morley*

*"Now that you know who you are, who do you want to be?"*

*John Lennon*

*"And what is a man without energy? Nothing — nothing at all... Sum all the gifts that man is endowed with, and we give our greatest share of admiration to his energy."*

*Mark Twain*

*"He has achieved success who has lived well, laughed often and loved much; who has gained the respect of intelligent men and the love of little children; who has filled his niche and accomplished his task; who has left the world better than he found it, whether by an improved poppy, a perfect poem, or a rescued soul; who has never lacked appreciation of earth's beauty or failed to express it; who has always looked for the best in others and given them the best he had; whose life was an inspiration; whose memory a benediction."*

*Ralph Waldo Emerson*

Ultimately the purpose of a career is to give a person a sense of success. Erikson's dilemma at mid-life and later between integrity and despair points directly at this issue, that is, how do you define success? If you're not clear on that, you may find that at mid-life, things aren't coming together as you hoped they might. Will that be because you didn't know what you were really looking for? Or because you couldn't make it happen? Actually the data suggest that the more people know what they want, the more likely they are to make it happen. This is in part because when people are clear on their goals and vision of a personal future, they are more likely to invest in those activities (learning or experiential) that will get them there.

So what is success to you? In a broader sense, the question is, "What do you want?" I taught a second year MBA elective by that title, "What do you want?" offered in the fourth quarter of the second year, just before they graduate. The idea was to help students think more than passingly about what they're going to be working for. In that course, we examined several definitions of success, including wealth, power, fame, health, family, materials goods, big houses, retirement, salvation, and personal satisfaction. We'll examine these briefly here in order to stimulate your thinking, before you read the stories that follow, about how to judge the effectiveness of these various lifestyles you'll see. In the end, someone else's definition of success is not likely to work for you.

One of the issues that one must be aware of here is "benign self-deception." Actually, self-deception is not so benign since if one makes decisions based on a more superficial criterion and then later in life after decades have passed comes to confront a deeper level criterion that doesn't match the earlier criterion, one can be devastated. The challenge is to know what you want — sooner rather than later. This was the issue described above in Erik Erikson's notion of "integration vs. despair."

Many will say but what we want *changes* with the chapter in life. You can see some of the research on that premise in the previous chapter. But take note of the following. First, people tend to progress through these predictable chapters in life. The issues and concerns that you have, and the way they change over time, might not be all that unique — in fact they are likely predictable. Second, if your wants change over time and you can't predict them, you'll likely be blindsided later in life. My thought is that some advance "warning" or at least awareness of the likely issues and dilemmas you'll face will help you balance your life in each chapter so that in the end, it will turn out in a deeply, or more deeply, satisfying way. Third, do your desires really change that much? Many of my MBA and executive education students are quick to say that they want to make enough money so they can retire early. Really? Do you dislike your work that much? Would you be happy with "nothing" to do? How much golf can you play? How many books can you read and how many ruins can you visit? Freud was once reported to have said that the purpose of life was "arbeiten und lieben," work and love. If you stop working, what will you do with yourself? If you win the gold medal at age 29, or if you sail around the world by yourself at age 19 (as one Scottish woman did), what do you *do* for the rest of your life?

With those caveats in mind, let's consider some of the basic issues that surround many of the common definitions of success.

**Wealth.** Let's begin with the most common definition, to be wealthy and financially independent. Most people seem to believe that if they had more money, things would be better, that is, that they'd be happier. Clearly this is true up to a point, but the data suggest clearly that money will not make a person happy. Yes, I know, we'd all like to *try* the premise! For those living below the poverty level in which ever country you choose, some additional funds would clearly help to provide food, shelter, transportation, and education. Beyond basic needs, though,

Frederick Herzberg[1] among others pointed out that money is a "hygiene factor," that is, we all need enough to have the basics in life, but after that money is not a good motivator. In fact, Alfie Kohn points out that money is in fact, along with other external rewards, a terrible motivator.[2]

> *"The more significant problem is precisely that the effects of rewards do last, but these effects are the opposite of what we were hoping to produce. What rewards do, and what they do with devastating effectiveness, is smother people's enthusiasm for activities they might otherwise enjoy."* (p. 74)

This effect has been demonstrated repeatedly in studies like the following: if you randomly select people from a population and put them in a room and invite them to play a board game for two hours, offering them a break in the middle, and then video tape what they do, some surprising things occur. If you don't pay the group, they tend to play through the break and you have to shoo them out of the room at the end of the two hours. If you pay them some nominal fee for playing the game, they take their break, come back late and want to leave early. This result happens not just once, but over and over again. When people pay us to do things we tend to think that the thing must not be valuable in and of itself. So, we try to up the input/output ratio by coming late, taking long breaks, and leaving early. In this way we can raise our "hourly wage." But it's really more about the sense of obligation rather than the hourly wage.

Consider the difference between two professional performers and their view on the value of an activity and the impact of being paid to do it. Tom Weiskopf was a professional golfer. He won a major tournament and was widely touted to have extensive natural and fostered talent. He once said that he remembered the day he stopped enjoying golf: "I stopped loving golf at exactly the time I decided to turn pro."[3] Contrast that with the statement of a Grammy award-winning musician who noted: People pay me a lot of money to go away from my family, stay in cheap motels, ride on the bus all night, and eat rubber chicken. But when the

---

[1] Herzberg, F. (1968). One More Time: How do You Motivate Employees? in *Harvard Business Review*, Jan–Feb. Reprinted multiple times as a classic article.

[2] Kohn, A. (1993). *Punished by Rewards*, Houghton Mifflin, New York.

[3] Weiskopf, T. (2004). *Golf*, July, p. 133.

curtain goes up and the light on the camera goes on, THAT I do for free."[4] For Mr. Weiskopf, the fact of being paid turned his joy in golf into an obligation. The musician was much more careful to protect that thing inside that was uniquely his. He was willing to "sell" the inconvenience of being away from home, but not his talent nor his joy in it.

Further, the data on people who win lotteries tends to be very mixed. Many of them declare that it ruined their lives and that, if they had it to do over again, they'd rather go back to the way they were. Perhaps this is because they were not prepared for the excesses that unlimited funds offered them. Perhaps they didn't have the training, the character or the discipline to manage their new wealth well, both personally and professionally. We'd all like to think we could handle it. Yet how many professional athletes, for example, wealthy at a young age, squander it away and end up in debt?

After the hygiene level (food, shelter, clothing, education), more money might allow one to buy more things or go more places, but the research is very mixed as to whether this will make one happy. Research conducted at the University of Virginia and elsewhere suggests that people have a "happiness setpoint" — that is, regardless of what happens, we all tend to return to our personal typical happiness level. The odds therefore are that more money will not make you happier. Martin Seligman at the University of Pennsylvania confirms that money will not make one happy.[5]

What is your "hygiene level" of income? I asked this question once to a group of entrepreneurs in Boca Raton, Florida. The seminar room by chance was long and thin, with an aisle up the middle, like a bowling alley. We were discussing a case about a successful Chief Executive Officer. I noted that the protagonist had retired with something like US$3,000,000 in the bank. Would this be enough, I inquired, for you? Would that be success? Interestingly, several voices on the right hand side of the room burst out spontaneously, "Heck, yes! That would be great! Wonderful!" At the same time, several hands went up on the left hand side of the room. Their owners commented, "What? That's *peanuts*. Not nearly enough!" Somehow, these people had scoped each other out by little, tiny subtle signals and chosen seats by their "peers" on different sides of the room. Apparently, you

---

[4] Name withheld by request of the musician. From interviews conducted by Douglas Newburg.
[5] Seligman, M. (2002). *Authentic Happiness*, Free Press/Simon and Schuster.

can "smell" (should I say "sense?") people with more or less money — and you gravitate towards those of similar wealth.

If you plan for your retirement, one of the questions your advisor will ask will be, "How much do you want to plan for on an annual basis adjusted for inflation?" I gave my advisor a number. What's yours? How much would you want to have annually to live on comfortably?

My dream to "live comfortably" annual income number:

If you don't identify your dream number, you may not know how to get there. But beware. Getting that number will be no guarantee, as the data show, of being happy.

What's more, two colleagues at the Harvard Business School, Paul Lawrence and Nitin Nohria have written a book in which they argue that all human beings are driven by four basic instincts. The first is the drive to acquire. They assert that no matter how much a person has, they always want just a little bit more. This genetic drive to improve one's situation in life may be a positive thing in the evolutionary sense; however, in today's modern world it could be a detriment to contented living.[6]

**Power.** Another segment of society seeks power as their focal definition of success. Of course, lots of money can equate to power — but only up to a point. In the political realm, money speaks, but it's not the last word. Country presidents may not be the most wealthy individuals, but they certainly tend to wield the biggest sticks. What drives a person to desire to influence not just a few hundred or a few thousand, but millions? The common saying is that power is the ultimate aphrodisiac. Visiting the Topkapi Palace one day in Istanbul and seeing the quarters of the Sultan's large harem, one could understand this connection. Is power about being able to mate with the most desirable others? It seems so in the animal kingdom where virtually every species has its mating rituals revolving around attraction and power. Think two male big-horn mountain sheep crashing into each other at full speed for the right to service the herd.

[6] Lawrence, P. and Nohria, N. (2001). *Driven*, Jossey-Bass, San Francisco.

Nigel Nicolson, a professor at the London Business School, asserts that there may well be a gene for leadership and dominance.[7] Some people he says just *have* to be in charge. Is this a genetic drive? Again, the drive to acquire might come into play with regard to power. Regardless of how much power we have, we may want just a little bit more. This tendency could well explain why seeking more money or power will never satisfy. Of course, many religious traditions have long since figured this out and argue that the path to happiness and serenity is to renounce the material world. Where do you come out?

One of the issues with power is the desire to be in control, to make the rules. How important is that for you? For example, if you had your own company and your name was on the door, how much control would you want to exert over your employees? I've asked this question of thousands of managers worldwide. Yes, I know, we could argue for some time about what does one mean by "control?" On average, though, how much control would you want to have where the relevant number is somewhere between zero and 100 percent? One man once said, zero. Really? That would mean that you wouldn't know if people were coming to work or not. You wouldn't know how much sales you had. How could you run a family much less a company or a country with zero control? Another woman once said, "110 percent!" Wow. Really? "Yes," she said. "If my name were on the door, I'd want to know what my employees were doing on Thursday nights and weekends and in all their leisure time and I wouldn't want them doing anything that would embarrass me or my company." Wow, indeed!

There are several problems with increasing power or control, of course, not the least of which is that this tends to stifle creativity and innovation. Carried too far, expanding control also tends to foment rebellion and violence. Unfettered control can also encourage cutting corners or making self-serving ethical judgments. The old saying that power corrupts simply means that if you have enough power to make the rules, why not make the rules to serve yourself? Most do that. We play educational simulations in business school that demonstrate this tendency.[8]

Some people seek power because of how they were treated when they were young, that is, seeking power can be a response to powerlessness experienced

---

[7] Nicholson, N. (2000). *Executive Instinct*, Crown Publishing, New York.
[8] Starpower™ is a game that demonstrates this tendency very clearly.

early in life. There's nothing wrong with that unless, of course, the reaction becomes an over-reaction that destroys the lives of others.

Reflecting on the literature on psychological development, I have come to observe two kinds of leaders in the world. The first, I'll call them Type I leaders, seek power because they like the power itself. They like the benefits, the influence, the chauffeured cars, the big offices, the prequisites that accrue to people in such a role. The second type, Type II leaders, seek power only because they want to do something they believe will serve their fellow man. (e.g. Sam Walton, founder of Walmart, who preferred to drive around in an old pickup or Warren Buffett who still lives in his original unassuming tract home.) They are not interested in the rewards of power other than the benefits they can provide to fellow citizens. In my experience, it's dangerous to trust Type I leaders. Type II leaders might become corrupted later on by their success — but in the short run, they have purer motives and are more likely to be trustworthy. This drama, the drama of corruption and power, plays out on stages large and small across the globe regardless of region, nation, culture, or industry in both the private and public sectors.

If success for you is about increasing your influence in the world, about expanding your power, are you clear why? Are you clear about how important this is to you? Do you understand what it's like to be in a powerful position? How much power do you want? What's your first impression there?

> I would like to be in control of things so that I could:

**Fame**. Others seek to be known. What is it that drives a person to do all they can to be recognized and singled out from the crowd? To be a celebrity? As we watch those who stand out in various parts of the globe, we see that some of them seem only to desire this public adoration regardless of their contributions. Others contribute much and seek anonymity. Is this desire to be loved by many a function of insufficient love received as a child? Or is there a genetic drive? Why do people jump and shout to be seen momentarily on television? Why do we look for our names in the newspaper? In a world of six and half billion people and counting, it's becoming increasingly difficult to stand out in any way. Yet we have whole segments of the entertainment, sports, and business industries that are devoted to making people *known*. The paparazzi feed on our desire to know and be known.

How important is it for you to be well known? If you had a lot of extra money and you gave it to your favorite charity, would you ask for your name to be put over the door of the new wing? Would you want to see your picture and name in the big newspapers? Do you seek the recognition of famous people? Do you drop names to impress others with how many people you know? Do you seek to be around famous others in order to bask in and perhaps steal a little of the limelight? These are not trivial questions for they drive large numbers of people to press to the front to be seen or photographed.

> To whom do I want to be known? How important is it to me to be well known and recognized?

**Craftsmanship**. Another definition of success is to become an artisan, an expert, a craftsman at your profession or talent. This is separate from fame in that one can be very good at what one does without seeking recognition for it. For the person who seeks to express their talent, fame is secondary and fleeting, but the self awareness of a job well done is deeply and internally satisfying in and of itself. Consider Eric Clapton, the famous guitarist, named by *Rolling Stone* as the fourth best guitarist ever. In Clapton's autobiography, he describes how painfully shy he was and how much he tried to avoid the limelight despite his well developed, self-taught talent. The joy it seems was in the playing, not in the spotlight.[9]

What is it that you do well, really well? What seems to come naturally to you? What do you enjoy doing above all else? How are you investing in your capacity to develop and express that talent? Do you have a plan to increase your skill set and when you practice your trade, do you take deep satisfaction in it regardless of whether you are paid, made powerful or famous because of it?

[9] Clapton, E. (2008). *Clapton*, Broadway Press.

> The thing I enjoy doing most in life is:

It is important to identify this thing, I think, because if you enjoy doing it, you'll want to do it again and the more you do it, the better you'll get. Malcolm Gladwell in his third book, *Outliers*, describes the 10,000-hour rule.[10] He says that to get really good at something one must devote roughly 20 hours a week for 10 years to really be good at it. This is consistent with the research of my colleague, Doug Newburg.[11] Lee Trevino reportedly was annoyed that people said he had so much "natural" talent — he said his natural talent was born of hitting a million golf balls.

**Salvation**. For very large numbers of people, the purpose of life is to be saved in the next life. The definitions and details around what this looks like vary from Christians to Muslims to Jews to Hindus to Buddhists to Sikhs to Shinto-ists and so on. The basic thought, though, that this life is preparation for the next life abounds.

I've met many a person at all levels of society who deep down focus their efforts in this realm. Sitting at an executive education dinner one night, the gentleman next to me declared that he believed the Bible to be the word of god, line for line, word for word. I hesitated to ask him about jealousy, genocide and polygamy included there (among other things) since I didn't want to disturb his dinner. Another friend looked me in the eye and declared with some vehemence that all apostates from Islam as well as those who tried to create apostates (missionaries) should be beheaded as he pulled his thumb across his throat. I didn't push the matter further. I read in the *Atlantic* about a young Jewish woman whose child was taken from her to a strict fundamentalist community. Elsewhere about young women stoned to death for being raped. I was standing on the sidelines of a soccer game when the gentleman next to me declared that he was sorry that I was going to hell. How did he know? I asked. He said that the judgment was all pre-determined and that since

---

[10] Gladwell, M. (2008). *Outliers*, Little, Brown and Company.
[11] Clawson, J. G. S. and Newburg, D. S. (2008). *Powered by Feel: How Individuals, Teams, and Companies Excel*, Singapore: World Scientific.

I was not attending his church, he knew that I was not one of the chosen ones. I think he was trying to express a tender thought for me, but it didn't come across that way. All of these incidents and millions more taking place very day reflect the importance with which people put on their future state in the next life.

What's your thought on the nature of the next life? Is there one? If so, what does it look like? What are the implications for your life here? How does that awareness shape the balancing decisions you make in life? Are you growing and developing yourself and those around you? Is this definition of success so important to you that you are willing to sacrifice many of the other definitions here for it?

> Is there life after death? If so, what does it look like? And what role does your behavior in this life have on your state in the next one?

**Health**. If you ask 30–50-year old managers in executive programs what "success" means to them, many will say to be healthy. They want to be fit, to be healthy, to be able to enjoy their physical bodies, even if they are completely honest, to be good looking. Who does not want to "look good"? Some will even say that their bodies are sacred stewardships given to them by god. For people that value health, the strategies for success include watching what they eat, exercising frequently, and getting enough sleep and recreation to regenerate and deal with stress.

How important is good health to you? In today's Web-based interconnected world, we can no longer feign ignorance of good health practices. Yes, our genes influence our health probably in ways we still don't understand well. Yet we know a lot. Americans in particular are in the midst of an obesity epidemic. Western cultures in general have high rates of self-induced illnesses caused by smoking, drinking alcohol, and poor eating and exercising habits. Yet we know what we "should" do.

How important to you is your health? Actually, I'm asking you more about your visible behavior than your words. Do you get enough sleep? Do you eat healthily? Do you exercise daily? Thomas Jefferson, the third President of the United States and the founder of my employer, the University of Virginia, noted

that two hours of daily exercise were very important because a healthy body was even more important than a healthy mind. How many of us in our frenetic world take time for two hours of exercise a day? It's almost a laugher. Some do. We admire them and their fitness. Then we enjoy our desserts.

What would you like your body to look like? What could you do to make that happen?

**Happy Family**. Is family the most important component of success for you? I remember having dinner once with a very successful Harvard graduate who was to become very influential in the world. He was traveling a lot in his job despite having a wife and several children. At dinner one night, I asked him how he did it, traveling so much. His answer surprised me. He said, "I do it for my family." I don't doubt that he believed that statement, but it didn't ring true. First, I know from talking with kids and reading the research that if they had a choice between a gold door knob on the bathroom door and dad coming to their soccer games, they'd take the latter every time.[12] I think deep down this individual really enjoyed being picked up at the airport in a limousine and being ushered into the mahogany paneled offices of CEOs and having them hang on his every word.

Another associate walked that "family" talk more dramatically. He left work every day at 3:00 pm so he could be home when his kids got off the school bus. He played with them, helped them with their home work, and put them to bed and then in the wee hours tried to catch up on work. Clearly for him, his first priority was "love at home." Unfortunately, as a result his productivity was insufficient and he had to leave for another institution.

How important is family for you? Again, I'm more interested in your walk than your talk. How many hours a week do you spend with your family? Do you enjoy those hours? Do you revel in what your kids say? Or do you believe like one person I met in Dubai who said, "Children should be afraid of their parents."

---

[12] See also Burke, R. and T. Weir (1977). Why Good Managers Make Lousy Fathers in *Canadian Business*.

Do you imagine spending more time with your family in the later years or perhaps in the next life? I was walking with my wife one morning recently. We walk three or four miles three or four times a week. We talk. I opined that I was getting closer to retirement and looking forward to slowing down and spending more time with her. She looked at me with a quizzical look and said, "Well, just don't think you're going to spend time at home and mess up my schedule! I've got things I like to do and people I like to spend time with, so you'll need to keep yourself busy." Huh? Oh. Okay. Maybe the vision I had of spending more time with each other in retirement isn't going to work out so well.

Another fellow I met told me that his father had dropped him (at age three), his two siblings and his mother off in a strange town with a bag of apples and left. His mother became an alcoholic, so he left home at age 16. Is it a surprise that he says with a tear in his eye that he wants to spend more time at home with *his* kids?

What's *your* plan? If you establish a set of habitual boundaries on your family relationships now and then later on try to modify those relationships, how will that work out? Will you anticipate spending more time with your adult children? What will you do? Will they be willing? Will your significant other?

My ideal family time would look like this:

**Contribution to Society**. This is a difficult one to sort out because so many of the other elements of success can creep in. There are those who want to better society and are determined to make a profit in doing so, the bigger the better. It may well be important to achieve positions of power in order to lever one's impact on society.

If this is a big one for you, how do you think about "making a difference"? I had one student who, for example, was determined to bring low cost electricity to rural regions in India. He was well on his way to making this happen as he had already set up two trial experiments of his plan and they seemed to be

working well. The odds are there won't be a lot of money in supplying a commodity to poor people, but he believes he can do this in a way to turn a modest profit and in the process, if the model works, have a major positive impact on his country.

Another student was determined to return to his home country in Southeast Asia and develop low cost housing alternatives for the poor there. He never once talked about getting rich. He may well become rich in the process, but it didn't seem to be his primary goal in life nor his definition of success.

What's your stance about contributing to society? Are there issues in the world or in your community that you feel strongly about, strongly enough that you are already doing something about them? Again, please be aware of the difference between talk and walk. How many hours last week, for example, did you spend working on these issues?

If I could make one change to society, it would be this:

What would I have to do in order to bring this change about?

**Retirement**. Do you imagine success to be being at leisure, able to determine what you do with every hour in the day? I was in an executive seminar this past week with a group of 35–50-year old senior level people. In the course of one discussion, a gentleman said that he wanted to make more money so he could retire earlier. "Hmm," I offered, "do you not *like* your job?" He was surprised by that question. His assumption, and that of many, is that they are working for the day they can retire. But if Freud was right and the purpose of life is "arbeiten und lieben" (work and love), of what will retirement consist? It seems to be a mixed bag as well. Some retirees I meet wish they'd retired sooner. Others can't seem to make it happen, they keep going back to work even though they long since had many multiples of what they needed to retire.

If you could retire tomorrow, what would you do? Can you list the top 10 things? What are you missing in your life now that retirement would bring?

---

Top 10 Things I Would Do If I Could Retire Today:

---

Don't misunderstand me. I'd like to slow down as much as the next person. Especially since I seem to have a bit of the workaholic gene in me. I understand the desire not to want to worry about how to pay the bills, or how to put the kids in good schools, or how to keep the creditors away. AND I'm inviting you to consider carefully what your image of retirement is, especially if that's your definition of success. Is it mowing the lawn and watching football? Is it painting? Writing? Traveling?

**Resonance**. Finally, I invite you consider another definition of success. It's an internal definition as opposed to an external one. We could have considered other aspects of success like big homes, nice cars, lots of jewelry, and so forth but they are in large part variations on the wealth theme.

**If you're wealthy and you're not happy, what good is it? If you're powerful and not happy, what good is it? If you're famous and not happy, what good is it?**

Resonance though is different. My friend and co-author, Doug Newburg, asserts, wisely I think, that it ALL boils down to feel. If you're wealthy and you're not happy, what good is it? If you're powerful and not happy, what good is it? If you're famous and not happy, what good is it? He'd say that success lies not in the achievement of goals (despite what our modern goal-oriented society and its proponents might say), rather in how one feels.

Do you know how you want to feel?

When he asked me that question at age 48, I did not. In fact, I couldn't sleep that night. How do I want to feel? NO one had asked me that question. Not my mother. Not my father. None of my teachers. Not god. None of my clients. No one. It seemed irrelevant because the whole world seemed oriented around goals and results. It's a goal-oriented, results-oriented world.

Yet if you ask people if how they feel affects their performance, every hand in the room goes up. Not just in North America. Around the world. Then, if you ask them how many times in their career has their boss asked them how they wanted to feel, they begin laughing. It's an absurd question! Never! The reason is that most adults believe that the very definition of adulthood and especially successful professional adulthood is to do what you have to do *regardless* of how you feel.

I've come to believe that this is a formula for mediocrity. But that's a story for another book.[13] For now, here, the issue is do you know how you want to feel? Can you describe it?

> How I Want to Feel:
>
>
>
>

If you can answer this question now, I commend you. It took me 18 months and 40 drafts to settle on "light, unhurried and engaged." Note that "happy" isn't good enough — it's too broad, vague and generic. And beware of "productive." That's a poor substitute for goal orientation which is about tangible output more than feel. When you're at your best, confident, productive, unaware of time, not self conscious, performing at your best in an easy way, and learning, how do you *feel*? Can you capture that?

[13] Clawson, J. and Newburg, D. (2008). *Powered by Feel: How individuals, teams, and companies excel*, World Scientific.

## Conclusion

Perhaps there are other definitions of success that you might offer. I invite you here to write your draft at the moment. What does it mean to you to be successful?

| My definition of success as of this date (                    ) |
|---|
|  |

Here's another way you might get some insight into this issue and before you begin reading the stories that follow. Fill out this little table assessing how important each of these dimensions is to you relative to the others. Note that I'm inviting you to develop a relative picture here, so your total score should sum to 100. If you believe that all of the elements are equally important, therefore, you'd give them even (10%) ratings. I've also included two blank lines in case you want to add some other criteria, a space for you to make some preliminary notes on what your thinking is about why you value one part of the definition the way you do.

| Dimensions of Success | My Rating | Notes |
|---|---|---|
| Wealth |  |  |
| Power |  |  |
| Fame |  |  |
| Expertise |  |  |
| Salvation |  |  |
| Health |  |  |
| Happy Family |  |  |
| Contribution to Society |  |  |
| Retire |  |  |
| Resonance/Flow/Feel |  |  |
|  |  |  |
|  |  |  |
| **TOTAL** | **100%** |  |

Whether you plan to or not, you *will* over the course of your life define what success means to you. The way

## The 168-hour week seems to be the building block of life.

you spend your 168 hours per week will build the *de facto* structure of your life. I say the weekly time frame is the important one because few people can fit every aspect of life into every day. On the other hand, if we were to exercise or spend time with our loved ones only once a month, that would be insufficient to strengthen either our bodies or our relationships. The 168-hour week seems to be the building block of life.

You also vote your values with your feet, that is, what you love you'll do and what you do is a reflection of what you love. You might, for example, keep a time log for a week and see where you spend your time. Several of the stories that follow are indeed weekly time logs that give us more data than a reflective summary. If you do this as well, you might sit down then at the end of the week and compare your "espoused" values with your "values-in-action" as indicated by your time spent. Surely you'll have some "shadow time," that is, time where you're doing more than one thing. You might be jogging with your spouse, for example, and be able to count the hour as both physical and social activities. Beware, though, as shadow time is not always quality time. Going to the kid's soccer game and working on the Blackberry the whole time wouldn't count much on the parental front.

On balancing your life, we've looked at three perspectives to introduce the stories that follow. First, we offered the Balance Wheel as a way of assessing how you're developing over time on the various "-AL" aspects of life. You'll note that I left a few of them out, "sexual" for example. Every man and woman has a sexual dimension and the data suggest that whether we are able to talk about it or not, it's a large part of life for every adult in some way.[14] Managers and executives are no different. You won't see much of that side of life in the examples that follow. There are little hints here and there, but nothing like a rich story about how executives manage their sex lives. Our global society doesn't seem ready for that, and certainly our subjects who were kind enough to tell their stories were not.

At 61, I'm saddened a bit by the years spent in superficial conversations. So many things seem "taboo" to talk about, and yet in my experience, those are the very things that we ought to learn to talk about more. Honest, authentic,

---

[14] See for example, Juska, J. (2004). *A Round Heeled Woman,* Villard.

transparent conversations have become for me like diamonds, jewels of truth that one can only find from time to time amidst the ocean of social interactions. Most people want to tell you what things *should* be like, and are unwilling to tell you how things really *are*. Because of that, many of us get a distorted picture of what the world is like.

The primary goal for me, developed way back in the 1970s, for this project was to develop a series of descriptions of executive lifestyles that included the personal as well as the professional. How do effective executives balance their lives? How do they manage to keep so many balls in the air? What kinds of support do they develop for themselves? What is their family life like?

Without answers to questions like these, students entering the business world may be well prepared for making a lease-buy decision, but utterly unprepared for the impact on their health and relationships of the demands of the jobs they take.

This is not a trivial issue. The media has often reported the number of divorces among senior executives, the "trophy wife" phenomenon, and the difficulty children of executives often feel in relating to their parents. I remember Stephen Covey telling us once in our MBA class on Organizational Behavior that trust was a pervasive concept and that if a man would cheat on his wife, he'd cheat in business. Several years later, I was having dinner with a CEO who'd built a billion dollar business from his garage and we got to talking about the Clinton-Lewinsky affair. I mentioned Covey's comment to him, and his reply was perhaps telling. He said that it wasn't true, that he knew lots of senior executives in his city who regularly cheated on their wives and he'd trust them completely in a business deal. Do wealthy, powerful alpha males naturally seek and get the most beautiful women even if temporarily? Newspapers reports this very week (Fall 2008) describe wild partying taking place even as Wall Street executives met to discuss the financial crisis. How does that all work? We cannot explore those issues here, but they are there, underlying and implied, in the stories that follow.

Second, I invited you to think about a longitudinal perspective, how adult lives unfold over time. There seem to be predictable stages. Careful scholars and researchers can and have gone beyond the mid-life crisis cliché. Surely there are individual variations, and yet for the vast majority of people, the patterns emerge. Do you see them emerging in your life? Can you anticipate, given the theory and

examples that follow, what chapters you'll be coming up on? Can you anticipate how to make the transitions? Can you anticipate how to handle the pitfalls? Can you anticipate learning more about yourself so that you can avoid the traps that others have fallen into?

Can you, in short, *lead* your own life? Can you balance your life in a way that will be satisfying for you? Or are you deceiving yourself into thinking, week after 168-hour week, that someday things will get better? Are you following an unproductive "path of least resistance" or have you established a vision for your life that guides and sustains you?[15]

> **Can you *lead* your own life? Can you balance your life in a way that will be satisfying for you? Or are you deceiving yourself into thinking, week after 168-hour week, that someday things will get better?**

Thirdly, in this chapter, I invited you to think about your definition of success. What does it mean to you to be successful? Can you do a little "future-perfect" thinking[16] and anticipate what you'd like to be able to say looking back on your life? Thomas Jefferson asked that three things be put on his tombstone, three things of which he was most proud of. The Virginia Statute for Religious Freedom, the Declaration of Independence and the University of Virginia. What would you like to put on yours?

What I'd want them to write on my tombstone:

The cases studies, shall we call them *stories*, that follow come from a variety of industries and several countries. They include men and women, traditionalists and moderns. Many professions are represented including business, academia,

---

[15]  Fritz, R. (1989). *The Path of Least Resistance*, Ballentine.
[16]  Davis, S. M. (1987). *Future Perfect*, Addison-Wesley.

and politics. My hope and invitation is that you read them with the conceptual frames already introduced in mind. Perhaps you can find a tip, an insight, a heuristic, a pattern that will provoke your thinking. Perhaps you'll find a practice that causes you to re-think some long-held assumptions about the way the world is or should be. That's happened for me as I've collected and written these stories. For example, I was trained that a mother's place was in the home and that no success could compensate for failure in the home. John Steinbeck's statement above challenged that assumption. Then I met a woman who in order to pursue her career hired a full-time nanny to care for her children. One day at a Halloween Party, I, in costume, "boo-ed" one of her kids and the child ran behind the *nanny's* legs to hide while mom was standing there. Aha! I thought. See! The child was attached more to the nanny than the mom. Whatever. I've since learned that the children are healthy, happy, well adjusted, smart, productive, and have very good social lives learning from their mom a host of wonderful principles as they grow up.

So, if you take the cross-sectional -AL aspects of life template and imagine it sliding over your life, week by week, through the various stages set up in chapter two until at some point you emerge in life with a sense of success (or not), you'll be able to apply all of the frameworks introduced here. (See Figure 3.1.)

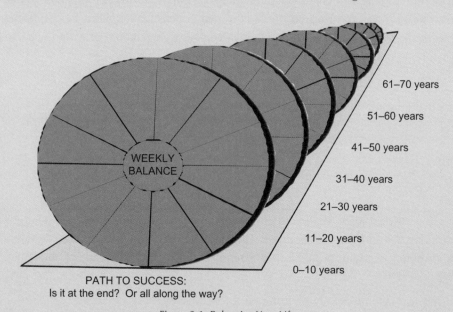

Figure 3.1. Balancing Your Life.

Whom can we learn from to gain insight on how to manage all of this better? Malcolm Gladwell and many others have picked the "outliers," those who have had extraordinary success and tried to describe the gardens from which they grew. Gladwell in his own right is an outlier, something he acknowledges. In fact, he noted that you could read his book about unusually successful people as "an extended apology for my success."[17]

What about the more accessible successful people, people closer to you and me? What about the attainable larger "hump" of people more toward the middle of the distribution? A dozen such people are presented here. Some of them you may have heard of, others perhaps not. All of them have been successful in their own way. Perhaps their stories will help you become more successful in yours.

## REFERENCES

Burke, R. and T. Weir (1977). Why Good Managers Make Lousy Fathers, *Canadian Business*.

Clapton, E. (2008). *Clapton*, Broadway Press.

Clawson, J. G. S. and Newburg, D. S. (2008). *Powered by Feel: How individuals, teams, and companies excel*, Singapore: World Scientific.

Davis, S. M., (1987). *Future Perfect*, Addison-Wesley.

Fritz, R. (1989). *The Path of Least Resistance*, Ballentine.

Gladwell, M. (2008). *Outliers*, Little, Brown and Company.

Herzberg, F. (1968). One More Time: How do You Motivate Employees? in *Harvard Business Review*, Jan–Feb.

Juska, J. (2004). *A Round Heeled Woman*, Villard.

Kohn, A. (1993). *Punished by Rewards*, Houghton Mifflin, New York.

Lawrence, P. and Nohria, N. (2001). *Driven*, Jossey-Bass, San Francisco.

Nicholson, N. (2000). *Executive Instinct*, Crown Publishing, New York.

Seligman, M. (2002). *Authentic Happiness*, Free Press/Simon and Schuster.

Weiskopf, T. (2004). *Golf*, July 2004.

[17] Quoted by Grossman L. in "Wise Guy," *Time*, 25 Noverber 2008, p. 48.

# 4

## CHARLES NELSON:
## A WEEK IN THE
## LIFE OF AN
## INVESTMENT
## BANKING INTERN

People often look at investment banking as a glamorous career which involves traveling around the world coordinating mega deals. What many people do not see are the sacrifices that investment banking professionals are forced to make every day in order to follow this career path. The time and energy required to be successful in investment banking severely alters a person's ability to have a passion for any activity beyond work. He or she also often finds him or her self a stranger to both their spouse and children.

They become consumed by the deal orientation of the business which stresses victory at every turn, and often forget to stop and enjoy the finer things **The stress and lack of balance in their lives eventually destroys them.** that life has to offer. This leads to the burn-out that so many investment banking professionals experience. The stress and lack of balance in their lives eventually destroys them.

However, the job is not without its rewards. The prestige and compensation of an investment banking job are what lures many young professionals to the business. The Wall Street firms pay almost double the average MBA salary in the first year out of school. The money does not come without lofty expectations as many first year associates will often work 90 to 100 hours a week.

In this essay, I will first make some observations on the recruiting process for investment banks, and then I'll outline a typical week for an investment banking associate based upon my experiences at a Wall Street firm during the summer of 1995. I hope you'll find this interesting and/or helpful.

### Recruiting Interviews

The competition for investment banking interviews on campus is fierce as many people are lured to the small number of interview slots. Students with previous investment banking experience are always invited to interviews with most of the banks, while those with no industry experience normally use their bid points to get on an interview list.

Interviews for investment banking jobs are notoriously difficult. Due to the aggressive nature of the business, the interviewer often puts the candidate in an uncomfortable position from the start. They believe this to be the easiest way to gauge how the potential employee will react in tough situations. While this demeanor often confuses and angers many candidates, I believe that it is somewhat effective at what it is trying to accomplish. While some interviewers want the candidate to cower in fear, others would prefer if the candidate took a stand against their aggressive behavior. For this reason, I have found that, as much as possible, a person must be oneself in the interview. This will most likely result in the best outcome for both the bank and the individual.

If a candidate is lucky enough to make it past the first round, you will often be called in the next day to be interviewed by new people. These interviewers are often senior to the interviewers from the day before. The protocol for this interview will be the same as the day before.

Finally, they will choose the finalists from your school and you will then compete against students from all schools for a finite number of jobs in the next year's associate class. This process is often held on a Saturday and will consist of seven to nine half-hour interviews. This is a grueling process, but I believe it gives the candidate a good opportunity to meet their future colleagues and let them determine if this is a place where they really want to work. Often times, the offer is made that day, and if you accept, you are now an investment banker.

## A TYPICAL WORK WEEK

My experience this past summer (1995) was in San Francisco, California, in the technology group of a major Wall Street firm. We were experiencing one of the hottest initial public offering markets in history. As always, the office had more work than could be done by the allocated staff. Therefore, we probably worked even longer hours than one expects for the investment banking industry. The following is a chronology of events over a one-week period. It could be any week as they all seemed to pretty much parallel the one which I have described.

### Thursday

**2:00 pm:** 400 pages of data providing details of the market for systems integration service providers have just arrived. I am learning all I can about an industry that I did not know existed before Tuesday. I must complete a 40-page book that analyzes the industry's competitors, clients and proprietary technology

for a customer looking to make an acquisition. That is the way things go around here; lots of information and work must be processed in very little time.

**2:30 pm:** A principal of the firm comes in and tells me that I have been assigned to work on the X corporation follow-on stock offering. The office is severely under-staffed, and I hardly have any time to get my current projects finished, but that doesn't matter because everyone else is just as busy as I am. A dry eraser board on the wall keeps track of the deals that each analyst and associate are working on, and there are several projects under each person's name. I am currently the least swamped, if there is such a thing, and that is why the project has been given to me. He tells me that the organizational meeting will be on Monday at 8 am in San Francisco.

I begin to think once again of the business which I had been working on before, but my mind keeps wandering to the new task that has been thrust upon me. I realize that I had better finish my acquisition proposal before Saturday because the weekend will be filled preparing for the X corporation meeting on Monday morning. As I sit in front of my computer downloading information, the time passes quickly.

**9:00 pm:** I look out from my cubicle and realize that it is already 9 pm, and the sun has just set. One would not realize this due to the amount of work that continues to occur in the office. It is just as busy now as it was at 10 am. We order "*Waiters on Wheels*" to deliver dinner at 10 pm. We have become such frequent customers that they know us by name. They deliver my dinner approximately five nights a week. I eat half of my meal and then lose my appetite while thinking about the amount of work that needs to be done.

**11:30 pm:** A fellow associate asks for help with a model that she cannot get to work properly. I politely oblige because we all realize that we are in this together and must help each other out.

**12:45 pm:** I put the finishing touches on her model and return to my cubicle. I have received three voice mails from the Hong Kong office while I was away. It is daytime there, and they need some information on an upcoming IPO. I wonder to myself why I am always here when they call in the middle of the night, but they are never there when I need to talk to them during regular business hours in the United States. Am I the only one working this hard?

**1:30 am:** I completed the e-mail of data across the Pacific and can finally get back to work.

> On my way to the car, I experience fresh air for the first time since coming to work almost 20 hours ago. It is the best that I have felt all day.

**4:00 am:** My computer screen has put me into a daze, and I decide that it is time to go home. On my way to the car, I experience fresh air for the first time since coming to work almost 20 hours ago. It is the best that I have felt all day.

**4:30 am:** I get home and play my answering machine. A college friend called to tell me some news, but I doubt that he would appreciate me returning his call now. I sit down on the couch to look at my mail, and I fall asleep instantly.

### Friday

**7:00 am:** I wake up on the couch and realize that I have not even made it into bed. There is a lot of work to be done today so I get up, shower and leave for the office.

**8:00 am:** It seems as if I never left the office except for the fact that I am wearing a different suit than yesterday. I must begin to assemble the data for the X corporation organizational meeting on Monday. I feel that getting a start this morning will make the weekend's work easier. A timetable for the offering must be decided upon and approved by both the management of X corporation and our investment bankers.

**10:00 am:** After numerous phone calls, I have been able to retrieve the names of the investment bankers, lawyers, accountants and X corporation executives who will be working on the project. This data has been given to the word processing department, to be formatted for the book.

**11:00 am:** I receive the preliminary timetable and begin to assemble a detailed schedule of filing dates and meeting times. I continue to think about my acquisition project which I am currently unable to work on.

**11:30 am:** I begin listening to the 19 voice mail messages that I have received while I have been away from my desk this morning. The messages inform me of

additional work that must be completed. It is important to prioritize because the timing of each assignment's completion is critical. I have three documents that must be updated and faxed to a vice-president who is on the road. I also must update all the market information in a proposal, which was initially prepared for presentation last month, for a Wednesday meeting in New York.

**12:15 pm:** Starvation is beginning to hinder my productivity as it seems that I have missed breakfast again. I eat a sandwich, potato chips, Snapple and cookie at my desk. It is not the lunch of kings, but the feast satisfies me. I am on the phone during the entire meal, making plane reservations for the "red eye" to New York on Tuesday night.

> Starvation is beginning to hinder my productivity as it seems that I have missed breakfast again. I eat a sandwich, potato chips, Snapple and cookie at my desk. It is not the lunch of kings, but the feast satisfies me.

**3:00 pm:** I fax the last document and return to the job of preparing for Monday's organizational meeting at X corporation. I must read several documents to learn more about X corporation and exactly what they do.

**6:00 pm:** Word processing returns the documents I gave them, and there are only about 10 mistakes. This is good for them, but I often wonder if I would not be better off typing my own documents. I circle the mistakes and send it back. This process will be repeated approximately two more times before it is all correct.

**9:00 pm:** I receive a call from the vice president working on the X corporation offering. He just got off the phone with X corporation's CFO, and they want to reduce the time until pricing from five to three weeks. I must now revise all the schedules and filing dates that I prepared this morning.

**12:00 am:** I have forgotten about dinner and have finally returned to my evaluation of acquisition candidates. I work well into the early morning with few distractions except for the custodial staff.

### Saturday

**7:00 am:** As the sun comes up, I go home and decide to rest awhile. I eat a hearty breakfast, my first meal since Friday's lunch, and sleep from 8 am until 12 pm.

**12:30 pm:** I begin revising the proposal that we will be presenting in New York on Wednesday. I must change 10 pages of financial information and over half of it is not readily available through our database. It will take me a few hours to retrieve and enter the data.

**6:00 pm:** I think that it is time for dinner, but I don't know what happened to lunch. I order a feast from "*Waiters on Wheels*", including numerous appetizers and desserts. The firm gives me a $50 allowance for food if I work over six hours on Saturday or Sunday. Lately, it seems as if I have been relegated to ordering food for fun because we have been so busy.

**7:00 pm:** I continue working on the book for Monday's meeting, inserting the standard sections which only require the changing of names and dates. It is a mindless task, but there is nobody else to do it.

**12:00 am:** A draft of the book for Monday's meeting is ready. It must be reviewed several times before Monday morning in order to make sure that all errors have been eliminated.

**1:00 am:** I go home and go to bed. I must get some sleep because there is a big week ahead.

My alarm goes off and I am so tired that my eyes hurt when I open them. I feel even worse when I think about the coming week. I go for a jog and enjoy some fresh air for the first time in a couple of weeks. It has a soothing effect, but I have to ask myself if there aren't some things that I am missing while I spend all that time in the office.

**Sunday**

**8:00 am:** My alarm goes off and I am so tired that my eyes hurt when I open them. I feel even worse when I think about the coming week. I go for a jog and enjoy some fresh air for the first time in a couple of weeks. It has a soothing effect, but I have to ask myself if there aren't some things that I am missing while I spend all that time in the office.

**9:30 am:** I am back in the office preparing for tomorrow morning's meeting. I review an enormous amount of relevant material, including 10-Ks, 10-Qs, and their amended S-1 registration statement.

**12:00 pm:** The managing director in charge of our group calls and informs me that the analyst who has been assigned to the X corporation offering will be unable to work on the deal at all. He has just been staffed on something else that has just come up. I realize that I will now be responsible for every mundane detail on this deal; however, this is neither surprising nor unusual considering the workload currently being done by this understaffed office.

**2:00 pm:** I have the book sent by courier to the vice president's house so that he can review it for mistakes or any changes that he would like to make. I then paged our word processing assistant to come in as the material for the acquisition proposal needs to be typed up.

**5:00 pm:** I am still working with the word processor assistant. I am trying to explain my notes and sheets to him, but I just cannot seem to make him understand exactly what it is that I want.

**6:00 pm:** I finally feel that I can leave him alone for a while to type up a few sections of the proposal. I return to the documents for Wednesday's meeting in New York and continue to update the information.

**8:00 pm:** I have set aside one hour to go out to dinner with my girlfriend. I arrive fifteen minutes late to the sushi bar, and she is exasperated as usual. She says that we just pass through the night like two strangers, and that she does not want to live like this any longer.

**8:45 pm:** I was paged by the vice president. I call him, and he screams that the entire timetable is wrong. He says that it must be changed for tomorrow morning. Evidently, they changed their mind a second time and did not bother telling me. He says that he is faxing the revised information to the office now, and he wants me to return there and get to work ASAP. I get back to the table with the bad news. I cannot even get away for one hour without my pager going off. I devour a few pieces of sushi and rush back to the office. It is going to be another long night.

**2:30 am:** The revisions of the book are complete and 30 bound copies of the book are ready for the 8 am meeting. I load them up for the trip to X Corporation tomorrow morning.

## Monday

**5:45 am:** I must wake up to get ready for the drive to X Corporation in Alameda. I am required to leave prohibitively early just in case any unusual traffic should delay my trip.

**6:30 am:** I leave for Alameda.

**7:15 am:** I arrive at the offices of X Corporation. I go to the meeting room and check to make sure that everything is ready for the vice president to run the meeting.

**8:00 am:** People are trickling in, but it appears that the meeting will not start on time. Unfortunately, I did not have the luxury of coming in late.

**8:30 am:** The meeting begins. In attendance are representatives from three investment banks, one audit firm, two law firms, and the senior management of X Corporation. Even though our vice president runs the meeting, the management of X Corporation is clearly in charge. They are the customer, and the client.

**10:00 am:** As the discussion moves to the timeline of the offering, I am struggling to stay awake. I know the timeline inside and out. As a matter of fact, I know everything that we are going to cover in this meeting today. I am basically just a "suit." A person from the firm who is just there to make the client feel that there are a lot of people working on their deal. My participation in today's meeting will be minimal.

**10:30 am:** I duck out of the meeting to answer three pages and check my voice mail. Tuesday's meeting with the company looking to make an acquisition, D. Corporation, has changed their meeting from 1 pm to 9 am in San Jose. Once again, it appears that I will not get much sleep as I prepare for the proposal.

**12:00 pm:** We break for lunch, and I go sit in the car and sleep for 30 minutes. These 30 minutes feel like eight hours as I am totally exhausted.

**1:00 pm:** We reconvene and start preliminary due diligence. We will interview each member of the management team and take notes on their discussion of the company and its current situation.

**6:00 pm:** The due diligence session concludes and we decide to convene again on Thursday at the offices of X Corporation's law firm in Palo Alto.

**7:30 pm:** I make it back to the office after stopping on the way home for some dinner. It is now time to put the finishing touches on the proposals for tomorrow and Wednesday morning in New York.

**10:00 pm:** The managing director in charge of the D. Corporation relationship calls to discuss a few details about tomorrow's meeting. He tells me that I need to use my knowledge of the acquisition targets to assist him in the meeting because he will not have time to learn all of the information before then. I decide to review the book another time in an attempt to make myself even more prepared for tomorrow's meeting.

**4:00 am:** The revision has continued late into the evening, but I must make sure that everything is ready for tomorrow. I finally get to bed at 4:30 am.

## Tuesday

**7:45 am:** I have overslept, but I should still have enough time to make it to the meeting on time. I get up and get dressed.

**8:45 am:** I arrive at D. Corporation.

**9:00 am:** The meeting begins, and we begin to discuss the current climate for acquisitions. Next, we review potential acquisition targets. I am very involved in the discussion, and I often add information that I have learned in my research but that is not contained in the book. My contributions are well-received by both the managing director and the executives at D. Corporation. At that moment, it makes me feel as if all my hard work is worth it.

**12:15 pm:** We decide to continue our discussion over lunch. As we end the meeting after lunch, I feel as if the prospects for a deal are very good.

**2:30 pm:** I return to the office to prepare for my New York trip. We are leaving on the red-eye flight at 9:15 pm, but I still have to complete the analysis for the books. I also find that I have accumulated 27 voice-mail messages in the past day and a half. I realize that it will take me at least 30 minutes just to listen to all of them.

**3:00 pm:** As I am still listening to the messages, a principal comes in and asks me if I could do him a favor. He needs a couple of modifications to a model for a dinner meeting tonight. I am the only person in the office, and I oblige even though I really do not have any free time.

**6:00 pm:** I have finished the model and taken care of most of the messages. I have three and a half hours left to get the books finished, pack, and get to the airport. I enlist the assistance of an analyst, who has just returned from a meeting outside the office. She helps me complete the books for the trip.

**8:00 pm:** The books are double-checked because any errors found after we leave cannot be changed. I hope that everything is correct. If this business only allocated more time and resources to each job, we would not have such worries.

**9:30 pm:** I barely make the flight as I arrive when they are doing final boarding. I look forward to my five hours of sleep in my business class seat.

## Wednesday

**5:30 am (EDT):** We land in New York's JFK airport. We are taken by limousine to the Pierre Hotel to shower and dress for the morning meeting. While the other meeting participants sleep, I call to double-check our flight back to San Francisco and our limousine pickup.

**9:00 am:** The limousine picks us up for the meeting.

**9:30 am:** We arrive at the meeting. I feel rested as my five hours of sleep last night was my most all week. I will not have to worry about falling asleep in this meeting.

**12:00 pm:** The meeting is over, and we go to our company's Wall Street headquarters to pick up some faxes. The faxes will provide more than enough work for me to do on the flight home.

**2:00 pm:** We have lunch at the 21 Club. This is one of the perks of the job. After a couple of drinks and a huge lunch, I am ready for a nap on the flight home.

**3:30 pm:** Our flight leaves for San Francisco without us on it because we have taken too long at lunch.

**5:30 pm:** We make the next flight for San Francisco. Unfortunately, the two hours lost by missing the plane will be costly later in the evening. I will have to stay later than I had expected to prepare for an all day due diligence session on Thursday.

**9:00 pm (PDT):** We arrive in San Francisco, and I go straight to the office. I find 20 voice mail messages and a note asking me to come by N Corporation's

closing dinner if I have time. N Corporation is a good client and I go directly to the restaurant for the closing dinner.

**11:00 pm:** I must sift through what appears to be reams of paper to find the draft of the preliminary prospectus for tomorrow's due diligence session. I will be the only representative of the firm at the meeting so I must make sure that the prospectus is published in the correct style. I must also check for errors and potential liabilities contained in the document.

**2:00 am:** I am not sure what time or what day it is. I only know that I have not slept in a bed in 48 hours. I decide to go home because the due diligence session begins at 7:30 am in San Francisco which means I have to get up at 5:45 am.

I am not sure what time or what day it is. I only know that I have not slept in a bed in 48 hours. I decide to go home because the due diligence session begins at 7:30 am in San Francisco which means I have to get up at 5:45 am.

## MY CAREER GOALS

After my summer experience, I took some time to reflect upon my investment banking job and how it related to both my skill set and my career goals. I needed to decide if it was something that I wanted to pursue full-time when recruiting began in the fall. I came to the conclusion that while the work was exhausting, I really enjoyed it. I also found that I missed the exhilaration that came with the narrow deadlines and frequent travel. I have decided to pursue a career in investment banking and will be going to work for a major investment banking firm in their technology group in San Francisco.

When matching my skill set with those required for investment banking, I found a pretty good match. Investment banking is very project-oriented which suits me well because I become bored with mundane, repetitive jobs. I consider one of my greatest strengths to be my interpersonal skills, and they are a key factor in the success of investment bankers. Lastly, my natural abilities are very quantitative in nature and these are necessary skills, considering a large portion of the workload is financial analysis.

As for my career goals, I believe that investment banking may fulfill some of my short-term goals, but it will not be an industry in which I plan to work for my entire life. I am not prepared to make some of the sacrifices which investment bankers must make concerning their families and their enjoyment of life. I have no fear of working hard, but I am also unwilling to let life pass me by as I sit engulfed by my work. My true desire is to have a loving family and to be able to provide for all of their desires. I am not concerned about the monetary desires, but rather that I will always be there for them, something that too many investment bankers cannot be counted on to do.

## QUESTIONS FOR REFLECTION

1. What surprises you about this story?

2. What are the three biggest lessons that jump out at you from this account?

3. How would you chart Mr. Nelson's Balance Wheel for this week in his life?

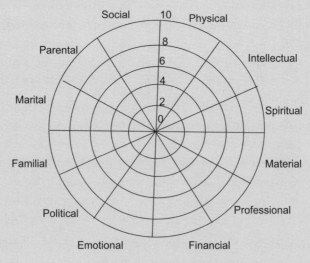

A Personal Developmental Balance Wheel.

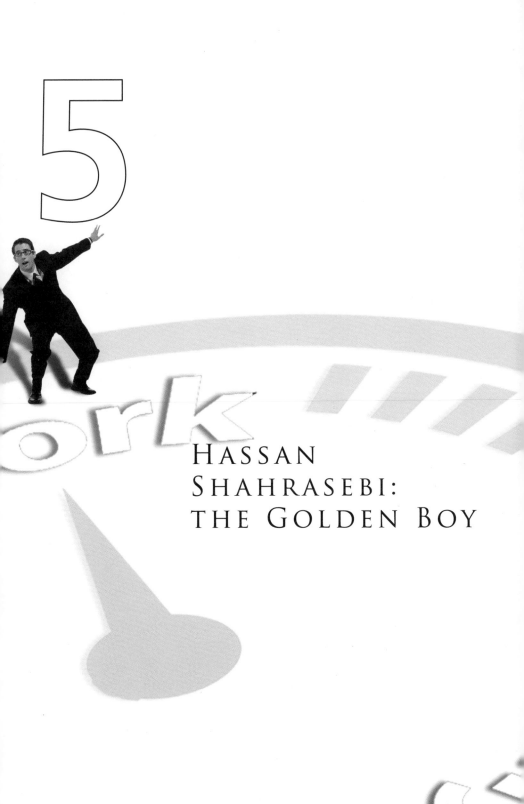

# 5

## HASSAN
## SHAHRASEBI:
## THE GOLDEN BOY

*"You go through life taking the path of least resistance.*

*We all do — all human beings and all of nature. It is important to know that. You may try to change the direction of your own flow in certain areas of your life — your eating habits, the way you work, the way you relate to others, the way you treat yourself, the attitudes you have about life. And you may even succeed for a time. But eventually you will find you return to your original behavior and attitudes. This is because your life is determined, insofar as it is a law of nature for you to take the path of least resistance."*

Robert Fritz, *The Path of Least Resistance, p. 4*

In early March of 1993 the executives at Iran Office Machines Center Company Ltd (IOMCo) were very busy. Office machines sales were at a peak before the end of the Iranian calendar year as government agencies rushed to spend the last of their remaining budgets. In addition, IOMCo's own fiscal year ended at the end of March which put the Accounting Department under extra pressure to close the books for the year. That particular day, however, was exceptionally frantic because the company's Chief Financial Officer, Hassan Shahrasebi, had had a serious car accident the previous night.

Around 9:30 pm, Hassan, as usual, had been the last one to leave the office building. He had said goodnight to the guard, entered his company car and started driving home. Passing over a highway bridge, Hassan had dozed off and the car had veered into the bridge's outside barrier at high velocity. The barriers had deflected the car which then rebounded for a second and a third impact. Immobilized with shock, Hassan had been dragged out of his car by passing motorists. Hassan was lucky that the car had not flipped off the bridge nor caught on fire. He escaped the incident with a few minor cuts and bruises even though the car was damaged beyond repair. This was Hassan's second accident in six months. The first had involved his wife and one year old son who had also escaped the disaster with a few cuts and bruises.

Despite the accident, Hassan had been the first one at work the next morning. He himself had informed the other executives about the previous night's incident. The Chairman, CEO and President of IOMCo had each spent time talking with Hassan that morning, expressing relief and concern at the same time — relief because he had escaped harm; concern because he was working himself too hard.

## IRAN OFFICE MACHINES CENTER CO. LTD.

Iran Office Machines Center Co. Ltd., a closely held family company established in 1964, was the oldest and largest office machines company in Iran. IOMCo represented in Iran exclusively a number of international manufacturers of office machines. Exhibit 1 provides the list of IOMCo's suppliers and the list of products marketed by IOMCo.

IOMCo imported, marketed, sold and serviced the office equipment of the companies it represented, selling directly to the government, using a network of approximately 750 dealers to distribute nationwide, and employing a direct sales force for its private customers. The company provided after-sales service through 120 service dealers and its own team of 125 technicians. Exhibit 2 shows IOMCo's installed machine population and service coverage channels. In all, the company employed 280 personnel and revenues from local operations reached a record $45.4 million in 1992.

IOMCo survived the Iranian revolution of 1978 and had maintained its leadership in Iran's turbulent environment since then by being innovative and flexible. For example, throughout the eight-year Iran/Iraq war when the import of non-essential products was restricted, IOMCo maintained its own critical flow of supplies and spare parts (especially for photocopiers) by using airline passengers as carriers from Dubai (in the United Arab Emirates). Since the process was costly, margins were low and the risk was high. Most competitors opted to cease operations altogether and a few limited their transactions to sporadic government orders only. The result was that IOMCo's SHARP brand copiers were the only operational copiers in Iran for eight years. Although IOMCo made no substantial profits during this period, it seized a leading market share in key products. When restrictions for imports were lifted in April of 1989, IOMCo had firmly established a 750-strong dealer network and developed a leading market share for nearly all its products. By 1993, IOMCo held an 85 percent share of the Iranian copier market, was more than triple the size of its closest competitor, and was the only company selling a complete line of office machines in Iran.

## HASSAN SHAHRASEBI

Hassan Shahrasebi was 37 years old, married and had a one year old son. He had joined IOMCo as assistant manager of accounting in 1980. After working

for three years, he had taken leave of absence for two years to earn a MBA in the United States at the University of Texas. Upon completion of his MBA, he returned directly to IOMCo where he had remained. His honesty, deep concern for the company and consistent hard work led to rapid promotions to his present post of Chief Financial Officer, the number four position after the President. The joint owners of the company — the founding Chairman and his brother the CEO — held Hassan in the highest esteem and considered him as one of the "central pillars" of the company. They privately referred to him as the "Golden Boy."

Hassan was responsible for all of IOMCo's financial activities. These included IOMCO's internal accounting, 750 dealer accounts, currency purchases, import administration, bank relationships, and all receivables and payables. His signature was required on every company check. He had six people reporting to him directly from the Accounting Department. Hassan also supervised the Warehousing and Shipping Departments with managers of each department reporting directly to him. In addition, he personally supervised the computerization of the accounting department by overseeing the design and implementation of the system by an outside software company. Hassan held a seat on the Board of Directors and worked closely with the Chairman, CEO and President in devising the growth and expansion strategies of IOMCo.

Hassan's work habits had become a legend in the company. He was always the first person at work, around 7:00 am, and the last one to leave, around 9:30 pm. He had refused to take a vacation in over three years and spent most weekends at the office. The Chairman, CEO and President had each asked him to take a vacation on numerous occasions but Hassan invariably refused to do so. There were always projects which needed his attention or tasks too delicate for others to handle.

**Hassan's work habits had become a legend in the company. He was always the first person at work, around 7:00 am, and the last one to leave, around 9:30 pm. He had refused to take a vacation in over three years and spent most weekends at the office.**

Hassan always had a number of important projects going on at the same time. In addition, he was a perfectionist. He had to work on a project until it was perfect.

The computerized accounting system was a case in point. In 1989 IOMCo decided to computerize its accounting system in order to maintain its speed and flexibility amidst its rapid growth. After reviewing existing software, Hassan chose a book-keeping package and decided to enhance it by developing a parallel information system with an outside software company. The information system was designed to record every sales transaction and maintain a current database on all dealer accounts and individual products. This was a formidable task considering that IOMCo distributed 600 different products through 750 dealers nationwide (excluding spare parts). The copier department alone ordered and distributed more than 70,000 items monthly. Spending many weekends and late nights, Hassan saw that the comprehensive computer system was operational within one year. He then continued refining it for the next three years, adding networking capabilities and countless other specifications.

The computerized information system became instrumental in the management's continuous speed and agility. The system itself, however, had become so complex that only Hassan and two programmers from the outside software company could maintain it; the software design had not been documented during its development. Some managers from the computer department expressed concern about the obsolescence of the underlying database engine used in the system but Hassan dismissed these concerns as unfounded. Incidents of software crashes and inaccurate information, however, had increased as IOMCo's operations continued to expand.

The information system also had become a crisis trigger for Hassan. If receivables were stretched or products turned over too slowly, Hassan would wage a battle cry against that particular evil and immediately warn other executives about the imminent dangers. Then, managers of the related department would be pressured continually to resolve the problem as soon as possible.

These crises became obsessions for Hassan. For example, when the calculator inventory reached the equivalent of seven months of sales one December, Hassan had declared that calculators had dramatically reduced the liquidity of the company and that their liquidation was a top priority. He had taken it upon himself to press the Product Manager of the Calculator Department to sell, sell, sell and not order anything more. The Product Manager obliged although he reported to the President and not to Hassan.

The other executives did not interfere with Hassan's crisis management style, but they were never as alarmed as he was. In that particular case, for example, calculators represented only about five percent of IOMCo's sales. The executives would joke that every time they asked Hassan how he was doing he would reply "These calculators, I don't know what to do with them! I dream about the damn things at night!"

Hassan always seemed to be facing a number of crises at once. During the calculator inventory buildup, he began to worry about low margins on computer printers. The fact that the Chairman of the company was responsible for the Computer Department did not stop Hassan from confronting him directly. He walked into the Chairman's office and asked angrily "Why don't you want to make money on printers? It's your company but you might as well just put the budget of printers in the bank and earn interest on it! Why bother paying salaries if you don't plan to make money?"

After calming Hassan down, the Chairman would explain that he was trying to penetrate the market preemptively and secure the best dealers before other competitors could do so. In addition, they were under the constraint of a minimum quantity contract with the manufacturers, etc. Eventually, Hassan would leave the room shaking his head saying "I don't know. It's your department, but I don't know ..." The Chairman knew that Hassan would be back again in a week but what could he say when someone showed so much concern and dedication towards the company? He would smile and shake his head thinking that Hassan was the only person in the whole company who raised his voice with him.

Despite Hassan's temper, everyone in the company liked him. The reason was his unconditional dedication to the company and his genuine concern for employees. Several months ago during a late night major delivery to the warehouse, one of the employees unloading the trucks had fainted. Hassan who was helping supervise the unloading that night, had rushed the employee to the hospital himself. By the time they reached the hospital, the employee had regained consciousness but Hassan insisted that he should stay at the hospital for the night. In addition, he was to be given a complete checkup the next day. The result of the checkup and the Doctor's recommendation were to be sent directly to Hassan and the company would bear all expenses. Later that night Hassan returned to the warehouse and personally filled in the position of the hospitalized employee. Actually, it wasn't uncommon to see Hassan help unload trucks on busy nights.

Hassan's dedication to the company even seemed to precede that of his family. About four months after his son was born, Hassan dropped by the office one morning to say that their refrigerator had broken and that he had to go buy a new one urgently. He said he would be back in the office as soon as he had the refrigerator delivered to his home. As he walked out of the office, he noticed a loose tile hanging above the fifth floor of the office building. He went back into the office and gave instructions that the tile had to be fixed immediately as it could break loose with the slightest wind and injure someone on the side walk. A manager volunteered to take care of it but Hassan insisted on making the arrangements himself. He called a contractor who then had to secure scaffolding in order to reach the damaged area. The repair took three days during which time Hassan oversaw everything while continuing his usual daily chores. After three days, Hassan himself joked that "I fixed the office building, but my wife and child are still without a refrigerator at home."

Over the last two years, Hassan had developed a number of unusual health problems. Despite his young age, he had high blood pressure, his skin flared up occasionally with rashes, and he complained about runny noses, headaches and backaches. In the beginning, Hassan associated these problems with the two packets of cigarettes he smoked daily. After a few attempts, though, he managed to quit smoking completely and hadn't smoked for over a year. After quitting, he put on some weight but claimed that generally he felt much better. However, although the headaches had diminished, he still had high blood pressure, and most of the other symptoms remained. Hassan believed that the remaining symptoms were a result of his sporadic eating habits. He said he was now trying to reduce the fat in his diet.

Contrary to Hassan, the Chairman and President believed that some of Hassan's health problems were due to excessive work. They insisted that he should take vacations and at one point banned him from coming to the office on weekends. Hassan had not cooperated with any of the above attempts, however, and continued his work behavior. The Chairman had even threatened to reduce Hassan's lucrative bonuses if he didn't take a vacation but never followed through on this as it seemed counter intuitive to reduce someone's bonuses for doing exceptional work. Everyone had given up changing Hassan — until that morning after the accident.

## Next Steps

The thought of losing Hassan shocked the executives. Hassan himself was very perturbed about the incident. After some earnest discussions during the day, Hassan had agreed, for the first time, to take a two-week vacation with his wife and son as soon as he had completed some pending projects. He also agreed to leave the office at the latest by 8:00 pm and stay away from work on weekends.

That afternoon, the Chairman, CEO and President talked amongst themselves after they sent Hassan home. The general consensus was that the accident had been a blessing in disguise for it had convinced Hassan to work less and relax a bit. That evening, the executives went home relieved that all was well and everything would be back to normal.

## EXHIBIT 1
## HASSAN SHAHRASEBI THE GOLDEN BOY

**IOMCo's Exclusive Agencies / Distributorships for The Iranian Market.**

**SHARP CORPORATION** — Osaka, Japan: Since 1964.

* Photocopy Machines.

* Calculators.

* Cash Registers.

* Facsimile Machines.

* Bank Teller Machines (Government orders only).

**GLORY CO. LTD.** — Osaka, Japan: Since 1986.

* Banking and Cash Handling Equipment (Government orders only).

**SEIKO EPSON CORPORATION** — Tokyo, Japan: Since 1991.

* Epson brand of computer printers.

**OLIVETTI S.P.A.** — Ivrea, Italy: Since 1991.

* Personal Computers.

* Notebook Computers.

* Banking Systems.

* Electronic Typewriters.

**MITSUBISHI PENCIL CO.** — Tokyo, Japan: Since 1980.

* Writing Instruments.

---

## EXHIBIT 2
## HASSAN SHAHRASEBI THE GOLDEN BOY

### IOMCo's Installed Machine Population and Service Coverage Channels

| PRODUCT | Installation 1985–1993 | IOMCo-Serviced | Dealer-Serviced |
|---|---|---|---|
| Copiers | 50,000 + | 40% | 60% |
| Facsimiles | 11,600 | 60% | 40% |
| Printing Calculators | 210,000 | 35% | 65% |
| Other Calculators | 2,400,000 | 30% | 70% |
| Cash Registers | 3,000 | 70% | 30% |
| Electronic Typewriters | 1,700 | 0% | 100% |
| Bank Teller Terminals | 8,300 | 100% | 0% |
| Bank Note Counters | 5,800 | 100% | 0% |
| Personal Computers | 17,000 | 90% | 10% |
| Notebook Computers | 1,900 | 90% | 10% |
| Printers | 29,000 | 95% | 5% |

---

## QUESTIONS FOR REFLECTION

1. Why does Hassan behave the way he does?

2. What underlying assumptions seem to drive Hassan's behavior?

3. How does an "achievement orientation" or a "goal orientation" affect one's overall lifestyle?

4. How does your lifestyle compare with Hassan's? What changes, if any, would you like to make in your lifestyle?

## EPILOGUE

Given the global political situation, we don't have an epilogue for the Hassan Shahrasebi case. What do you imagine the epilogue would look like? What would have to happen for Hassan to re-examine his life structure and priorities? If you were his boss, what action would you take?

We might speculate that Hassan had learned early in life that approval and affection were dependent on his performance and that this contributed to his goal orientation and workaholism. He may also have a genetic/bio-chemical slight to moderate tendency toward obsessiveness. His desire to be an indispensible asset to the company (by not documenting his work) may also be based on his experience with conditional approval early in life. The upside to conditional approval ("I love you more when you achieve") is a strong achievement orientation. The downside is exhibited in Hassan's story as his semi-or sub-conscious desire to be needed and approved of is dominating all aspects of his life. The real question is, "what can we learn from Hassan's story that might help us manage our lives?

# 6

## TETSUNDO IWAKUNI: THE LIFE AND CAREER OF A JAPANESE EXECUTIVE

In 1993, a national survey revealed that Tetsundo Iwakuni,[1,a] mayor of Izumo City, was the most popular of Japan's 656 mayors. Based on his strong, positive, national image, as well as his brief but remarkable term as mayor, by the spring of 1995 Iwakuni was running for the national Diet seat from Setagaya. His decision to do so testified to his varied and interesting career as a domestic busi-

nessman, an international investment banker, and a local politician with national prominence. His story sheds light on the nature of Japanese leadership and the challenges it faces today.

## CHILDHOOD

Iwakuni's story begins on the southern coast of Honshu in the Kansai Region. Iwakuni was born in Osaka in July 1936. In December 1943, in the midst of World War II, Iwakuni's father passed away: Iwakuni was only seven years old. In later years, Iwakuni would remember his father as a generous man who had taken him on business trips and to baseball games. After Iwakuni's father passed away, Iwakuni's mother determined to escape the imminent threat of the Allied bombing of Osaka by taking Iwakuni and his younger sister westward across the central mountain range to her ancestral home in Izumo City, Shimane Prefecture.

Iwakuni remained in Izumo for the duration of World War II. He remembered the day the war ended. He saw soldiers standing in a circle and crying while an officer explained something that Iwakuni could not hear. He knew that something disastrous had happened, since soldiers never cried. When he heard the emperor announce on the radio that Japan had been defeated, however, he understood.

After the war, the young Iwakuni worked hard helping his mother. He cultivated land for growing tomatoes, cucumbers, squash, and other vegetables. By the time he was in the fifth grade, he was working part-time delivering newspapers and milk. Although it was unusual for a boy his age to work, he did not feel

[1] Japanese vowels are all pronounced the same: a = ah, I = ee, u = oo, e = eh, and o = oh. Hence, Mr. Iwakuni's name is pronounced, tets-oon-doh ee-wah-koo-nee. Likewise, Shimane = shee-mahn-eh and Izumo = ee-zoo-moh.
[a] Please view video clips of interviews at http://store.darden.virginia.edu/business-case-study/japanese-leadership-the-case-of-tetsundo-iwakuni.

burdened. His father's early death meant that his role, as the oldest son, was to become the leader of the family. Although he sometimes cried himself to sleep recalling his father, he accepted his obligation to support his mother and to take care of his younger sibling.

Even though Japanese people, especially in the countryside, tended to keep a distance from strangers or newcomers, Iwakuni made friends with ease. He had a knack for drawing and enjoyed teaching the other kids to play baseball. He spent all his spare time playing baseball. "I played baseball all the time probably because it made me feel closer to my father and would remind me of my days with him," he recalled. "I had a dream to be a teacher like my father. I was also interested in becoming a journalist or politician. Inspiring people by pen or organizing society through politics was attractive to me."

Iwakuni worked hard in school and after taking the competitive Japanese entrance exam was admitted to the best high school in Izumo. He commuted two hours each way to and from school. His schedule meant that he had to give up baseball, but he continued working part-time. He also studied diligently, finishing the advanced curriculum a year early. No one was surprised when he passed the entrance exam for Tokyo University, the best university in Japan. Armed with four scholarships, Iwakuni left Izumo for Tokyo.

## COLLEGE LIFE

Tokyo University offered a powerful experience for the country boy from Shimane. If Japanese universities were famous for stiff entrance examinations, they were also notorious for lax academic discipline among admitted students. As a freshman, Iwakuni fell into this pattern and did little but play baseball. He skipped all his German classes for two years until he realized that the law program he intended to enter in his junior year required German. He petitioned the school administration to allow him to take all the required German tests for the two-year curriculum. Fortunately, the administration authorized him to do so and set the test date for a week later. "I studied like a madman all day long for a week. It was quite fortunate that I passed all the tests. Naturally, I forgot everything I had learned within a week," he later recalled.[2]

---

[2] Tetsundo Iwakuni, *When a Man Makes a Decision*, PHP laboratory, Tokyo Japan, October 1990, pp. 136–139.

Iwakuni's desire to become a teacher had diminished by the time he was ready to graduate and choose a career. He considered taking the public service exam and entering one of the Ministries of the national government. He explained:

*"I could have taken the exam to become a public servant, but to take the exam, I would have had to stay in Tokyo for the summer. However, I longed to return to Shimane to see my family. It was a family tradition to have a summer get-together, and my mother usually prepared a big feast for us. I could not resist this family tradition and opted not to take the exam."*[3]

He had also considered becoming a journalist. But after speaking with an alumnus of Tokyo University who had become an executive of Nikko Securities, Iwakuni decided to enter the world of finance.

Right after graduation, Iwakuni married a classmate from Izumo High School. "Initially, ours was not a passionate love; we were more like high school buddies. In fact, we did not even date while in high school. Since Ginko also went to college in Tokyo, we started to get together and gradually fell in love. It was more like a natural process that we got married," he explained. Iwakuni noted that he expected that his career would occupy most of his time and there would not be any chance to build and maintain a relationship with Ginko if he had not married her at that time. He commented, "I remember that I told her a few conditions for our marriage which were very old-fashioned ideas. As I expected, I devoted myself to my work and often did not make it back home. I was probably not a good husband at that time."[4]

## CAREER AT NIKKO SECURITIES

Early in his career at Nikko, Iwakuni was asked to go to New York. Even though he could not speak English, his boss's considerable support and encouragement convinced him to take the assignment, and he and his wife moved to New York. For a while, he was a little disoriented at his new office; as much as possible, he avoided speaking English. When the telephone rang, he hoped someone else would take the call. Eventually, however, he saw that people spoke English with pride even if they were not fluent. He realized people spoke Spanish-English,

[3] Ibid. 143–144.
[4] Ibid. 144–148.

French-English, and Italian-English, so he might as well speak Japanese-English. This realization helped Iwakuni to learn English.

Iwakuni became addicted to the dynamic business activities in New York and, later, in Europe and worked harder and harder. He became an acting branch manager in London and then played an important role in opening a new branch office in Paris. He successfully lobbied for a building in a prime location in Paris and then persuaded Nikko's president to invest in it. That building eventually became the standard for Japanese security companies in Paris, since other Japanese security firms followed Nikko's lead and established offices nearby. Soon, Iwakuni became branch manager of the Paris office. His career in Europe was also impressive. After he had created innovative financial products, including a tax-free small-sum savings system and bond-investment trusts in Tokyo, he successfully introduced a completely new convertible bond with options in the Middle East market.

Ginko was a very supportive wife. She followed Tetsundo wherever his career led. They had two daughters, Mari and Eri, both of whom did their schooling in London and Paris. In addition to learning English and French, the children had to master their native Japanese, something difficult to do while not living in Japan. Whenever Iwakuni visited the head office in Japan, he brought back video tapes of popular TV programs to help the girls in their Japanese studies. Because he'd lost his father early in life, Iwakuni paid as much attention to his family as he could. Although his weekdays were full until late with business, he spent every weekend with his family. He often arranged for them to travel together around Europe.

Then, quite unexpectedly, in 1977 Iwakuni received an order to return to Japan to manage the Ginza Branch in downtown Tokyo. By that time, both 15-year-old Mari and 13-year-old Eri had their own dreams of attending Cambridge University and Oxford University respectively to pursue their studies, and Iwakuni worried about disrupting their international experience. He was also concerned about the fact that Japan's educational system was less than accommodating for students who had been educated abroad. He saw four available options. First, he could go back to Japan alone. Second, the whole family could go back to Japan and Mari and Eri could attend the American School there. Third, the whole family would go back to Japan and Mari and Eri would attend Japanese school there. Fourth, he could resign from Nikko Securities and stay in London.

His family meant too much for Iwakuni to choose the first option. Taking the second and third options would put Mari's and Eri's dreams at risk. Iwakuni seriously considered the fourth option. Resigning from Nikko Securities, however, could be a fatal career choice. In Japan, where life-time employment was given and expected, the strong conflict between company loyalty and family ties was usually resolved in favor of the company. Iwakuni had never imagined the possibility of resigning from Nikko Securities when he took their original offer. He was wracked by the implications of the decision facing him and realized that no matter which option he chose it would affect his career and the lives of his children in major ways. He recalled this time as one of most stressful periods in his life.

Iwakuni chose the fourth option. He resigned from Nikko Securities and stayed in London, even though he had no idea whether or not he could find another job.

Subsequently, however, rumors began to circulate that Iwakuni had left Nikko Securities not to support his daughters' education but to further his personal career in Europe. There was also speculation that Iwakuni had regarded the assignment to the Ginza Branch office in Tokyo as a downgrade. In his book, Iwakuni described this episode:

*"I understood the company's concern about my career development. They realized my lack of experience in Japan would hurt my career as I climbed the ladder at Nikko Securities. The Ginza branch office had a good reputation and solid customers and could provide a great opportunity for me to learn the Japanese market. I really appreciated their consideration."*

To quell speculation that he had left Nikko for personal gain and not because of family obligations, Iwakuni hesitated before actively undertaking a job search. He eventually received an offer from the investment bank Morgan Stanley.

## INTERNATIONAL CAREER

Ironically, Morgan Stanley soon required Iwakuni to return to Japan. Ginko and Tetsundo went back to Japan and left their daughters in Britain to continue their education. Whenever Mari and Eri visited them in Japan, Ginko and Tetsundo would meet them at the airport. On the way to the airport, Tetsundo's heart would dance thinking about Mari and Eri: How tall had they grown? How beautiful had they become? On the other hand, when he and his wife would see Mari and Eri off at the airport for the return trip to England, Tetsundo would feel his heart sink in despair.

One day, while driving back from the airport, Tetsundo asked Ginko, "Shall we go back to New York so that we could live together as before?" Eager to reunite his family, in 1984, Iwakuni left Morgan Stanley and joined Merrill Lynch in New York. He soon became the chairperson and president of Merrill Lynch Japan. In 1987, Iwakuni became the first Japanese Senior Vice President of Merrill Lynch Capital Markets (the parent company of Merrill Lynch Japan).

As a new international leader, Iwakuni was the subject of many journalistic inquiries. He repeatedly explained his career and responsibilities during many interviews. He was also often asked to discuss racial issues. He recalled one incident at a train station when a stranger accosted him and accused Japanese soldiers of cruelty during World War II. Iwakuni tried to explain the Japanese side of the situation, but the gentleman remained angry. Iwakuni asked, "What do you think about Germany, then?" "It's OK because they are Christian," replied the man. The incident left Iwakuni with a sense of the deep underlying racial distance still lying between the East and the West.[5]

Many Japanese people looked up to Iwakuni as one of only a handful of Japanese who had become truly international businessmen. Iwakuni, too, felt the significance of his rare accomplishment. He once said to an interviewer, "Sometimes in this office, viewing the scenery of Manhattan, I feel personal pride for achieving this position as an internationalist. Then I just bubble up with Enka, the popular music of my generation." The interviewer closed the article by noting, "It could be his being a Japanese country potato that made him [so successful as] an international business man."[6]

In September of 1988, Iwakuni received a phone call from an influential friend in Japan who asked him to run for mayor of his home town, Izumo City. After that, the number of telephone calls increased each day. (For some of the people of Izumo, it was their first experience making an international telephone call.)

[5] Minoru Sato, *President*, Tokyo, Japan, June 1987, pp. 292–305.
[6] Ibid, pp. 292–305.

Iwakuni received many enthusiastic calls asking him to become the mayor; a few voiced opposition to the idea. Those against the idea said that becoming the mayor of Izumo was too small a task for Iwakuni and if he wanted to enter politics, he should consider becoming a Diet member.

Iwakuni was overwhelmed by the political passion of the people in Izumo. He knew that becoming mayor would mean that he would have to return to Japan and live there. Mari and Eri were attending Stanford University and Harvard University respectively, and the family would again be separated. Iwakuni again faced a tough decision. Sensing his frustration, his wife reminded him that they could come back to New York again someday, but Iwakuni knew that despite these kind words, they would probably never return to New York if they left. Nevertheless, after much thought, he decided to run for mayor of Izumo.

## MAYORAL ELECTION

Some people said that Iwakuni's bid for the mayorship in Izumo would merely prove to be a short-term stepping stone to the Japanese Diet. Iwakuni, however, viewed the mayorship as a four-year commitment — an opportunity to satisfy his public service calling — and so did not look beyond the immediate term.

Iwakuni did not satisfy any of the four generally accepted tacit requirements for the mayor's job. The mayor in Izumo was supposed to be a person who had been born in Izumo, had grown up in Izumo, had been living in Izumo, and intended to live in Izumo afterward as well. Iwakuni's intention to enter the race was a new experience both for himself and for the people of Izumo.

At the outset, Iwakuni identified some conditions on which he wanted to conduct his campaign. First, he wanted to win the mayoral position in an open and fair election. In the countryside, it was not unusual to perform "spade work" prior to an election and effectively appoint a mayor by discouraging other candidates to run. Secondly, he demanded that he would not be limited only to LDP's[7] policy recommendations. He wanted to receive recommendations from all other parties. Finally and most importantly, he made it clear that he would run his campaign in his own way.

Iwakuni won the Izumo City mayoral election on March 26, 1989.

---

[7] LDP stands for Liberal Democrat Party, the dominant political force in Japan following World War II; it was Iwakuni's supporting party at the time.

## MAYOR IWAKUNI

By all accounts, Iwakuni's service as mayor of Izumo was remarkable. He introduced a number of practices that re-energized and transformed municipal governments not only in Izumo but by example in numerous other cities as well. He had an unorthodox style, creative ideas, and a curious tendency to break precedents while still maintaining a strong traditional belief in the Japanese people. Personally, he was rather shy, not given to emotional outbursts, and projected a professional but reserved presence both on and off camera. His creative thinking, however, was evident from his first day on the job.

As soon as Iwakuni had won the election, his staff began planning the traditional first day ceremony, which was always held at nine-thirty or ten o'clock in the morning of the first business day that the new administration took office. Iwakuni, however, decided to have the ceremony between seven fifty and eight twenty am, so that city office staff could start service at their regular hour of eight thirty am. He felt that the municipal office should be considered one of the biggest and best service industries in Japan and he didn't want to inconvenience the citizens with a celebration in the middle of regular service hours.

After the celebration, on his first day in office, Iwakuni outlined many of his plans for the city. He notified his staff that he would reorganize the whole organizational structure within two years in order to make it more responsive to citizen needs. This plan was a major undertaking since Iwakuni would have to learn the existing system and also give the municipal workers the opportunity to review their own practices.

He also declared that in order to minimize exposure to bribery attempts, senior officers, including himself, should resist attending wedding ceremonies, funerals, and other unofficial receptions. Iwakuni wanted to wipe away the unfair custom of using personal influence to find a government job.

He also outlined plans to improve the quality of service to the citizens. To many city employees, who were used to doing just the minimum needed to get by, these changes were considered overwhelming. Eventually, his policies designed to reduce bureaucratic overheads and improve service came to be known as "Small Office, Big Service." He felt that this concept was an easier one for citizens to understand than the more technical terms used in the newspapers, like *gyousei kaikaku*, "administrative reform."

Iwakuni had three immediate goals: improving citizen orientation, increasing efficiency, and maintaining commitment to deadlines. He felt that the city government should be the model of high quality service and began applying business procedures and processes in city hall. Iwakuni claimed that nobody at the municipal office should use the previously common expression, "We are giving it some thought," which often ended up meaning, "We are not going to do this." He permitted only two answers to a citizen's request: either "We will answer by this date," or "We cannot do it." This policy put a large amount of pressure on the workers who were used to the more leisurely pace of the traditional bureaucracy.

As a part of this quality-improvement program, Iwakuni also launched a "manpower dispatching system" that borrowed personnel from large companies such as Mitsubishi Chemical and Yamaha Motors for short periods and employed them in city hall. These short-term employees set examples for and motivated municipal office workers.

As a part of his citizen focus, in May 1989 Iwakuni initiated a plan to develop a high-tech social-service card system. The card would use an integrated circuit chip that would contain all necessary social-service information. For example, the card would include administration, benefit, and health information that would ensure swift medical treatment in case of an emergency. Iwakuni planned to target the citizen ID card first to senior citizens and then to all Izumo citizens.

One of Iwakuni's most shocking proposals had to do with making municipal services available during non-business hours. Most Japanese work Monday through Friday and half-days on Saturday. Since the city hall was open the same hours, it was difficult for working citizens to conduct their municipal business. People who wanted to obtain municipal documents or handle other city business had to coordinate their schedules to go down to the municipal office on weekdays. Iwakuni felt that this was tremendously inconvenient, especially given the increasing numbers of working

His proposal to open branch offices of the city office building in shopping malls during weekends stunned people in Izumo City and earned nationwide attention.

women. His proposal to open branch offices of the city office building in shopping malls during weekends stunned people in Izumo City and earned nationwide attention.

Of course, there were many complaints from municipal office workers at the beginning of this new procedure because they did not want to work on weekends. Iwakuni's plan to alleviate employee resistance turned out to be not only acceptable to his staff but innovative. He established several groups of five people. Each group was assigned just one Saturday and one Sunday a year at the weekend service center. In the end, his idea to locate the desk in shopping centers was welcomed by everybody — citizens and employees alike — in Izumo.

Iwakuni also had a strong belief that the Japanese people had a close connection to nature and its resources. For example, in contrast with Chinese architecture, Japanese architecture was simple and used very little ornamentation and paint. Out of respect for nature, artists would intentionally leave a flaw in their work to show their regard for the original that they were imitating. In addition, the national religion, Shinto, taught that the gods, *kami*, lived in various places and dens of nature. Building on this theme, Iwakuni announced plans to rebuild the public schools out of wood and to construct an all-wood, all-weather domed sports arena.

Many thought these ideas odd. At the time, most schools in Japan were two- and three-storey concrete structures with external hallways overlooking all-dirt playing fields. The typical school design was reminiscent of the thousands of modern, concrete blockhouse *danchi* or apartment buildings throughout the country. Iwakuni, however, believed that Japanese culture was based on paper and wood and that these features were reflected in traditional architecture and construction materials. He noted elements like *washi* paper, *shoji* doors, *fusuma* paper room dividers, post and beam construction, *kotatsu* and other features of premodern Japanese houses. Iwakuni maintained that the concrete blockhouse construction of the "modern" schools desensitized students to their rich national culture and inured them to the fine arts. He wanted the citizens and students of Izumo to be encouraged rather than alienated by their surroundings. He instituted regulations that all new school buildings were to be designed and built with a much larger wood content than before.

# I W A K U N I

Iwakuni's love of natural materials and his belief that the Japanese people had a close association with trees and wood extended to his concern for the environment in general. He established a "tree doctor certificate" and a tree service so that anybody could inform the municipal office of a sick or dying public or private tree. He gave licenses to six "tree doctors" and charged them with keeping the district's trees healthy. The idea took root, so to speak, and gained rapidly in popularity. Other municipalities began calling to find out about the program, and the national news media picked up the story and made it a national public interest story. Even Iwakuni was surprised at the number of inquiries received from all over Japan. It soon got the attention of the Ministry of Agriculture and Forestry and became a national project.

Based on his living experience in Paris, London, New York, and Tokyo, Iwakuni was also concerned with the problem of waste disposal. Several talks with women's groups resulted in a new measure for garbage treatment in Izumo. In order to decrease the amount of garbage the citizens of Izumo produced, the municipal office decided to adopt a fee system. Each January, the municipal office provided one hundred garbage bags to every household. If those bags were not enough, households could purchase additional bags. By the same token, the city would re-purchase leftover bags at the same price. It was mandatory to use these specially designed bags and to write the household name on them. Though the name requirement was controversial at first, after just six months, 80 percent of Izumo citizens approved of the policy.[8]

Iwakuni participated in community group meetings as much as possible. He found that women's study groups and organizations were tremendously innovative and often developed interesting ideas. Since Iwakuni was actively involved in the women's participation movement, whenever he could he worked with women's groups instead of groups consisting of mainly men. He even went as far as discriminating against men in some ways so that he could have more time to exchange ideas with women. He wrote in his weekly magazine article, "Women tend to be more verbal than men. They constantly communicate with their children or mothers . . . They are more responsive as well. . . . Women are the majority, too. Fifty-two percent of Izumo citizens are women and 53 percent of the eligible voters are women as well . . . " He also gave higher-level positions to women in the municipal office.

[8] Saburo Nagao, *Friday*, Tokyo, Japan, pp. 48–51.

Iwakuni also tried to have close contact with children. He visited many elementary schools and high schools to encourage the children to think about Izumo City's future. He would explain things as plainly as possible so that the children could understand. In his book he described their enthusiasm:

*"They listen to my stories with their eyes wide, openly showing their curiosity about what is happening in their city. Often, they would write a letter to me after the lecture. Even though their letters are not that sophisticated and their writings were somewhat hard to read, reading their letters is one of my favorite activities."*[9]

By July of 1990, most of Iwakuni's plans were in full swing. Many of his programs had multiple purposes: to build on Japanese culture and cultural values, to teach, and to benefit the citizenry. For example, he promoted a national event, a 42.195 kilometer foot-race, in Izumo. He called the race "Izumo Kamiden" (the "god marathon") to invoke the ancient myth and held it in October, the month when legend held that the gods congregated in Izumo. The race enabled people to remember their national heritage, to learn more about Japanese culture and Izumo, and also to undertake a healthy exercise program.

Another manifestation of Iwakuni's appreciation for Japanese culture was his instruction to limit the number of English-based terms used in public office. Japanese borrowed many foreign terms and even had a script, *katakana*, set aside just for foreign terms. Iwakuni set the example and invited others to avoid using these *gairaigo*, or foreign terms, as another means to build national pride. Paradoxically, Iwakuni also believed that rural Japanese cities should know more about world affairs.

Rural cities in Japan like Izumo tended to have a primarily domestic orientation and were generally ignorant of international affairs. This was, in many respects, a holdover from the isolationist policies of the Tokugawa Government that had kept Japan separated from the rest of the world for 300 years. Thus, many rural Japanese were unaware and distrustful of foreign affairs and people and customs. But Iwakuni, because of his experience, saw the importance of introducing world events to his district. He felt that the lack of international exposure in the

[9] Tetsundo Iwakuni, "Three promises II," *Yomiuri Newspaper*, (July 14, 1993), pp. 239–243.

countryside accelerated the movement of young, ambitious people to Tokyo, a phenomenon that had been encouraged by the national government since the Second World War and which had deprived the outlying prefectures of youthful talent. To change this myopic focus, Iwakuni energetically promoted the existing "Sister City" program with Santa Clara, California.

He also changed the official calendar from the traditional Japanese calendar (which counted the years of each emperor's reign) to the Western calendar. Izumo was the only municipality in Japan to do this. He then organized a goodwill trip to China. Iwakuni found it fascinating that housewives were very open-minded about this trip and enthusiastically attended in part based on their respect for him, saying, "There was nothing to worry about because Mayor Iwakuni is here with us."

Education was one of Iwakuni's most important community platforms. Iwakuni launched a plan to establish a women's junior college in the Izumo region.[10] Iwakuni was also concerned about the traditional Japanese educational system. Students tended not to learn such subjects as world history because they knew these subjects did not have much significance in the national college entrance exams. At the same time, the world was becoming smaller and smaller, and there was an increasing need to understand global affairs. Iwakuni believed that learning another country's history was the first step in understanding its culture and spirit. To give credence to his ideas, Iwakuni declared that anybody who did not study world history in school would not be eligible to become a municipal officer in Izumo.

## REACTIONS

Most of the reactions to Iwakuni's innovations in Izumo were positive. Not only did local citizens applaud his efforts, but news reporters and municipal officials from other cities constantly contacted him for more information on his new approaches. Not all of the reactions were positive, however. One journalist who attended a meeting at the Izumo municipal office in September 1990 wrote the following critique:

*"Thirty-four workers resigned from the office within a year. ... Izumo City's budget was increasing. ... In his first year as mayor, the budget was*

---

[10] The college was completed in March, 1995.

*$219 million; a 13.1 percent increased from the previous year's budget.*
*This year's budget reached $251 million; a 14.7 percent increase from the*
*previous year's budget ... "*[11]

Iwakuni's popularity grew quickly throughout Japan. In his first year, he lectured over 150 times around the nation. He was a frequent guest on TV and radio programs. In March of 1991, Izumo City was given the "Marketing Excellence" award by Japan's *Noritsu Kyokai* as one of the best service organizations among prestigious electronics, automobile, and cosmetic companies. It was the first and only time a governmental agency had received the award.

By April 1991, most of Iwakuni's projects were reaching fruition. The IC social-service card system had been introduced and was the first of its kind in the nation. The Izumo Cultural Museum was established with the mandate of passing on Japan's precious traditions to future generations. Plans for a senior citizens' exercise facility were well under way. In 1992, the Izumo all-weather athletic dome was completed. It was the world's biggest wooden dome, reaching 48 meters high and equalling the legendary height of the original Izumo shrine. The dome, which was designed to glow at night when lit from the inside, received an award for the beauty of its lighting. To celebrate the city's growth and innovation, the Prince of Japan even paid a goodwill visit.

In the elections of March of 1993, Iwakuni garnered 87 percent of the vote and was re-elected Izumo City's mayor. The vote clearly demonstrated that the people of Izumo approved of Iwakuni's policies. During this time a survey conducted by a popular magazine revealed that Iwakuni was regarded as one of the top eight people likely to become Japan's Prime Minister in the 21st century.[12]

Iwakuni's political ideas concerning Japan at the national level were well-recognized; they became even better known when his co-author, Morihiro Hosokawa, became the first non-LDP Prime Minister in 36 years. When Hosokawa was governor of Kumamoto Prefecture, Iwakuni and he had written a book, *Hina-no-ronri*, outlining their views on national policy. In their book, Iwakuni and Hosokawa discussed what they considered to be government misconduct; they were particularly concerned about the central government's heavy-handed

[11] Kazuko Takai, *Seiron* (September 1990), pp.172–179.
[12] Shuichi Kondo, *Weekly Post,* (May 1993), pp.62–63.

control over local municipal offices. They claimed that projects with strictly local impact were severely mired in central government red tape.

Iwakuni was widely recognized as one of the main advocates of decentralization. At the 10th Congress of Secretaries in Asia, he remarked:

> *"In the postwar period, Japan accomplished remarkable economic growth by centralizing all of our economic and political control in Tokyo. We, the local governments, now advocate decentralization. We need more autonomy in terms of authorization for decision-making in our respective cities and towns, rather than having to always rely on Tokyo. Tokyo is not Japan."*

## NEXT STEPS

Recounting the successes of his five years of service, Iwakuni noted, "I have not approved any plans to build schools based on concrete construction. The tree doctor system, adopted in 1989 in Izumo, was extended to a national program in 1991."

In 1994, Izumo City was chosen as the best city in Japan for the second year in a row. The "best city" award was based on 15 criteria including security and convenience. Iwakuni took pride in saying that the award was won by combining Izumo's natural resources with the efforts and contributions of the municipal office's staff and leadership. Moreover, Iwakuni was named the most popular mayor in Japan.

In 1994, Iwakuni wrote another book, *Rin Toshite Nihon*, about the reforms that he thought were necessary to move Japan into the 21st century. The list of some 70 recommendations that he put forth in the book are shown in Exhibit 1.

Meanwhile, in Izumo, Iwakuni announced that he would not run in the next mayoral election. He believed that nobody should be in public office for more than 10 years because

**He believed that nobody should be in public office for more than 10 years because 10 years should be more than enough time to achieve whatever one set out to accomplish.**

10 years should be more than enough time to achieve whatever one set out to accomplish. Iwakuni stated that he was satisfied with his service and believed that all the projects he had planned had been realized.

Shortly thereafter, Iwakuni declared himself a candidate for the office of Mayor of Tokyo. The mayor of Tokyo enjoyed a large public forum, influence among the vast majority of the country's business leaders, and close connections with the national government. Iwakuni thought this might be the appropriate next step in his endeavors to reform Japanese institutions. Thus far, Iwakuni's career had been a series of surprising, major changes, and if he were able to win the mayor's post in Tokyo, this pattern would continue. In the spring of 1995, Iwakuni established his residence in Tokyo and began an intense one-month campaign.

As it turned out, a television comedian won the office from among a dense field of candidates. A similar result in Osaka, where another comedian won the mayor's job, was taken by most observers as a statement of how little respect and trust Japanese had for their established political community. Scandals relating to bribery, pay backs, indecision during the Gulf War, and other events had undermined the public trust. Iwakuni was heartened, though, that he was able to win 820,000 votes during the short campaign period. In early 1996, he announced his plans to run for the Diet seat from Setagaya-ku, one of the 23 *ku* or districts in the Tokyo metropolitan region. In October, he was elected with a wide margin.

## EXHIBIT 1:
## JAPANESE LEADERSHIP:
## THE CASE OF TETSUNDO IWAKUNI

**Reforms Proposed by Tetsundo Iwakuni in his book,
*Rin Toshite Nihon*, A Mature Japan Pursuing Real Wealth
for Co-Existence Translated by Yuichi Kamoto, edited by
Jim Clawson**

### Economic Reform

1. Disassemble the Ministry of Finance and redefine its role into clear and smaller functions.

2. Protect depositors' rights from financial crisis and disclose full information on financial institutions to general depositors.

3. Apply disciplines of capitalism to banks.

4. Put the Japanese version of SEC under the jurisdiction of the Ministry of Justice.

5. Japanese companies relocating to headquarters could solve trade friction and the rise of the Yen.

6. Allow Japanese companies to buy back their own stock so that they would restore the confidence of investors and so that the companies would have more alternatives in carrying out their capital structuring strategies.

7. Develop and invigorate small- and medium-sized companies which contribute more to the development of the local economy:

8. Allow easy transaction of real estate and land in order to make full use of these for economic activities by loosening and tightening relevant taxes.

9. To invigorate Japanese economy,

    a. put fixed annual salary system for compensating business people,

    b. reintroduce Stock Option plans,

    c. deregulate and delegate powers to local governments.

10. Detach the triangle relationship between politicians, bureaucrats, and businesses. Japanese exporting companies are actually buying Yen, which raises the value of Yen. Japanese import businesses get the benefits of high-valued yen and keep its products' and services' price high by regulations.

11. Arrange the return of the U.S. base at Yokota and turn it into the Japanese International Airport and establish three hub airports. (Yokota, Narita, and Haneda)

12. Merge Tokyo and Saitama prefecture into one entity to realize the New Capital Area Plan.

## Immediate Anti-recession Policies

13. Elect a Prime Minister and Minister of Finance who understand economics and the stock market.

14. Save agricultural and financial institutions with public funds because of their importance and emergent issues.

15. Do not lower real property tax (tax imposed on land). Rather, raise it in order to increase the flow of land.

16. Lower the land sales tax.

17. Establish a public "Land Bank" in order to stabilize the rapidly falling land prices.

18. Acquire lands worth 300 trillion yen for the next 10 years (until year 2004).

19. Lower taxes related to buying and renovating housing.

20. To invigorate smaller- and medium-sized companies,

    a. zero housing-loan interest,

    b. not increase public utilities rates (postal service, telephone, highway, etc.),

    c. abolish the consumer tax (sales tax).

## In Harmony with Bureaucrats

21. Stop "Amakudari" (literally, "angels descending from heaven," bureaucrats finding jobs in subsidiary organizations after forced retirement from major institutions). This happens way before they become 60 years old.

22. Do not elect bureaucrats and ex-bureaucrats in the administrative reform committees. If this reform proposal cannot be kept, do not set up the committees. Use anonymous votes in the decision-making processes in the committees so that bureaucrats would not know who voted what.

23. Set up systems where Diet representatives can control the bureaucrats.

24. Business leaders should say "good bye" to politicians and bureaucrats.

## Agricultural Reforms

25. Government should help establish large-scale agricultural business by owning lands and leasing them. Financial resources should come from Zero-Coupon Bond.

26. Support farmers who are financially weak and small, but contribute to preventing natural disasters such as floods and landslides. (Japan is a very mountainous country.)

27. Invest in agricultural business in spite of the fact that Japan will not be able to feed itself, because this business is not only important for national security, but is also a benchmark for how friendly our country is to nature.

28. Establish a "Rice Bank" in Japan and make it the center for production and sale of rice in the world. Start helping to solve food shortage problems in the world.

29. Help Japanese farmers farming abroad and exchange agricultural know-how.

## In Harmony with the Rest of the World

30. Introduce referendum for major issues and speed up decision-making process in our country.

31. Elect Prime Minister directly.

32. Amend the Constitution, especially the ninth article (which renounces war and prohibits Japan from establishing its own military forces).

33. Clearly state our right to defend our country with our military force.

34. Decrease the number of both Upper and Lower Diet members by 50 percent.

35. Diplomacy, defense, education, and culture should be solely under the jurisdiction of the Upper house.

36. Voters should have multiple and negative votes to elect representatives to reflect their opinion more precisely.

37. Introduce an electric voting system that allows voters to cast votes anywhere.

38. Apply more rigid discernability criteria against economic criminals. Do not give them leeway to escape from indictment by letting them say, "I was not aware of the situation, or the regulation."

## Correct Things that are in the Way of this Harmony (Coexistence) Process

39. Establish a sound monetary administration and transparent disclosure system of company performance.

40. Build up grass-root relationships on the municipal levels such as prefecture-state and city-sister-city relationships. This would greatly contribute to Japan's national security.

41. Build water-pipe lines covering the African continent to prevent famine, poverty, and war in the continent with Japan's technology and financial might.

42. Establish an International Peace Squad in Japan for peace-keeping operations in the world.

43. Japan has, from its own historical experience, an obligation to contribute to world peace by making its economic might and technological know-how available to the world.

44. Establish "Terakoya" all over the world. Japan should help countries all over the world set up schools for the general public and help them invest in education in their country. This would lead these countries to be more stable and help them understand more about Japan.

45. Invest in cultural exchange. Accept workers and students from foreign countries in Japan.

## Create Happy Communities

46. Give financial incentives (zero or minus loans) for families in big cities to build three-generation houses (grandparents, parents and children) and financial incentives for families who live close to their parents (for example, within a 500-yard radius). These would help reduce the health-care cost for elderly citizens, by saving the huge cost of construction and maintenance of aged people's accommodations by local government.

47. Establish an elderly-care system where neighbors can mutually take care of elderly families.

48. Introduce Personal Identification Cards for every citizen. This would help identify the person when he or she can not identify himself or herself in a disaster such as the Great Hanshin Earthquake.

49. Establish a police organization that covers interprefectural, nationwide, and international crimes such as Oum Group.

50. Establish "Anti-disaster" headquarters to develop and implement rigid and reliable contingency plans for disasters.

51. Eliminate vending machines of alcohol and adult magazines on the streets.

52. Introduce deposit system for merchandise such as automobiles, soda cans, batteries, and so forth.

53. Eliminate regulations that are causing high consumer prices in Japan.

54. Make donations deductible for income tax.

### In Harmony with Women, Elderly Citizens, and Children

55. Staff government and public offices with 30 percent women.

56. Intertwine volunteerism to reduce the healthcare cost, especially for elderly citizens.

57. Introduce a Comprehensive Welfare Card for each citizen. (Medical information, blood type, pension history, insurance, and so forth.)

58. Utilize elderly citizens' skills and experience in business and social contexts by establishing seminars and schools to support these intellectual and social assets.

59. Fight against discrimination. (Discrimination against foreigners, disabled citizens, voting rights, women.)

60. Introduce curriculum for religion that does not advocate one specific religion, but facilitates students' understanding of religions in their historical contexts. This would prepare young Japanese people to make better judgments on their beliefs.

61. Make senior high school education mandatory. Unleash students from "examination hell" and focus on real education that prepares them to be global citizens.

62. Emphasize and ask continually where we are from, historically and culturally. One of the ways to do this is to realize how close we are to trees and tree cultures. (Wooden schools, houses and buildings).

63. Set up "Green-Keeping Operations" for the world.

### Locals Coexist with the National

64. Create a small central government and large local governments.

65. Encourage local governments and businesses to import from the United States and the other parts of the world to solve trade deficit issues.

66. Hand over authorities to the local governments except policies such as defense, diplomacy, and monetary policies. These authorities would promote and develop businesses in the local community, employment, welfare policies, environmental policies, and education.

67. Scale down local government and reduce costs as well.

68. Impose restrictions on terms for mayors and governors.

69. Design a Japan that consists of 300 city states as seen in ancient Greece. (Japan now consists of 3,300 cities, towns, and villages.)

70. Maintain the current pricing system where any person anywhere in Japan can purchase newspaper and books at the same price. This system would help keep our education stable and equitable throughout Japan.

## QUESTIONS FOR REFLECTION

1. How was Mr. Iwakuni able to maintain his creativity throughout his career?

2. How did he balance work and family life?

3. What principles seemed to govern his life?

4. How would you chart his balance in life?

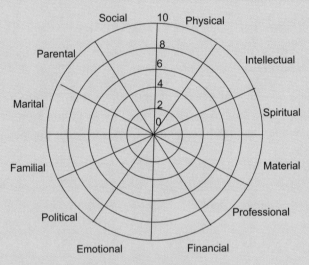

A Personal Developmental Balance Wheel.

## REFERENCES

"Be a Strong and Gentle Corporate Worker," *Tokai*, May 15, 1994.

Kazuko Takai, "Applause and Conflict: Mayor of Izumo," *Seiron*, September, 1990: 172–179.

Ken Taki, "What Should Current Leaders Do?" *Pinnacle*, date: 3–14.

Kiyoshi Otani, "Tetsundo Iwakuni," *Nikkei Business* (May 30, 1994): 60–63.

Koichiro Sakai, "Tetsundo Iwakuni-Mayor of Izumo," *Nikkei Business*, June 4, 1990: 82–86.

Masakiyo Nakayama, "International Businessman Coming Down to a Mythical Country," *Weekly Current Topics*, (April 29, 1989): 38–41.

Minoru Sato, "Tetsundo Iwakuni's My Fight," *President*, June 1987: 292–305.

Saburo Nagao, "Tetsundo Iwakuni," *Friday*, date?: 48–51.

Shuichi Kondo, "Tetsundo Iwakuni Runs for Tokyo Mayoral Election?" *Weekly Post*, May 7, 1993; 62–63.

Tetsundo Iwakuni and Morihiro Hosokawa, *Theory of Region*, (Tokyo: *Kobunsha Publishing*, January 1991).

Tetsundo Iwakuni, "Another Textbook of Mine," *President*, July 1994: 94–97, III 1994, IV 1995.

Tetsundo Iwakuni, "Changing Our Way in Japan," (Tokyo: *NHK publishing*, January 1993).

Tetsundo Iwakuni, "Creating New Generations," *Gakushu Kenkyu sha*, (Tokyo, April 1993).

Tetsundo Iwakuni, "Three Promises II," *Yomiuri Newspaper*, July 1993.

Tetsundo Iwakuni, "Three Promises," *Yomiuri Newspaper*, July 1992.

Tetsundo Iwakuni, *A Message from the Mayor of Izumo — New Regionalism*, (Tokyo: *NHK Publishing*, October 1991).

Tetsundo Iwakuni, *Current & Surges: Is any breakthrough of the Status Quo Possible for Japan?* (Tokyo: *World Culture Publishing*, July 1991).

Tetsundo Iwakuni, *New Japan from Wall Street*, (Tokyo: *Kodansha Publishing*, October 1988).

Tetsundo Iwakuni, *Rin Toshite Nihon*, Kobunsha, Tokyo, 1995.

Tetsundo Iwakuni, *When a Man Makes a Decision*, (Tokyo: PHP Laboratory, October 1990), 136–139.

**7**

DEE DEE FISHER:
THE LIFE AND
CAREER OF A
FREE SPIRIT

*Destined to be an old lady with no regrets.*

*A saying posted on Dee Dee Fisher's refrigerator*

*When we begin to see that our identity was put together in response to something that we had determined shouldn't be, the result is a new freedom in saying who we are — a fundamental shift in what we see and know as possible.*

*The Landmark Forum*[1]

*It's not the truth you know, it's the truth you create.*

*Another of Dee Dee Fisher's favorite sayings*

Dee Dee Fisher was wondering what was next. In January 2006, her long-time partner was up for promotion on the faculty at a major business school. Despite four years of a stretching, growing, often blissful relationship, he had not proposed. Fisher had a product on the shelves of GNC (a national chain selling vitamins and supplements), but it was in need of upgrading. She didn't particularly like where she was living. And she was growing increasingly impatient and antsy. She wondered if she should end the relationship and move on. Should she go back to Phoenix or Philadelphia, two cities in which she had lots of friends and kindred spirits? Should she write a book based on her philosophy of life? Should she get back into the health supplement business? Should she herself propose? In some ways, the world was full of options and possibilities. In other ways, she felt trapped, and she didn't like that feeling.

## THE EARLY YEARS

Fisher grew up in the small town of Ririe, Idaho, where she wrestled with self-esteem and acceptance. Her father was not a physically affectionate man, but demonstrated his devotion to Fisher by attending every one of her school activities, including four years of varsity volleyball and basketball. Fisher's father owned and operated a gas station that primarily serviced local farmers near the family's home. Fisher helped out at the station, and early on, she learned that if the farmers had a bad year, so did the Fishers. In the midst of that somewhat emotionally flat

[1] http://landmarkeducation.com (accessed 16 March 2006).

family life, Fisher's maternal grandmother treated her like an adult and became her confidant and friend. Fisher recalled:

> *"She never said this is what you are supposed to do or this is how it is, instead talking me through my questions asking, "What do you think you should do? How do you feel about that?" She actually would have a communication with me — regardless of my age."*

Mormonism had a marked influence on the community Fisher grew up in. Generally, the community encouraged adherence to Mormon standards of behavior in social and religious matters. People were expected to refrain from drinking and smoking, premarital sexual relationships, and foul language. Reading the scriptures, praying, encouraging non-members to join, and attending church were virtues. Fisher's father was a member of the Church of Jesus Christ of Latter-day Saints, but her mother was not. Because most of the people in the community were Mormons, Fisher and her brother grew up in the midst of a highly conformist environment. Despite that, Fisher exhibited an independent spirit — and often found herself challenging the local cultural norms. For example, Ririe High School required students to take a Mormon seminary class as a regular part of the curriculum. Fisher told the administration that she would not take the class, pointing out that because the school was state-sponsored, they could not make her do so. She held her ground against school administrators and agreed to become a teaching assistant for seventh- and eighth-grade girls' gym class instead.

## GRADUATION, MARRIAGE, DIVORCE, AND MOVING AWAY

Through her teenage years, Fisher's main thought was leaving home. That goal and her free spirit led her to decide to graduate from high school early in January of her senior year. Her mother's pleas to reconsider the decision, however, dissuaded Fisher, and she remained in school for her final semester. In retrospect, Fisher regretted that she did not stand up for what she believed to be right for her at the time.

> In retrospect, Fisher regretted that she did not stand up for what she believed to be right for her at the time.

*"I appeased my mother and stayed in school. I completed the basketball season and graduated with my classmates. I suppose I am not very senti- mental but I found it all to be a bit much, all the pomp and circumstance, since we were all going our separate ways."*

The night of graduation in May 1987 brought another surprising turn for Fisher in that her high school boyfriend asked her to marry him. In her heart, Fisher realized that was not the right thing for her, but she believed it was what she was expected to do. Right up to the wedding date, she had severe doubts:

*"I didn't want to go through with it. I remember standing at the end of the church aisle after everyone had already gone into the sanctuary and turning to my maid of honor. I told her, "I don't want to go through with it. Get me out of here!" She only replied, "The whole town is out there. They will be so upset!" So, again in an appeasing fashion, I went through with the wedding. I found myself only a few days later on my honeymoon thinking of how I was going to get myself out of the marriage."*

Fisher's graduation and wedding decisions brought her to a personal realiza- tion, "If I continue to make decisions based on what somebody else wants, I am going to get to a point in life where I realize I am living someone else's life and not my own."

So at 18, and newly married, Fisher began work as a dental assistant to earn enough money so that she could afford to separate from her new husband. When she realized the job would not provide adequate financial support long-term, she decided to begin college. By the time Fisher enrolled in fall classes at the state university 90 miles away in Pocatello, she had decided that divorce was the only option. The decision proved unpopular with her family:

*"My father came to my house before the divorce and told me essentially, "Stay married. Get pregnant. Your mother cried the first year we were mar- ried. You'll get over it." It really sounded like something I wanted to sign up for! [Not!] I realized coming from his world it was good advice, but it wasn't good for me."*

This time, Fisher was not dissuaded from her plan. The divorce was finalized during her second semester in college. For her remaining years at Idaho State University, Fisher lived in Pocatello and worked to support herself while she was in school. She found college to be far too similar to high school and longed to finish college to move on to "real" life.

*"In college, everyone's life experience was so limited. Most of the students were on scholarship or supported by their family. They were going home in the summers. There was no reality of life. I found college to be a lot like high school. For me, college was my means to leave."*

At the same time, Fisher began struggling with her weight and feelings about her personal appearance. At one point, she ballooned up to more than 160 pounds, which on her five-foot-three-inch frame made her feel heavy and plump. Fisher continued studying and finished college with a BA in mass communications with an emphasis on advertising and public relations. Shortly after graduation, a friend said, "Let's go to Arizona," and they left for Mesa almost immediately. She had finally achieved her first big dream: to leave Idaho.

## OUT OF IDAHO

In Mesa, Fisher found an interim job as a cocktail waitress until she got a position with a company called Microage, where she worked as a phone salesperson. She found she didn't like the disconnection from the customer so she began looking for alternative employment. The search ended during a conversation at the gym where she was working out. There, she met a consultant with a company that sold "human development products" to corporations. Those products gave employees "permission and action plans" to "own" their jobs and their lives. Fisher felt a connection with the company's message and product and decided she wanted to work with them. The face-to-face nature of the sales job suited Fisher's social nature and personality.

*"I remember when I was a senior in college my advisor asked me what I wanted to do and I said I was unsure — but I was sure of one thing: that business left out the human aspect of life and since humans are the heart of*

*companies, I wanted to help change that. So, I went to work for the [human development products] company [TimeMax Inc.] on straight commission. I ended up making the most commission in the shortest amount of time of any salesperson they had brought on. The job was great. I loved sales. I was teaching people about strengths that in some respect I had not fully realized I had: the ability to say I want that and to go get it, the ability to say no to authority, the ability to own my life and not let other people take away my power."*

In 1996, a year after beginning her sales position, Fisher was introduced to a man at work and they went out on a date. Surprisingly, he proposed on that first night! Perhaps even more surprisingly, Fisher accepted:

*"At that point I had dated enough to realize that you are going to have the same things come up in marriage with any human being. Who is to say just meeting someone and getting married will not work? There are plenty of dating relationships that go for years, they marry, and it doesn't work."*

Six months after their engagement, the couple was married in a picturesque and dramatic ceremony overlooking the Grand Canyon. The ceremony had a Native-American theme and was conducted by a Winnebago chief who was also a Presbyterian minister. Fisher recalled the experience:

*"My family thought I was out of my mind. For me it was being able to say that we created out of nothing a wedding ceremony overlooking the Grand Canyon. There was a lot of drama we had to go through to get married in a national park. It was fun creating it."*

The marriage also offered a new business opportunity for Fisher. Her new husband had just started a company with two friends. They were brokering raw materials, specifically enzymes, to contract manufacturers for making vitamins that were then purchased by retailers such as GNC. Eight months into their marriage, Fisher left her sales position and joined her husband's company. She felt this was a better use of her time and talent: "If I was going to do sales, I figured why not do sales so that all the benefits went toward our family?"

The change proved stressful on their new marriage as it quickly became evident that Fisher was more of a people-person than her husband. Her outgoing vivacious nature served her well in sales. She quickly established connections with key people in the vitamin/supplement industry. Everywhere she went, she was eager to meet new people, to learn their names, to hear their stories. The connections proved valuable as Fisher discovered a new world of healthy living and alternative medicine.

## DISCOVERING CONTROL

The world of supplement manufacturing opened up a new perspective for Fisher on personal health care. Growing up, she was exposed only to traditional medical practices. She recalled:

*"In my family growing up, if you were sick you went to the general practitioner. For me, I had always been frustrated by my female problems and later, after high school, struggled with my weight. I actually had an OB/GYN tell me as a teenager that I was upset about nothing. That I needed to deal with my female problems, and that this is how it is for women. I learned very quickly in the natural industry that I did not have to suffer with my problems and that there were things I could do besides just take a pill."*

At the start of her second marriage in 1997, Fisher weighed 160 pounds — which she considered overweight, and which was, indeed, at least 20 pounds heavier than the medical standard for the ideal body weight for her height. Throughout high school, an active lifestyle helped her body maintain a high metabolism, so weight was not an issue. Graduation from high school, a stressful first marriage, and the start of college marked a transition in her lifestyle that promoted a quick weight gain. The weight remained despite her best efforts to exercise.

Soon after beginning work in the natural food/supplement industry, she experimented with different supplement formulas and became more dedicated to watching what she ate and working out. Fisher talked about this period of experimentation:

*"I had met someone in the industry who was a food chemist. He had a small facility where he made private label products for doctors and*

*chiropractors. I would take a symptom, find a herb that was defined to aid in this symptom and then ask my friend to encapsulate it. He agreed, and I began to experiment on myself. Soon, I found a combination that helped me control some of the problems I had experienced as a woman, including weight gain. My weight dropped to 125 pounds and the negative effects of my monthly cycle decreased."*

The change for Fisher was dramatic. She felt better physically than at any other point in her life and she reached a new level of self-discipline that gave the changes permanence. She learned from that experience that, "I alone am in control of my life, no one else. I alone can improve my life for my benefit."

The results of her physical change motivated Fisher to talk with other women about her health struggles. She found that many women identified with her story and wanted to see similar changes in their own lives. Fisher wanted to help them fulfill that desire and began to realize that her story was a vehicle she could use to empower women to change. As a result, Fisher began to craft and polish her story. She had professional photos taken to demonstrate the "before and after" of her personal physical changes. And she became much more comfortable with her body and her sense of independence. Fisher found that she liked, very much, being in control of her life.

## TRYING CHOCOLATE CAKE

During this time, her husband's business thrived. A great deal of the success was attributed to Fisher's outgoing personality and her gift at connecting with people in the industry. She found that people contacted her for help even in areas of the industry outside her expertise. She found herself playing a matchmaker/broker's role, connecting people who could help one another. That networking skill helped her to create a web of goodwill for Fisher and the company, but it also deepened the tension in her marriage.

Two years into their marriage, Fisher's husband approached her with the confession that he'd been involved in extramarital affairs. He wanted to keep their marriage together, but he didn't know if he could be monogamous. Fisher recalled this time period:

*"He asked me if I would work with him on the issue. He was raised in a household where monogamy was not demonstrated, so that was the only*

*lifestyle he knew. How could I say no to someone who was serious about working on their problems? We decided that we would change our initial marriage agreement and give him time to work on the issue. We tried it for a year and a half.*

*Many people think I'm crazy for staying with him for the year and a half, but who can say because I was raised in a monogamous household that means monogamy is the correct way to live? There are plenty of places outside the United States where people live in non-monogamous relationships. It turns out it didn't work for me, but it would have to be true for each person in this type of situation.*

*The way I look at it, if I do not eat chocolate cake, how do I know whether or not I like it? I do not know what is right for me until I try it."*

The marriage ended on good terms, without tears or emotion. Fisher simply asked to take the rights to her story and her supplement formula with her, to which her husband agreed. Fisher had a story she wished to share with the world, and she knew, from her advertising background, that it was a sellable story.

## THE LANDMARK FORUM

Large parts of Fisher's story dealt with the issue of taking responsibility for her life and discovering why she did what she did. She heard about and signed up for Landmark Education's Landmark Forum seminar, which promised to help her learn more about herself. The experience had a major impact on Fisher:

*"The Landmark Forum is mostly based on Eastern philosophy and believes there are events that occur in your life that make you who you are. The Forum helps you break down significant events in your life that help shape who you are. They say in the Forum, "Something happened and you failed in a way of being and then you made up something to make up for that failure."*

The Landmark Forum helped Fisher see more clearly several incidents in her life that shaped who she became. The first incident related to an event when she was a child and was punished for bad behavior by her brother.

*"There was one time when I was spanked for something my brother did. Because we were four years apart, there was no way I could physically have stopped him from what he was doing. So since I got in trouble for that incident, I "made up" that I wasn't big enough, so I had better be responsible, and I wasn't smart enough to communicate with him to make him stop, so I had better be responsible for everyone. After that moment, I would be terrified if someone else was going to get in trouble for something. This probably made me a very responsible teenager. The event was very impactful and it turned out, useful."*

A second life-shaping event for Fisher occurred when she was in sixth grade. She was in a scuffle with a girl from school who had challenged her to a fight:

*"I had decided prior to the incident that I was just going to be cute, but that did not stop the fight. As a result of the event, I "made up" that if I couldn't be cute I had better be tough. I learned from the event that I had to be tough with my emotions. Life was going to happen, and I could either let my emotions cripple me or I could choose to use them."*

While at the Landmark Forum, Fisher also reflected on her father's advice to stay married and get pregnant — advice that preceded her first divorce.

*"I said to myself after that event, 'I cannot conform so I had better be outrageous.' I decided that if what I am doing is not the norm then it had better be out there, outrageous, against all odds, and it doesn't matter what other people think, just go do it."*

Fisher credited the Landmark Forum with helping her to see the importance of those events and how they had shaped her life. At the Landmark Forum, she explained, the instructor talked about "choosing your response."

*"Once you have had an emotional experience, your psyche will say, 'I don't want that to happen again. So, we are going to respond this way and not this other way.' But once you see the way you are conditioned to*

*respond, you can choose to respond in a certain [other] way, rather than the way you are conditioned. This is a very powerful tool, to **choose** to be cute or tough; to be smart or responsible."*

That ability or power to choose became central to Fisher's story.

## FINDING AN OUTLET FOR HER STORY

After her second divorce, Fisher used her network in the industry and found a company in Northern California that was looking for a consultant to assist with personnel issues that had grown out of a recent restructuring. As a result of the restructuring, the company had recently consolidated a number of manufacturing facilities into a single site. Fisher interviewed with the owner and was offered the consulting position. That meant living in Napa Valley near San Francisco and starting up her own consulting firm, Discover Response. She explained her choice for the company name:

*"Discovering what you are responding to in life is the first and most important step in creating a life you love. There are many learned behaviors that we respond to as human beings. Some of these are chosen beliefs but most are learned from the generation before us and then lived as truth by us. There is another way; by questioning all of our behaviors and beliefs we can create our own truths and our own lives."*[2]

The consulting job also allowed Fisher enough free time to begin pitching her weight loss story in the nutrition industry. She found little receptivity at first, but she kept pitching. Eventually, she found a sympathetic ear in an unusual place.

## BODYONICS PINNACLE

While she was consulting, Fisher had continued to attend the nutrition industry tradeshows. One person she kept running into was Mel Rich. Rich had a PhD in pharmacy from MIT and in 1996 had started a company, Bodyonics Pinnacle,

[2] http://www.deedeefisher.com/consulting.html (accessed 15 March 2006).

which provided supplement formulas directly to distributors/manufacturers like GNC, but also produced a line of supplements under its own brand name.

During the time Fisher and Rich began talking, Rich was working on a project for a company called Twinlab. The project involved formulations containing enzymes with which Rich had little experience. Rich found Fisher's background and knowledge of enzymes valuable and asked her if she would come to New York City to help him complete the project. Fisher accepted the offer, and two months after her consulting contract was completed in California, she went to New York to meet with Rich.

While in New York, Fisher helped Rich complete the enzyme-based formula and also introduced him to the leading broker of enzymes, someone she'd met before and who happened to be in New York at the time. At one point, Rich asked Fisher what her plans were following her time in New York. Fisher recalled the conversation:

*"I told him I was actually on a road trip and was heading to Florida to pitch this story. He asked, "What story?" So, I told him about my weight loss story and showed him my before and after photographs. I also showed him the formula I had developed. He couldn't believe it. It turns out he had a formula that he was trying to pitch to GNC that was very similar to my formula. He just didn't know how to market his formula. As a result, he asked me if I was interested in partnering to release the supplement.*

*We renegotiated the formula [and the advertising pitch] so it was factual. He agreed that I should write the ads and use my pictures. He would put up the money to pay for advertising and would also manufacture the supplement through Pinnacle's own line. We then pitched it to GNC. Within 45 days of our first discussion, we had our first purchase order from GNC."*

## ESTROLEAN

As Fisher thought about her new partnership with Rich, she focused on several important details. She wanted to control the advertising and the content of the campaign. She also wanted to use her story as the main thrust for the campaign. A big part of that for Fisher was owning her own photographs:

> *"I took one more photo shoot so we had pictures from 1996, 1998, and 2000 to show the progress over time. I used my own photographer and owned the pictures — which was different from [the norm in] the industry. Nobody could do anything with my pictures without my permission. That was the only way I was going to put my story out. I wanted to keep control."*

Another aspect of the advertising that concerned Fisher was the integrity of the ads. With the recent changes to her supplement formula, other less scrupulous ad writers might find an opportunity to push half-truths or inaccurate implications in the ads. Fisher was unwilling to accept that.

> *"I needed to write the ads so they were factual. Even after the new herbs were added that Mel recommended from his experience, I was able to honestly say that when we had the full product together, all my symptoms went away. [I could say that] because I still had some female problems that were alleviated with the changes in the formula."*

In addition to being able to control the advertising, Fisher also considered the financial benefit of releasing her story.

> *"Since Mel was willing to front the cash for the project, I was only entitled to a certain percentage of the sales. I honestly had no idea what this percentage should be, but I had former clients who knew agents who worked with people in my situation. I called the agents and based on my being a "friend of a friend" they gave me some free advice on what the percentage should be."*

When Rich agreed to allow Fisher to control all aspects of the advertising and offered her the top percentage she was told was standard in the industry, Fisher agreed to release her story in partnership with him. They named the new diet supplement: Estrolean. Estrolean was manufactured by Pinnacle and distributed by GNC. For Fisher, the release of Estrolean was a means of sharing her story with women in the hope some would choose to change their lives. (Exhibit 1 shows an excerpt of Fisher's story from her personal Web site that advertises Estrolean.)

## WAITING FOR THE ESTROLEAN RELEASE

After Rich and Fisher signed an agreement, the actual release of Estrolean took several months. Fisher grew increasingly impatient:

*"There was a process of having to make the pills before they hit the shelves at GNC. So, there was a huge wait. So Rich said, "Go away, go on vacation. You are driving me crazy. There is nothing for you to do until the pills hit the shelves."*

So, to take her mind off the waiting, Fisher flew to Hawaii for several weeks and stayed with a friend who owned a place on Kauai. And something happened on the way to the gym:

*"I was in a tiny gym on Kauai, and I saw this guy, and he saw me. We were checking each other out as I went back to my workout. I then noticed a woman that I thought I recognized. We asked each other if we knew each other from somewhere, and it turned out that we knew each other from Phoenix. She was on the island for her wedding and the guy I was checking out was the best man in the wedding!*

*She pulled me outside and excitedly asked me to come to the wedding. She said 'There are all these Harvard guys and nobody has dates. You must come! It will be so much fun.' So, I went to the wedding with the guy from the gym, as his date. After the wedding we started seeing each other."*

At the time they met on Kauai, the "guy" was finishing his PhD at Harvard. So, returning to the United States, Fisher found herself with two strong eastward pulls: business and romance. She looked for a home in Rhode Island, but the terrorist attacks of September 11, 2001, persuaded her to keep her home out West.

## THE AMERICAN PSYCHE

Shortly after Estrolean was released, Fisher was again living in Arizona. She found that the schedule she had kept over the past few years remained relatively intact. Her mornings consisted of a one- to two-hour workout followed by work followed by either an additional workout or a more vigorous activity like rock climbing. The biggest change was that "work" now consisted of staying connected with Rich in New York and answering e-mails from Estrolean customers. What she found in the e-mails often surprised her:

*"I learned a lot about the American psyche that I had no idea about. I thought if women just knew that if they simply changed a few things, everything would be fine, that they would want to take responsibility to change these things. For example, I tried to show them that they could take responsibility for their health and be healthy, that women do not have to depend on their doctors to keep them healthy as we are programmed to believe. I quickly learned this was not what the American psyche wanted.*

*I would actually get e-mails from women who would ask, 'Can I eat whatever I want, take this pill, and still lose weight?' I would look at these e-mails to see if people might actually be joking and I found out they were not joking. This was what they actually wanted. They wanted to eat what they wanted and look like a model."*

In addition to battling the "American psyche," Estrolean was competing against a number of diets, including ephedrine-based products (popular at the time) and other supplements that promised quick results with very little effort. The majority of consumers flocked to those products. From 2000 to 2004, the sales of ephedrine-related products soared. Fisher saw the success of the ephedrine diet as an insight to dieting consumers' philosophies. In an attempt to provide a more realistic and effective alternative, Fisher put together a whole healthy living program revolving around Estrolean.

*"Every packet of Estrolean came with an insert telling the purchaser what to eat and how to exercise in addition to taking the pill. We even hired nutritionists to write diets. We gave the consumer everything they needed to be successful, to lose weight, and to feel better. All they had to do was*

*take responsibility, but all they wanted was to just take the pill and lose weight."*

Despite the responses of so many women looking for a miracle pill and the competition, Estrolean still experienced a successful launch. Fisher was able to live comfortably from the proceeds she received from Estrolean sales. At the peak of Estrolean sales, Fisher enjoyed a six-figure income. Sales remained strong for almost two years, the average sales/product life cycle of a dietary supplement in the nutrition industry.

In the meantime in 2003, the Harvard guy asked Fisher to move to Philadelphia, where he was teaching on a one-year post-doctorate at the Wharton School. He had been involved in two successful IPOs and was serving on the board of a major corporation, and was quite capable of caring for her financially. He enjoyed the enviable position of starting his career with a seven-figure income. By that time, sales of Estrolean had slowed enough that Fisher's income did not cover all her expenses. The couple decided to move in together in Philadelphia.

At that point, she wrote a business plan that proposed a line of six supplements developed around the idea of personal responsibility. She pitched the plan directly to GNC, where she personally knew one of the executives. The executive argued that the market was not ready for products based on a personal responsibility message. They still wanted low-carbohydrate, low-effort diets and programs.

## MOVING TO THE COUNTRY

After her partner's year long post-doctorate came to an end, he accepted a position at another major business school in a much smaller, suburban environment. Fisher had grown to love him so she went with him, but she hated the small, confined atmosphere of the conservative community. During the last three years, Fisher had allowed herself to rely more and more on her partner's support for her lifestyle and interests. They traveled to the far reaches of the world together scuba diving, partying, attending college reunions, fraternity reunions, and major entertainment industry events. Life on one hand seemed carefree and a barrel of fun. Her partner was coming up for promotion on the faculty, but the outcome was not yet known. It was clear that he loved the teaching, but he wrestled with the writing and publishing aspect of the academic life.

And there was another thing: after living with her boyfriend for more than three years, he still had not asked her to marry him. Fisher wondered if she was wasting time. Should she restart her entrepreneurial interests in the nutrition industry? Should she write a book with a more detailed version of her story? Should she find a coauthor or ghostwriter to help? Should she bag her lingering relationship and move back to Phoenix where there were more opportunities? Or was the East Coast a better bet? What about children? And how would she support herself?

---

**EXHIBIT 1:**
**THE LIFE AND CAREER OF A FREE SPIRIT: DEE DEE FISHER**

### Excerpts from Fisher's Web site[3]
### (accessed 16 March 2006).

Using natural ingredients, she experimented with different combinations of herbs and extracts, and created her own nutritional and exercise program. She lost 40 pounds and 23 inches. She was a size 4.

However great being the right size was, it was not enough. The painful, debilitating menstrual cramps and intestinal pains still plagued her. Looking to go further, she knew she needed to add a safe, natural, effective hormone-balancing ingredient. Dee Dee took her quest to Pinnacle, a leading natural supplement manufacturer with a women-friendly brand, Pinnacle for Women. Incorporating natural hormone phytoestrogens into her already existing nutritional regimen worked its magic. For the first time in 24 years, Dee Dee lived without constant intestinal pain and exhausting monthly periods. She felt like her own woman. And Estrolean was born!

And there are more products and projects in the works. Dee Dee is out to help women worldwide find the inspiration and courage to do what she has done, take her own life in hand and improve it for her benefit.

A letter from ME!

[3] http://www.deedeefisher.com/story.html

---

To answer before you ask, 'yes' it is me in the pictures, 'yes' everything above is true, and 'yes' you can do it. There is a quote; "Nothing is yet to be said that's not been said before,' (Terence). That means that the information I give you is already out there to find. I've only made it easier for you by putting it all in a logical order.

We women are very smart. We know that burning more calories than you eat causes weight loss. We know that we suffer every month at least once because of our unique systems. And we know that there is no magic pill or recipe... Or is there?

Well, there are answers so simple that, when combined with a little effort, they work like magic. I am excited to take you on this process. And I will be here for you as you learn to do for yourself as I learned "to rely on myself to do the difficult, to understand and take my supplements, to eat foods that are satisfying yet nutritious, and to exercise." Whew, with all this going on it needs to be simple and logical.

— Dee Dee Fisher

## QUESTIONS FOR REFLECTION

1. What lessons do you think Ms. Fisher has learned or should have learned from her life so far?

2. What chapter of life is she in?

3. What aspects of the way that Ms. Fisher has managed her life do you admire and why?

4. What aspects would you have done differently and why?

5. If you were in her position, what would you do and why?

## EPILOGUE

About six months after the case was written, Ms. Fisher and her significant other were married on a catamaran in the Caribbean surrounded by their closest friends. Thereafter, they moved to Boston where he had accepted a position with a large, well known private equity firm. Within a year, Ms. Fisher delivered a healthy baby girl on whom she doted. She said she loved being a mom, but sometimes she felt crazy and bored. A year later, her husband accepted a position in the Pacific Northwest, so she was planning their move and wondering what life would be like on the "left coast" again.

## REFERENCES

http://www.deedeefisher.com/consulting.html (accessed 15 March 2006).

http://www.deedeefisher.com/story.html(accessed 15 March 2006).

http://landmarkeducation.com (accessed 16 March 2006).

# 8

ERIKA JAMES:
THE LIFE AND
CAREER OF
A TENURED
PROFESSOR

People who met Erika Hayes James[a] tended to be impressed. She was tall, slender, vivacious, well-groomed, immaculately dressed, and she exuded energy. The more you learned, the more she seemed like a woman who had accomplished what many, if not most, just dream about: having her complex life-act all together and well balanced. She was a successful professional, a loving spouse, an adoring parent, physically fit, emotionally upbeat, socially polished, and seemingly cool, calm, and collected. After a while, they would begin to wonder: How does she do it all?

> She was a successful professional, a loving spouse, an adoring parent, physically fit, emotionally upbeat, socially polished, and seemingly cool, calm, and collected. After a while, they would begin to wonder: How does she do it all?

## Erika Hayes

Erika Hayes was an only child born in Bermuda in 1969 to William and Gloria Hayes. Both her parents worked as school music teachers. The Hayes family felt constrained and isolated in Bermuda, so they moved to Pennsylvania in the United States in 1971, where William Hayes continued his career as a jazz musician, music teacher, conductor, and composer. A few years later, the Hayeses divorced. The day her dad moved out was one of Erika's first and most poignant memories in life.

Erika's father remarried soon thereafter and moved to Michigan. Gloria Hayes took Erika to St. Louis, Missouri, where she took another job teaching music. Within a year she married a prominent psychologist with an active practice and professional influence, and the three of them worked to create a new, biracial family. Erika believed that from the age of five or six up until she left to go to college, she had "sort of a traditional family" in that there were both a mother and a father in the household. Erika also maintained a long-distance relationship with her biological father in Michigan. She often went to visit him for the summer months.

Erika's mother was very active and worked the whole time Erika was growing up. She had taught music in Bermuda, but when she arrived in Missouri, in addition to

---

[a] Please view video clips of interviews at https://store.darden.virginia.edu/business-case-study/erika-james-the-life-and-career-of-an-associate-professor-2350

135

teaching music, she went back to school and earned two master's degrees, one in education and one in education administration. She continued working in school administration and mental health at the high-school and community-college levels for a number of years.

With both parents working, Erika spent a lot of time by herself. When she was young, she would go to a babysitter's house. When she was old enough to be alone, she would come home from school and let herself in. Although she was a latchkey kid, Erika said she never felt lonely. She learned to entertain herself. Eventually her mother left her career in education to work alongside her husband. Their work together had the couple traveling around the world. Erika described her early family model like this:

*"My experience growing up was seeing a working mother who managed work and family responsibilities. One of the things that I learned from her experience, and she was very explicit about this, was that she always carved out time for herself. My mother would do things that would make her happy. She would travel and do any number of things that were important to her. I think that allowed her the space, the freedom and the joy in her own life to then do for the family.*

*I never felt neglected. I never asked, 'Why isn't she staying home with me?' I grew up knowing my mother took herself seriously. She took care of herself and that, I think, enabled her to take care of family responsibilities as well.*

*So I did spend time alone taking care of myself, and I think I grew up a very adult child in some respects."*

Erika's parents moved on occasion, so that by the time she was in middle school they had arrived in the small town of Sherman, Texas. Erika was a curious child who liked learning and really enjoyed school, which no doubt helped her adjust to all the changes. By middle school, though, Erika was getting annoyed with the moving, so she let her parents know she had had enough, and they agreed to stay in Sherman until she graduated from high school. Erika continued to do well academically. She recalled an incident that occurred when she was in middle school:

*"I didn't know what the honor roll was. I remember my mom coming home and saying to me, 'Erika I thought you were doing well in class.' And*

*I said, 'Well, I think I am.' And she said, 'Then, what's this?' And she put this newspaper down on my desk. I looked at it and read about something called an honor roll and my name was there. So I said, 'I don't know what this is.'*

*She explained to me that this was people who were performing at a high level in their classes so they were honored in the newspaper. I picked up on how proud this made my mother and every semester from that point through graduation I made the honor roll."*

When Erika was in seventh grade, her English teacher wrote in her yearbook, "It was such a pleasure having you in class; you have such a sunny disposition." That was the first time that Erika became aware of anyone noticing anything about her personality. She liked being referred to as having a sunny disposition.

Erika began managing multiple roles when, in middle school, she took up running as an extracurricular activity. She realized that she was pretty good at it. Her neighbor, who was also a runner, coached her. Then, Erika wanted to become a cheerleader like all of her female friends. Her mother very much discouraged her from becoming a cheerleader, which was a sore subject for quite some time. Rather, her mother encouraged her to be the one they were watching and cheering for instead of standing on the sidelines cheering.

In high school, Erika continued her academic achievements, making honor roll and studying Spanish, and joined the track team. She also picked up basketball and volleyball. Track was her best, though, and she ran for four years, excelling in the 400- and 800-meter and the mile relay. Then, she added politics to her list of "balls in the air" when she was elected to the student council; in her senior year, she was elected class president. "It was fun being in charge then," she recalled.

When it came time to think about colleges, Erika felt as if she were ready for a change in venue. Her parents had been talking about moving to California when she graduated from high school, so Erika decided to explore California schools. When she went to Pomona College in Claremont, California, Erika was one of only three people in her high school class to leave Texas or go any farther away than Oklahoma. She decided to follow in her stepfather's footsteps and major in psychology. In the meantime, her parents changed their minds about relocating and stayed behind in Texas. (Years later, one of her colleagues commented that it seemed like an interesting way to get the children out of the nest.) Erika enjoyed her undergraduate years and continued to have a reputation for bright cheerfulness. One of her classmates began calling her "Sunshine".

Erika loved her time at the small liberal arts college and wondered if someday she wouldn't like to be the president of a similar institution. She also concluded at Pomona that if she wanted to have a career that had a good financial return, she needed to pursue something other than psychology, so she decided to attend graduate school. She searched for a field of study that would allow her to utilize her natural curiosity and her love of reading, writing, and learning. She chose organizational psychology and went off to the University of Michigan, where she earned a doctorate she planned to use in the private sector, perhaps in consulting. Though Erika worked part-time during her doctoral program, she completed her five-year schedule in less than four years.

## ACADEMIA

Working part-time and completing a five-year program in four years would be stressful for anyone. While Erika certainly had times when she was feeling overwhelmed and sad, those times didn't last very long. By and large, her natural tendency was to be happy, to be cheerful, and to be pleasant.

Near the end of her program, as Erika was thinking about postgraduation career options, Erika's dissertation advisor suggested she apply for an academic job at Tulane University in New Orleans, Louisiana. She recalled:

*"They hired me literally five minutes after I gave my job talk presentation and proceeded to sort of wine and dine me the rest of the weekend. At that point I had several opportunities with corporations in New York City and consulting opportunities I had thought I would pursue. What I realized was the business recruiters didn't treat me the way that Tulane had treated me. So, I decided to go to Tulane and try it out for a year or two. If I didn't like it, I thought I could always go back to the corporate world."*

Erika spent three years as an assistant professor at Tulane and then moved to Emory University in Atlanta, Georgia, for the next three years.

## JIMMIE JAMES

One day she was in the Dallas/Fort Worth International Airport, waiting for a flight and reading John Grisham's *The Firm*, when a tall, handsome stranger sidled up and asked her what she thought of the book. They were on the same plane, so they continued their conversation while waiting to board the flight. When they arrived at their destination, they said goodbye and parted ways.

The young man, Jimmie James, a promising executive-to-be at Exxon living in Houston, Texas, tried to muster his courage as he walked away. He recalled:

*"One of the things about being a male in our society is that there's the expectation that the guy's going to take the lead. And one of the things associated with that obviously is that we end up taking a certain amount of risk. But I think that people understand, too, the relationship between risk and reward. So if the reward looks great enough, then certainly your desire to take that risk is higher."*

*So, here was this exceedingly beautiful woman sitting there looking so pleasant. And on Erika's behalf, if you notice, she has in general a very pleasant, inviting disposition; so I don't think you feel threatened immediately, and you say: 'Well, the worst thing that can happen is that she says no.'"*

Jimmie convinced himself, spun around, ran down to her connecting flight departure gate, and found her just as she was about to board. He asked for her phone number. They exchanged contact information, Erika boarded, and Jimmie, smiling, went on his way.

They began to call each other daily. Despite the odds, they began to develop a long-distance relationship. In time, Erika and Jimmie discovered some similarities, among them their being comfortable with time alone. Neither worried about being accepted or being a part of a group. "I think that (ability to enjoy being alone) helps Erika and me in our relationship and the time that we spend apart," Jimmie said. "It's an opportunity to reflect and think and then really enjoy and appreciate the time that's spent together."

Gradually, the relationship grew. They would talk for hours on the phone while living in different cities. They discovered that they were both planners. "In order to have the life that we have and make it work requires a lot of planning and a tremendous amount of trust," Jimmie said. "Trust that we know that when we say we're going to do something that we're going to follow through and trust that we're both committed to making this work." As time passed, they became closer and closer.

## MARRIAGE

In 1999, they were married in Houston. After their honeymoon in Italy, they separated as Jimmie flew off to Baton Rouge, Louisiana, and Erika headed for Atlanta. Erika admitted to feeling sad: "I thought, 'This isn't how it's supposed to be.'" Yet the rhythm of their long-distance relationship quickly resumed.

> **They continued to have separate careers in separate cities, she in Atlanta and he in Baton Rouge, connecting on weekends in one city or the other. With limited time together, they learned to make the most of what they had.**

They continued to have separate careers in separate cities, she in Atlanta and he in Baton Rouge, connecting on weekends in one city or the other. With limited time together, they learned to make the most of what they had. Jimmie noted that he and Erika shared something in their family backgrounds that helped make their relationship work: They were both raised to believe that it was the big picture that counted. "You learn to really tolerate little things that really aren't significant," Jimmie said. "Because, living apart, if you started an argument over something small, by the time you resolved the argument it would be time to leave." Coming to grips with being two professional people who were very interested in having both a family life and a career required a tremendous amount of discussion, agreement, and understanding. Their mutual respect grew in these early years. Jimmie said:

> *"I would characterize Erika as amazingly efficient. I'm really fascinated at times by how much she's able to get done. So I would start off in a*

*characterization of her as amazingly efficient; I would say that she is very positive — confident, but not arrogantly confident. Confident in knowing that if she puts her mind to doing something that she's going to be able to do it. And in the time that I've known her and what I've known from her background, there's not been a goal that she's set for herself that she's not achieved."*

Erika said of Jimmie:

*"Jimmie has a great sense of humor. Even when he's not funny, his efforts to be funny are hilarious. He definitely makes me laugh and smile. He has the utmost integrity and I appreciate someone who takes that seriously. He's really smart and I've always been attracted to smart people."*

## MAKING IT WORK

Erika and Jimmie spent the first three years of their marriage commuting to spend time with each other. One or the other would fly in on a Friday evening, they'd spend the weekend together, and then separate on Sunday night or Monday morning. Erika commented:

*"I always say that even for couples who are in the same place, living in the same state or city or house, there is a way in which you can take that for granted and never really have to talk because you're together and you assume that the relationship is on solid ground.*

*I think given that we were living in separate states, it really forced us to develop a relationship based on communication. So over the years, we knew that we had careers that were important to us, that we wanted to both continue in those careers, and that we wanted to be together as a couple. And so we've just made very explicit decisions that we were going to try to operate in a way that worked for that."*

Technology helped Erika and Jimmie stay connected. Jimmie had two cell phones, one for work and the other for personal use. "My work colleagues note that I will ignore my work phone at times," Jimmie said. "But when my personal phone rings I become very attentive because there's a 90 percent chance that it's Erika."

**Erika's upbringing and lifestyle forged her into a careful organizer and planner who had high expectations for follow-through.**

Erika's upbringing and lifestyle forged her into a careful organizer and planner who had high expectations for follow-through. At times she became impatient when plans didn't work out. "If someone drops the ball or we're making plans to do something, even if it's a fun activity, and then it never goes anywhere or it just kind of sits and meanders, I get irritated," she said. "I'm rarely angry, but just have a lot going on," she said, describing her emotional reactions to her increasingly hectic lifestyle. "Jimmie helps to put me in perspective and helps balance me in that regard."

From time to time, the couple would arrange to fly from their separate cities to some exotic location for their weekend rendezvous. This change in their normal routine added some spice and energy to their long-distance relationship.

Then, after three years of marriage, Jimmie was transferred to the ExxonMobil head offices in Washington, D.C. Erika began looking for jobs in the Northern Virginia region so she could be closer to him. There were plenty of schools at which Erika believed she could get a faculty appointment in the Washington metropolitan area, which included Northern Virginia, Washington, D.C., and Maryland. The position she accepted was well outside the metro area in Charlottesville, Virginia, a two-hour commute. But she took the job and joined Jimmie in Northern Virginia, commuting two hours each way to the Darden Graduate School of Business Administration for the next three years.

## PROFESSOR ERIKA JAMES

Erika believed that going into the world of academics was one of her best career decisions. That choice sent her work in a direction she truly enjoyed:

*"The research that I do is on topics that I find interesting and compelling. I love being in the classroom — the engagement, the experience in the moment that you're in the classroom with students and you're asking the*

*right questions that get them thinking and you're seeing how moments go off for them. That just brings me a great deal of joy.*

*I can't imagine there being another field or career that works so well for who I am and what's important to me. So a couple of years ago, I went through the tenure process and that went successfully, thankfully, and it allowed me the opportunity to continue in this field. For some people who are in this field, I think tenure is the thing that they strive for. And it's to some extent the end for them. I always thought of tenure as the means. I wanted to get it because it was an acknowledgement that I could achieve at this level. But I didn't see it as the end in and of itself — just the opportunity to continue to do something that I loved in a school, at a university, that I loved."*

At Darden, Erika became a respected colleague and developed numerous friendships. Mary Margaret Frank, assistant professor of accounting, believed that Erika had a unique ability to relate well to students, faculty, executives, and other colleagues from all walks of life. "I think that barriers are created when you have a gift, and she's definitely got a gift," Frank said. "I think she has a unique ability to break down and reach beyond those barriers."

Although they taught in different functional areas, Frank and Erika worked on committees together. One in particular, the academic standards committee, was a very difficult assignment. Faculty had to make hard decisions that had the potential to adversely affect students' futures. "Erika is really good in committees at synthesizing different opinions," Frank said. "So she may feel strongly in agreement with one person, but she's very good at hearing and brokering a discussion between somebody who has a different opinion and trying to get us to talk together to come up with a mutual solution." In addition to their professional interaction, Frank and Erika became friends at Darden. Erika was the first person to approach Frank about taking better care of herself. As Frank described:

*"When I had my first daughter I tried to do it all. And I think part of it had to do with the fact my mother stayed at home, and I thought: 'Well, I will do her job, stay at home, and I'll do my job, work.' And that didn't work very well. Erika was very in tune with that. She saw that tension in my life, walked into my office one day, and said, 'You need to make some decisions*

*about things that you are going to do and how you're going to handle all these balls that you have in the air.'"*

Erika encouraged Frank to recognize that one person couldn't do it all and that she needed to know when to ask for help. Erika's philosophy, learned from her mother, that taking care of oneself would translate into being better able to take care of those one loved, emboldened Frank to make several changes in her efforts to balance work and family life.

Perhaps Erika's closest colleague at Darden was Martin Davidson, associate professor in leadership and organizational behavior, who also served as a mentor. Not only did they share a common intellectual pursuit — Erika was an organizational psychologist and Davidson a social psychologist — but they thought about the world and people in a similar manner. That created a connectedness between them, which allowed them to use a common language to talk about ideas, concepts, colleagues, the profession, and how they were going to teach. Davidson described one aspect of their association:

*"We share our personal lives and talk to each other about what we deal with: the reality of being a minority and African American in a predominately white elite business school. We are a small community in that regard. We share a role on faculty. I've spent most of my career as the only one, so having Erika share that with me is meaningful. Dealing with, having fun with, the trials, and tribulations of... I can't do that with anyone else in the same way as I do with Erika. And I've learned a lot from Erika — what we do as faculty members at a business school, our scholarship, and what we do to generate knowledge. Erika is socially intelligent and has a high EQ. She's tuned into how people think and feel, are motivated, and demotivated."*

As Erika become increasingly successful, she took on a larger role as mentor to others. Davidson described a conference for incoming women MBA students where he watched Erika from the sidelines discuss how to participate in case discussions:

*"I'm in a room full of women serving as a coach. It was powerful to see her lead the conversation and help them think about what their experience was*

*going to be like moving into the MBA classroom There were 50 women of all colors and ethnicities with Erika standing in front of the room leading a case discussion on Martha Stewart. 'What can we learn from each other in this process?' she asked, 'What can we learn from each other about how things went?' She had them think about what their experience would be like in a predominately male classroom. How they want to carry themselves, handle themselves, speak, and express themselves to be successful and influential. For me it was powerful to see Erika not just as teacher and successful professional, but as mentor to other women."*

## FAMILY

During their courtship, Jimmie and Erika had talked about having two children. They were married three years when Jordan James came along. "For the first nine months, I was commuting two hours each way pretty much on a daily basis — pregnant, getting bigger and more uncomfortable," Erika said. "Fortunately for me I had a very easy pregnancy so there wasn't a lot of morning sickness or fatigue or anything of that nature."

How does a couple manage two careers in different cities and raise children at the same time? Before the baby was born, the Jameses looked at their lifestyle. Erika was working two hours away from where they lived. They wanted their child to have as much opportunity in as nurturing an environment as possible. They knew daycare required making sure one of them picked Jordan up on time at the end of each day. Those factors helped the couple decide to hire a live-in child-care provider — a nanny.

Finding a nanny was an educational experience. The Jameses contacted several different services in the Northern Virginia area and did a lot of Internet searches to learn what possibilities were out there. Erika described their search:

*"We settled on a particular firm, and told the woman who was working with us what our needs were and that we were new parents with a father who traveled and a mother who commuted two hours to and from work. And she asked us what kind of person we were looking for. I don't know that we really knew that. So I honestly don't remember what the criteria*

*were that we said at that point. There weren't a lot of people who could accommodate the schedule that we had.*

*She sent several people to our house to interview as options. All of the applicants were female and generally older. One woman who was very much the professional nanny took out a dossier of her life as a nanny. But she felt very strict and regimented — almost corporate in the way that she approached her job. I thought if someone was going to be living in my house, I wanted to feel comfortable with the person. Although I thought she would have been very professional in her responsibilities, she wasn't someone who I would have felt warm and cuddly with. There were two applicants who just really stood out for us."*

They chose a woman who had been a nanny for many years and was accustomed to living in. The nanny had raised her own family, knew how to manage a household, and was nurturing to a newborn.

Erika taught her MBA class the morning Jordan was born. She did take seven weeks off after Jordan arrived and then traveled back and forth from Northern Virginia to Charlottesville with baby in tow because the nanny didn't drive. Eventually the Jameses bought a small condominium in Charlottesville for the days when Erika had an early or late class to teach.

About a year and a half later, Jimmie was transferred to a large Exxon facility in Texas. At that point, they sold their home in Northern Virginia and bought a home in Charlottesville. Because their nanny was not able to relocate to Charlottesville, the Jameses had to start the nanny-search process again. In the meantime, Jimmie became the commuting spouse/parent.

This time they had more experience, knew what worked and what didn't, and had learned about au pairs — young women students who came to the United States from other countries to work as live-in child-care providers. "It's an educational program (for them), so they do need to take courses while they're here," Erika explained. "But their primary responsibility is to care for your children." The Jameses also realized they wanted someone in the house who could introduce their children to Spanish, which was becoming an increasingly important language in the United States. They chose a young woman from Costa Rica.

In 2005, daughter Alexandra James joined the family. Her parents and her older brother were thrilled. And the stress level jumped another notch. On the one hand, Erika said, "They light up my life, to be honest." Yet there were times when she really felt pressure at work with deadlines and her heavy travel schedule. On occasion during those stressful times, she noticed herself being short with the kids — "not short-tempered," she said, "but anxious and wanting them to hurry up when they're just being who they are, and they're taking five minutes to put their shoes on." After those moments, Erika would remind herself that her mood wasn't about them, but rather it was about not having managed the morning well enough to build in that time for the children to do what they needed to do. So when she found herself in those spaces, Erika realized she had to take something off her plate — change something so the children didn't think what they were doing was problematic or troublesome. She needed to plan better.

## A TYPICAL WEEK AT THE JAMESES' HOUSE

In 2007, Jimmie was promoted to a new job back in Washington, D.C. Now the smaller apartment was in Washington and the main house was in a gated, golf-oriented community in Charlottesville. They developed a mirror image routine of the one they'd had before. Jimmie would arrive in Charlottesville on Friday evening, and the couple would generally spend time with the kids before they went to bed. The Saturday routine was typical of that of many other parents with young children. They drove the children to ballet lessons, basketball or soccer practices and games, and maybe swimming. If possible, Jimmie played a round of golf, and the pair did errands. Saturday evening was for family time, and often, they made sure they had some couple time together without the kids. Sunday mornings were spent at church, with a relaxing "at home" time in the afternoon. Jimmie described this ritual:

*"I joke with Erika about the fact that when I was a kid Sundays were completely about church. We would start out at Sunday school at about 9 in the morning and we'd go into the 11 o'clock service. Then we'd take a break to have Sunday dinner, which took place around 1 o'clock. You know, dinner was the country version of lunch — but on Sundays it was dinner. And then we'd go to an afternoon service around 3 and then we'd have a 6 o'clock*

*service at someone's church around 6 and we'd get home about 10 pm on Sunday nights. What we saw there were a lot of honest people and a lot of integrity. It was very clear that we wanted to be the people who were what you actually saw. And so for my family, for all of us, integrity is a key value and very important. I think that's a trait that growing up in a family of eight with similar and shared values — it seemed natural and not out of the ordinary."*

Erika enjoyed cooking Sunday meals herself, so the family usually had a sit-down dinner together. Jimmie usually left the house in Charlottesville around 4:30 or 5 on Monday mornings to head back up to Washington, D.C., for the week. Every night, and probably once or twice during the day, Erika and Jimmie exchanged e-mails or talked on the phone. He called the children every evening.

The Spanish-speaking au pair was on duty when Erika left for work each morning Monday through Friday. She had been instructed to speak to the children in Spanish. Erika arrived home between 5:30 and 6 pm and released the au pair. The children were usually having dinner or just finishing up by then, so Erika read books, played games, and spent time with them. After bath time each night, the children went to bed by about 8:30 pm. Erika then spent the next two hours getting things done, doing household chores such as laundry or schoolwork such as reading, writing, and answering e-mails.

Before they had children, Erika and Jimmie had used vacations as a way to build energy in their relationship. They continued this practice after the children arrived. After one trip to Disney World, Erika remarked that the sight of watching her daughter meet Mickey Mouse for the first time, standing there mouth agape, speechless, timid at first, then amazed, and then gently hugging his leg, was the "sweetest, sweetest thing I could imagine." That said, Erika's mother's advice to take care of herself continued as a legacy. She and Jimmie made a point of still taking couples-only vacations as well as trips that included the children.

## MAINTAINING ENERGY

Erika had learned in middle and high school how good it felt to be physically fit and strong. She also admitted to being highly competitive and driven. "Exercise makes me feel good," she said. "I like the achievement, the accomplishment of having done something."

After Jordan was born, Erika was uncomfortable with her weight gain and felt compelled to do something. So, six weeks to the day after Jordan was born, she started an exercise program that was new to her — Pilates — twice a week for an hour. Rachel Bryce, her instructor, explained the exercise:

*"Classical Pilates is defined by the method that Joseph H. Pilates invented in the 1920s. He had developed a method or system of exercising that he called Contrology and also invented several apparatuses to go with it.*

*In 2000, the trademark name Pilates was overturned. It was a large court case in New York and since then there have been many offshoots. Anybody can kind of create a series of exercises and call it Pilates. Maybe it's Pilates-based, maybe the principles align themselves with Pilates, but it doesn't really have anything to do with the original method or sequencing of Joseph Pilates's work."*

In general, Pilates involves a series of movements that results in poses held briefly, perhaps repeated, on flat surfaces or furniture/equipment designed for the proper posture. As in *tai chi*, Pilates requires proper posture, muscle control, and breathing control as the muscles are strengthened and lengthened. Bryce observed of Erika's demeanor as she came to class and used that information to structure her one-on-one classes. "If she comes in very stressed, rushed to get there, and has a bunch of bound-up energy," Bryce said, "then we push a little harder to release some of that stress." Although Erika found Pilates challenging, she had to prove to herself that she could do it. "Pilates is very important for focus," Bryce said. "The utmost concentration and focus is required to be able to get your precision, your flowing motion, and your breathing executed."

Erika also arose early several times a week and power-walked for 45 minutes with a friend and colleague through their neighborhood. She admitted that she did this exercise primarily so she could satisfy her sweet tooth and have her nightly ice cream. She often brought doughnuts to her faculty teaching meetings. Her colleagues were amazed that she could eat doughnuts, have ice cream for dessert at lunch, and sip smoothies during the day, yet still maintain her athletic physique. Her attitude on exercise perhaps explained how she could do it:

*"In addition to my Pilates and walk, there's another little place that I go to do a quick gym exercise a couple of times a week — and I bring my children with me to that. They have this little gym with a trampoline, and so while I'm on the machine doing what I'm doing, they will jump on the trampoline. They think it's fun, but they also know that Mommy is there to exercise and so that's their form of exercise.*

*I'll come home from work and my son will say, 'Mommy, let's do sit-ups.' And so I think they recognize that exercise is a part of life, and I think them seeing me do that has just made them curious and interested. At this time they don't see it as work or something that you have to do, it's just sort of fun for them. So one of the things that I hope is they continue to have that attitude about exercise that it's not a chore. It is something just fun to do."*

## MANAGING CAREERS

Clearly, Erika and Jimmie's desire to build a two-career family gave them a somewhat unusual, although increasingly common, lifestyle. They spent much time talking with each other about their respective careers, and she realized that, on a daily basis, she taught what he practiced. Although unsure what it would look like, they both wondered if there was an opportunity at some point in their careers to pursue a business or vocation together. They also noted they were in different phases of their respective careers. Jimmie said:

Clearly, Erika and Jimmie's desire to build a two-career family gave them a somewhat unusual, although increasingly common, lifestyle. They spent much time talking with each other about their respective careers, and she realized that, on a daily basis, she taught what he practiced.

*"Erika and I are in two different stages in our careers, and I think that as she takes off more, my current one will be winding down by design. I believe*

*that I have about eight to 10 years with my career as it is today. I'm pacing myself so I'm going to be completely burnt out by then. If I'm not burned out in eight to 10 years, then I've not done my job effectively. The next part, or Act II if you will, will be a continuation of time with the kids and more focus on them and what they want to do with their lives."*

Both Jimmie and Erika wanted to serve others through their careers. They asked themselves, "What is this achievement allowing me to contribute?" They wondered if they were positively influencing peoples' lives — positively influencing the community as a whole. Jimmie explained:

*"Even in the pursuit of financial value, you really have to look at it in the overall context of economics. Money is just obviously the tool for rationing, but it's not in itself a true measure of value — you can't just put a dollar number to get to total absolute value. So, if we're not doing something that really is advancing mankind as a whole or this community of which we all are a part on this planet, then you really have to stop and question yourself. Are you really truly going to be satisfied and feel content with yourself after it's all over?"*

## New Opportunity — or Straw that Could Break the Camel's Back?

Erika had been in academe for nine years and had gotten tenure as an associate professor at the Darden School when she was asked to be the Associate Dean for Diversity, a new position at the school. She discussed the offer with her colleagues and contemplated the matter thoroughly. The position would bring with it a sizeable increase in pay, much more responsibility, and many more administrative meetings, with a continued requirement to meet her teaching responsibilities. All in all, the job would mean more work. The job would likely cut into her available consulting time in the summer, and require her to create an initiative and strategy for the office from scratch. She was not yet a full professor, but she did have tenure. She had several research projects under way and was partway through her first book manuscript. She had a husband who was a busy executive and lived two hours away during the week — and who was likely to get more promotions. She had two small children full of energy and enthusiasm. She had a full-time au pair and a personal Pilates trainer. She had always been known for her cheerful, can-do attitude. Could she bear the additional strain?

## QUESTIONS FOR REFLECTION

1. What do you find interesting and noteworthy about how Ms. James structures her life?

2. What choices have she made that run counter to your own values, assumptions, beliefs and expectations about the the world is or should be?

3. What chapter of life is she in?

4. If she takes the new job, what issues do you think she will encounter?

5. If she doesn't take the new job, what would be the consequences?

6. How would you diagram Ms. James' balance in life?

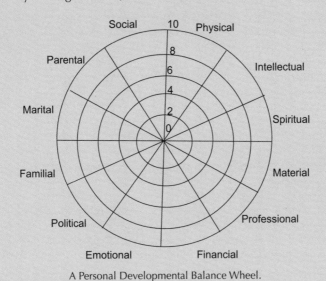

A Personal Developmental Balance Wheel.

## EPILOGUE

Professor James accepted the invitation to become the Associate Dean for Diversity at the Darden School. She served in that capacity for three years. Her schedule seemed to be even more hectic. Her husband received a new assignment at Exxon/Mobil which took him to New England frequently. In order to be closer to her husband, Erika decided to accept an offer from the Harvard Business School to visit and teach for a year, so she took a leave of absence from the University of Virginia. The Jameses moved to Boston in the summer of 2008, but kept their home in Charlottesville.

# DONNA DUBINSKY:
# THE LIFE AND
# CAREER OF A
# HIGH-TECH
# ENTREPRENEUR

Donna Dubinsky had spent the last 10 years of her career working in the high-tech industry with Apple Computer Inc. She had seen leaders come and go, been on the ground floor of new product distribution, support system implementation, and product promotion and forecasting. Dubinsky had come and gone herself — not outside the company, but to Apple International in Australia in 1986. Returning stateside a few months later, Dubinsky took on the role of vice president of international at Claris, an Apple subsidiary. When the parent company decided to incorporate Claris under Apple governance in 1991, Dubinsky thought it was time to break away from the only company she had worked for since graduating from Harvard Business School.

After spending a year in France thinking about what she wanted to do with the rest of her career, Dubinsky returned to Silicon Valley to search for an inviting opportunity. She found two exciting prospects. One position meant joining a seasoned team with someone she had worked under before and whom she greatly respected. The other was to push hard to be considered for the job of CEO at an up and coming technology company.

## FROM BENTON HARBOR TO HARVARD BUSINESS SCHOOL

Dubinsky grew up in southwest Michigan in Benton Harbor, where her father worked at a local scrap metal foundry and her mother was a homemaker. During her youth, the area changed rapidly as industrial plants closed their doors, releasing thousands of workers. Economically, the region also changed, with many middle-class families moving to more affluent regions closer to Lake Michigan, creating a largely lower-class population in Benton Harbor. With few jobs available and race-related tensions flaring, Benton Harbor lived under a pressure dome that exploded into violent riots several times in the 1960s and the 1970s, during Dubinsky's high school years.

After one of the 1970s race riots, security guards patrolled Dubinsky's high school hallways. It was a difficult time to be a student. Dubinsky reflected on her final years at home:

*"My mother hates it when I say I left Michigan without a diploma. I had an interesting high school experience in what could be considered a tough high school and I won't say I walked away with much academic preparation.*

*The school actually let me go to the junior college for my senior year. I started going to the junior college, the junior college faculty went out on strike, the administration fired them, and they never went back, and I never had an opportunity to complete those courses, so I actually never had enough credits to complete high school. So I went and worked full-time. They did end up giving me a diploma, so that is why my mother hates it when I say I never received my diploma, although I never really did complete high school."[1]*

Despite her academic background in Benton Harbor, Dubinsky applied to and was accepted at Yale University in New Haven, Connecticut. Yale took her more than 800 miles from Michigan, but in many ways she crossed a far greater social distance when she arrived there. "Socially," she said, "I found Yale a totally amazing place. I didn't even know what a 'preppy' was. In some sense, I was your typical yokel from the country with no idea about many of the things that went on."

The academic rigor of Yale also took a toll on Dubinsky. In her first year she averaged Bs and Cs, which was far below her high school average. A professor and some friends helped Dubinsky to learn the art of writing college papers. Dubinsky's supportive family also helped her persevere. They saw her taking new trails that were uncharted for them:

*"I was the first one in my family to attend Yale. I am second-generation American. All my grandparents came from Russia, came with nothing. My grandfather actually grew up around Yale, so when I was accepted he was so stunned. He had arrived here with nothing, and here I was going to Yale. It was so unbelievable to him, it seemed extraordinary."[2]*

Dubinsky graduated from Yale still wondering what she wanted to do for a living. When she received a job offer with Philadelphia National Bank, she jumped at the opportunity:

*"I decided I needed to work a couple years to figure out what I wanted to do. So I took a job as an entry-level financial person at Philadelphia*

[1] Gergen, David, *Yale and the Frontier of Technology: Donna Dubinsky and the Handheld Computer,* Yale300 Alumni Leadership Convocation. Yale University. April 19–22, 2001, http://www.yale.edu/yale300/aprilweekendvideos (accessed 12 October 2005).
[2] Ibid.

*National Bank. I remember they called and offered me a job for $11,500 a year. I just couldn't believe it. I sat back and thought, 'What am I ever going to do with all that money?' I quickly accepted the position and spent the next two years in Philadelphia — essentially in banking training."[3]*

At Philadelphia National Bank, Dubinsky discovered another new world: business. Prior to starting with the bank, Dubinsky had considered law school. While at the bank, she worked with lawyers on a number of transactions, and she had a revelation:

*"I loved business. It was a big puzzle, and I loved solving lots and lots of puzzles. I saw very quickly that as a junior banker, not having any clue what I was doing, I was giving directions to these lawyers on what sort of deals I wanted done. I liked that part of it! I decided I wanted to be in business."[4]*

Dubinsky set out to enter business school and conducted a short search; in the end, she applied only to Harvard Business School. She later laughed at her approach and said, "Fortunately I was accepted." In 1979, two years after starting with the bank, Dubinsky said goodbye and headed for Cambridge, Massachusetts. She found her first year at Harvard to be among the most stressful and difficult of her life. One of the primary contributing factors was the thought of constantly being on the edge of failure. Yet she believed it was the possibility of failure that drove her to succeed.

## THE DAWN OF THE PERSONAL COMPUTER AGE

About the time Dubinsky finished the third year of her undergraduate degree at Yale, two early pioneers of the personal computer industry, Steve Jobs and Steve Wozniak, finished work on a preassembled computer circuit board. They called it the Apple I. At the time, the only people who used personal computers or minicomputers were hobbyists who assembled computers from components and developed programs using a wide variety of low-level programming languages.

[3] Ibid.
[4] Ibid.

The creation of the Apple I led to the formation of Apple Computer in 1976 in Cupertino, California, an area that came to be known as Silicon Valley.

A new wave of computing was born that would catch many people in its wake, including Dubinsky.

## The Discovery of Apple

In January of 1981, Dubinsky started her final semester at the Harvard Business School. She seriously wondered what lay beyond her Harvard experience in four short months. She felt strongly about working with a manufacturing organization where she would have an opportunity to help create a product. Her goals were counter to those of most of her Harvard classmates, who were looking for high-paying consulting jobs. She recalled:

> During my final semester at Harvard, I saw Dan Bricklin and Bob Frankston give a demo of an Apple II. It was a very early Apple II and very early personal computing. They demonstrated it with Visicalc. This was the sort of analysis I had done at the bank over and over again. So, I really lit up because I knew this was going to be big. Everyone was going to want one of these computers. At the time, I didn't know much about hardware or software but I saw the Apple logo. Shortly after the demo, Apple went public and it was in the news a lot. The combination of the two things made me focus on Apple."

Getting Apple's attention turned out to be more challenging than being noticed by larger companies. Dubinsky's initial attempts to contact the company about employment were all turned down. Then, Dubinsky learned that Apple was visiting the Harvard campus during the semester to recruit — with a hitch. They were only recruiting Harvard engineers. Undeterred, Dubinsky attempted to sign up for the interview schedule. Due to her nontechnical background, she was turned down. Dubinsky remained determined and showed up at the recruiting office early on the day Apple conducted interviews.

> "I went and sat outside the recruiter's interviewing office, and every time she came out with someone who was interviewing, I would say, 'Hi, I need

*to talk to you for a few minutes.' She would say that she couldn't because she needed to talk with the next student. I sat there the entire day until finally at the end of the day she came out, gave in and said, 'Okay, I'll talk to you now.'*

*I walked into her office and said, 'I know you are looking for technical people. I am not a technical person, but you are going to need nontechnical people too. You are going to need people who understand your customers, and I am one of those people.' I effectively launched into my sales pitch. Eventually she allowed me to interview. I went to California and interviewed with Apple. In the end, I pitched them on the idea that I could understand their customers. They ended up offering me a job in customer support."[5]*

## Stepping into the Tornado

Dubinsky arrived at Apple to find a company growing at nearly 300 percent year after year. Revenue increased from $117 million in 1980 to $335 million in 1981.[6] Apple IIs were flying off the shelves at local dealers, and Apple was struggling at times to push enough units out the door to keep up with demand and also manage the flood of requests from computer shops wanting to sell Apples.

Being aware of Apple's growth, Dubinsky thought she had a clear idea of what customer support would entail. She envisioned herself working with professionals in banks and other financial institutions, helping them fully utilize this new technology. Instead, Dubinsky was presented with a much different job description:

*"When I got to Apple, I discovered that customer support was all about supporting the retail channel. I spent my first year building the dealer channel, which was in its infancy when I started. This meant I put in all the support systems needed to support a dealer channel."*

Initially a little surprised, Dubinsky quickly found her stride working with the retail dealers. The culture at Apple helped tremendously. Although it felt like

[5] Gergen, David.
[6] "Graphic indicating Operating Revenues and Net Income for Apple Computers," *USA Today.* 19 September 1985.

stepping into a tornado, her coworkers' creativity and enthusiasm for their jobs and the future was contagious.

## The Early Years: 1981 to 1983

The first years at Apple were a blur for Dubinsky. The company's revenue continued to soar and new hires nearly doubled Apple's work force between 1981 and 1983. During that period, Dubinsky found effective ways to work in Apple's high-growth environment. Her methods allowed her to manage the growth in her area and adapt her skills to be more effective. "This time period was chaotic," she said. "Apple was growing at an extraordinary pace and had relatively little management structure. The company was striving to do things differently."

One thing that changed was her approach to decision-making. Both the bank and Harvard stressed a quantitative approach to decision-making. Without the numbers, a decision could not be reached. Such was not the case at Apple. Managers routinely made large decisions with limited understanding of the numbers and more from a "gut instinct." The philosophy was, if it made sense for the company, then "go for it." Due to that approach, middle managers at Apple, like Dubinsky, found themselves making decisions that in most companies would require senior level approval.

Dubinsky was able to adapt to that way of thinking and thrived on the freedom she had to make difficult decisions. That freedom helped her as she strove to incorporate more discipline into the operational processes. Due to its rapid growth as an organization, Apple had not taken the time to formalize many procedures. Instead, the company acted more in a reactive fashion, allowing systems and procedures to grow organically with the company. In many cases, the creation of those procedures was put off to focus on more pressing needs. Dubinsky believed strongly that having formal systems would alleviate many of the common problems that the distribution and the retail channel experienced. In many ways she believed it was a discipline her group could not afford to put off.

## The Two Faces of Apple

Apple rapidly thought beyond the Apple II and started projects to create the next great computer — this time designed for business users. In the fledgling computer industry, new PCs had seen at most a two-year life cycle in the market before being replaced by an entirely different design.

As Apple pulled resources from the Apple II projects, several new computer projects were created within Apple. Jef Raskin and a four-person research team developed one of the early projects in 1979. Initially the venture received very little attention internally at Apple. That changed in 1981 when Jobs recognized the potential of the project, code-named Macintosh, and took over management of the group.

Jobs brought to the Macintosh project an unending drive for perfection. He believed very strongly that he was an artist and that each of the designers on his team was also an artist. He encouraged and often demanded changes to designs, not because of technical shortcomings but because the design was not visually pleasing. He also believed the Macintosh team was building the best computer in the world and was not afraid of sharing his pride with anyone, including members of other teams within Apple. Jobs instilled in the Macintosh team a sense that they were renegades within Apple.

The Macintosh group's rise within Apple took place while sales for the Apple II continued to beat expectations. Except for minor hardware modifications to the Apple II in 1979, no further changes were made until 1983. During this long development hiatus, the Apple II customer following grew to well over a million users. Hundreds of independent third party hardware and software developers created plug-in boards and software applications for the Apple II. The Apple II became the first personal computer to capture and hold the attention of a large customer base.

Jobs believed that the future of Apple Computer lay with the fate of the Macintosh group. Therefore he strove to bring the best people into the group either through external or internal hiring. One such star hire was Debi Coleman, who arrived late in the fall of 1981 to act as the controller for the Macintosh group. Jobs also saw Dubinsky as a rising star at Apple and asked her to join the group in the first part of 1983 to help with their upcoming launch of the Macintosh. Dubinsky turned down the position:

*"There were two reasons I turned down the offer. First, the Macintosh people were arrogant. I really enjoyed the down-to-earth aspects of*

*Roy Weaver and his organization. Also, I never viewed myself as a product person. Instead, I viewed myself as someone who helped the product groups get their product to market."*

While Jobs built the Macintosh group, the company was fighting another battle, the rise of the IBM personal computer.

### The Rise of IBM

While Apple was succeeding with the Apple II, new competitors began to appear on the market. IBM introduced the IBM PC in August 1981. The IBM PC became the first PC to feature an open architecture, which meant only off-the-shelf components were utilized. Initially, Apple's response to the IBM threat was muted, but by late 1982 it was clear the IBM PC was creating a wave in the computer industry and Apple needed to formulate a response. Jobs believed it was important for Apple to find mature CEO leadership to battle against a more established technology competitor like IBM. So in the spring of 1983, Apple announced John Sculley as their new CEO.

Other executives came to Apple after Sculley, including Bill Campbell, a former college football coach. Campbell entered the company and filled a position that included managing Roy Weaver and the distribution group.

The new management changed very little of the day-to-day operations as Apple began the ramp up to the Macintosh release, an event that was scheduled for late 1983.

### "1984": THE TURNING POINT

For Dubinsky and Apple, 1984 was a pivotal year that began with a flourish of success and optimism. Dubinsky was promoted in the first part of the year to distribution manager, which made her responsible for Apple's field warehouses, sales administration, inventory control, and customer relations. Dubinsky remembered:

*"I didn't have time to think about promotions. Things were totally chaotic. At any point in time 20 percent of the employees were considered new,*

*having been there less than six months. It was insane growth. So it was very hard to keep a pulse on things."*

For Apple, the year kicked off with a memorable, first-ever prime-time commercial during the Super Bowl. The Super Bowl spot was quickly followed by the official release of the Macintosh 128K at the annual shareholders meeting. Sculley introduced Jobs to investors by saying that the most important thing that had happened to him in his first nine months with Apple had been the opportunity to develop a friendship with Steve Jobs. The meeting concluded with Jobs introducing the Macintosh to the audience.

Jobs had made huge predictions for the Macintosh all along. He predicted that Apple would sell 50,000 Macs in the first 100 days. To back up his optimism, Jobs unveiled a new manufacturing facility in Fremont, California, designed specifically for the Mac. The plant opened as one of the most automated plants in America and was designed to produce 80,000 Macs a month.[7] Apple reached the 100-day sales goal, but problems quickly arose at the manufacturing plant. They were having difficulty reaching full capacity. To address the problems in manufacturing, Steve Jobs asked Debi Coleman to step in as manager of operations at the Fremont facility.

## THE "JUST-IN-TIME" PROPOSAL

In the fall of 1984, Steve Jobs met with the CEO of Federal Express, Fred Smith. During their meeting they discussed details of "Just-in-Time" (JIT) manufacturing, which was a Japanese manufacturing process beginning to catch on in the United States. The process meant manufacturing goods in a real-time fashion based on actual orders, which reduced the need for inventory and warehousing. Manufacturing at Apple was based on sales forecasting, which had proven difficult for Apple to do accurately. Jobs thought the JIT manufacturing process was a perfect fit for his newly launched Fremont plant and could save Apple millions of dollars. Much of his conclusion on the monetary savings came from the information he had received from Coleman's earlier study.

---

[7] Amanda Hixson, "The Reshaping of Apple," *Personal Computing* (April 1987): 123.

From Dubinsky's perspective, the Mac group's actions seemed sudden. The only warning Dubinsky had that something was brewing, beyond her conversation with Jobs, came in September during the presentation of her group's business plan to the Apple executive staff. During the meeting, Jobs brought up a number of points challenging the plan she presented.

The debate escalated and took more and more of Dubinsky's time and attention during the first three months of 1985. Finally, she reached the end of her tolerance for the issue. She had started to consider options outside Apple when a company event changed her perspective on what had been occurring.[8]

## The Splitting Apple

By the time the Macintosh computer was released in early 1984, Jobs had managed to alienate a number of people involved with Apple II and the Lisa projects. Jobs's candor regarding the Mac's superiority to all other computers, and his desire to cut back funding to the Apple II projects, created the perception to many insiders, and also to investors, that Apple was a company split and fighting internally. The perception was not helped when, in early 1984, Apple consolidated operations by product into two groups, the Apple II and the Macintosh. This consolidation brought the now-released Lisa computer into the Macintosh group.

The issue of operational responsibilities became more heated as 1984 wrapped up. Apple's share of the PC market was shrinking, revenue growth slowing, and the overall PC industry moved into a slowdown as the PC became more of a commodity product. The result was that only the top players, IBM and Apple, were able to squeeze out a profit in 1984 while many others ran deep in the red. Jobs's insistence on managing the Macintosh group and the declining market conditions were two major factors in the rapid deterioration of the top executives' relationship throughout 1984 and 1985. Outside investors observed that major changes would have to be made inside Apple. Otherwise, the company had only a small chance to survive in the changing marketplace.

For Dubinsky, the distribution world was not sheltered from the political infighting since her group serviced both product groups within Apple. Dubinsky's

---

[8] Mary Gentile and Todd Jick, "Donna Dubinsky and Apple Computer, Inc. (A)." *Harvard Business School Publishing*. February 21, 1986.

primary concern, however, had been keeping the dealers' shelves stocked with both Apple IIs and Macintoshes:

*"It was all I could do at the time to keep up with the critical needs of my job function. I tended to prioritize things and I was never very good at politics. I was known as the one who liked to put her nose to the grindstone to get the job done, while all this political stuff was happening around me that I was somewhat oblivious to."*

Because of her focus, she was unaware of the impact the rapid cultural splits were having on other parts of the company. Dubinsky's eyes were fully opened to the splitting at Apple at a "Leadership Experience" seminar in the spring of 1985.

### The Team Takes Sides

Dubinsky attended the seminar for middle managers with hope dwindling on whether her area would even exist in a few months' time. With that attitude, she worked through the exercises the seminar organizers had created to help foster greater teamwork and unity within Apple. Through her interactions with her colleagues, she began to see a pattern emerging in their responses and attitudes that explained more clearly what had been happening to her over the past six months. Seminar participants were expressing in a number of ways their perception of a split at Apple. Jobs and Sculley were tugging the company in two different directions. When Sculley later appeared before the group, she decided it was time to say something about what she was observing.

*"I stood up and confronted Sculley in front of the group, saying how this division at Apple was pulling us apart and we could not go any further. I wanted to convey to him this observation and this was the opportunity I had. I was at the end of my rope and felt he needed to hear about the problem. I didn't really care what it meant for my professional career at the company. He, Sculley, reacted very badly at the time, but I felt it had to be said. I personally felt relieved by speaking out."[9]*

Dubinsky left the seminar with a renewed vision of what she needed to do. She immediately set a time to meet with Bill Campbell to discuss her thoughts.

[9] Todd Jick (1986).

After a weekend of thought, Campbell gave Dubinsky the time to prepare the distribution strategy.[10]

## Apple Reorganization

A few weeks later, Dubinsky was again called into Campbell's office. This time it was so that Campbell could tell her that Apple was embarking on a major reorganization and would now be organized along functional lines. In addition to shifting organizational lines, Apple would lay off more than 20 percent of the work force. Dubinsky survived the cut and moved into an entirely new role, but before transitioning, she released a number of the employees she had helped to hire. This action proved difficult for her.

Her new role as the director of sales support had responsibility for sales training, sales communication, sales administration, and technical support. She now managed a $28 million budget and more than 200 employees. She would also report directly to Bill Campbell. Dubinsky had mixed feelings about the new role:

*"It was a surprise and, in a sense, a promotion. I reported to a higher level and I had more people working for me. I was out of operations and was more in sales and logistics. It was a surprise given that during the last six months I had been involved in the distribution conflict — it could easily have been said I didn't do a great job. So it was a pleasant surprise to me when I came out okay after the reorganization."*

Many in Apple were upset over the reorganization, especially when it was released that Jobs was being relieved of all operational duties. He would continue as chair but with no direct influence on company operations.

## Transitions

In September of 1985, Jobs officially resigned as chair of Apple. Apple computer sales continued to suffer as the computer industry continued in a downward trend and competitors like IBM continued to take market share. Revenue was only modestly higher, and the company reported the first losing quarter in the company's history.

[10] Mary Gentile and Todd Jick (1986).

Dubinsky found that her transition into her new role was overshadowed by the seismic organizational shifts taking place all around her. "Despite the changes," she said, "Apple continued to be very unstable from the top, reorganizing every few months." A year after her transition, Dubinsky decided to pursue other opportunities within the company. "The idea was I would go to Australia for six months, gain the field experience, and help their marketing department. After the experience I would come back to corporate. I was excited by the opportunity."

## Dubinsky in the Land Down Under

Dubinsky arrived in Sydney, Australia, late in 1986. She found an office lacking in process and rigor and Apple Australia as a bit of a "cowboy operation." She focused on distribution strategy and managing the dealer network, which were roles she was very familiar with from her time at headquarters. The work proved rewarding and she found she loved the freedom of a smaller office where she felt each day she was able to have an impact.

The office culture was much different from the one at the California headquarters. Many of her Australian officemates were married and held to rather strict schedules both at work and outside of work. She found they generally did not extend much hospitality to newcomers like her.

Australia itself offered a number of attractions for Dubinsky to explore, including the famous Sydney Opera House, which Dubinsky was able to view from her apartment on the north side of the harbor. One of Dubinsky's favorite interests proved to be the Great Barrier Reef north of the city. In her spare time, she became certified as a scuba diver and dove at the reef. But as more and more time was taken up by work, Dubinsky's diving opportunities dwindled.

Dubinsky's original six-month commitment in Australia came and went. When she returned to California for a short business trip, Dubinsky met with Del Yocum, a senior executive. Dubinsky recalled, "I told him I really wanted to talk about what was next for me, where I was going to go, and what I was going to do. Yocum had replied, 'Don't worry, something will come up.'"

After that trip, Dubinsky felt the only way she was going to make her next move was if she pursued openings at Apple headquarters. Among the new e-mails awaiting her return to Australia were several that quickly drew her eye. Describing personnel changes within Apple, the messages reflected Apple's almost constant state of reorganization that seemed to be unending. Dubinsky had grown used to that reality but what frustrated her was the stream of promotions that were announced back at headquarters. Many of the promotions were into positions that she was qualified for but had never been contacted about.

Just when Dubinsky thought Apple's executive management had forgotten about her. Campbell offered Dubinsky the opportunity to be VP of operations and report directly to him. Her responsibility was to develop a new venture's worldwide distribution strategy. Campbell gave her two weeks to decide.

## What's Next?

Dubinsky decided to join Campbell at Apple's new subsidiary, named Claris, in the spring of 1987. She liked the idea of being part of a founding team, and she respected the other members of the team that Campbell had already selected. She also definitely wanted to return home to the United States. So Dubinsky joined the Claris team:

*"I enjoyed working with Bill Campbell at Apple. He and I had a great relationship — despite what many would consider a rough beginning. He grew to respect my honest, up-front attitude. He knew when I said something, there were no hidden agendas. So, I was excited when Campbell started Claris. It was the best of both worlds. I was joining a startup. A business I could get in on at the ground floor. Also, it was Campbell who was going to be building a new team. The weekend after receiving his initial inquiry, I was back in California participating in the founding team meetings. I was employee number three at Claris."*

Joining Claris proved to be a great decision. Dubinsky successfully built an international distributor network for the Claris software products. She traveled nearly 50 percent of the time to all areas of the world. Within four years, Dubinsky's group made up more than 50 percent of Claris's total revenue.[11] In addition to gaining further experience with international sales and marketing,

[11] Pat Dillon, "The Next Small Thing," *Fast Company* (June 1998): 97.

Dubinsky also learned a great deal from Campbell on building a management team:

> *"Claris was an amazing experience. I was traveling a lot, and I was mainly setting up distributors for our products. I had a small team back in California that serviced those distributors and a management structure I built out. We were very successful selling those software products to the international markets.*
>
> *Bill handpicked an amazing executive staff. This was when I really learned the basics of management process, watching Bill run Claris that close up and build it from nothing into something pretty significant. I really enjoyed the experience."*

## The Apple Takeover

After four years of functioning like an entrepreneurial venture, Claris lost its spinoff status as Apple reacquired a controlling interest in it. Despite their best efforts, the Claris executives were unable to persuade the parent company to restore its independence. Rejoining Apple raised issues for Dubinsky:

> *"I was at the end of my rope with Apple. I really had not wanted to be there anymore. Claris had been the opportunity to do this new thing and we planned to do it as an independent company. It was when Apple said, 'No, we are not going to spin you out,' that I made the final decision that I did not want to work for Apple anymore. I wanted to do something else."*

Dubinsky and Campbell left Claris at the same time. Dubinsky decided to head to Paris to take an extended period of time off to think about what was next:

> *"In Paris, I thought a lot about what I wanted to do. Did I want to go back into the computer industry or do something totally different? In the end, I decided I was good at technology and that I should get back into it. I also really wanted to work on a startup. I enjoyed the Claris startup experience and I did not want to do the big company thing. So after a year in Paris, I came back to California focused on finding a technology startup to join."*

## Choices: to Go or to Palm?

When Dubinsky returned to Silicon Valley in the early summer of 1992, she talked with a number of small startup companies. None of them presented the kind of growth opportunity she was looking for. So she decided to start calling some contacts to see what they were up to. Dubinsky was in contact with Bruce Dunlevie, a well-known Silicon Valley venture capitalist who had invested in a startup called Palm Computing. That entrepreneurial venture started in 1992 when Jeff Hawkins, a bright technologist with experience in the handheld industry, approached Dunlevie with an idea for a handheld computer. Dunlevie immediately loved the concept and helped Hawkins get started with a first round of venture funding.

Jeff Hawkins and Palm were now at a point where they needed a CEO to help organize the company. Dubinsky's recommendations impressed Dunlevie, but he had reservations about her lack of CEO experience in the valley. He told Hawkins:

*"I liked her enormously. I thought that she was very intelligent. She doesn't want to be a CEO for the wrong reasons — a lot of people want to do it because they want to have power. She just wants to fully use her skills. But she was the least qualified of all the people we talked to."*[12]

Despite Dunlevie's initial assessment, Hawkins agreed to meet with Dubinsky. During their first meeting, they clicked immediately. Hawkins showed her what Palm was trying to accomplish: create a palm-sized computing device. She was impressed:

*"I liked Jeff immediately. He was straightforward and said he needed someone who would respect him as a product guy. He showed me a device similar to what Palm was helping to develop. I had never seen anything like it, electronics in the palm of your hand. It was the first time, in a long time, that I'd been really jazzed. It was like the first time I saw the Apple II at Harvard."*[13]

After the meeting, Hawkins called a number of Dubinsky's references. The comments reflected his initial impressions, that she was the "real deal." He did

[12] Andrea Butter and David Pogue. *Piloting Palm* (New York: John Wiley & Sons, 2002): 37.
[13] Pat Dillon (1987).

receive some "glass ceiling" comments, challenging him to think twice before hiring a female executive because in the words of the responders, "You're going to have to deal with a lot of people who will not understand how to handle a woman executive."

Another longtime contact on Dubinsky's list was Bill Campbell, who was with GO Corporation. Lotus Development Corp. founder Mitch Kapor and Jerry Kaplan, one of his leading software engineers, had started GO with $25 million in early venture funds in 1987. One of their product ideas was to develop a pen-based computer. They believed it would be a huge hit in a number of market segments, replacing the bulky, portable computers of the day. Over the first few years of development, they narrowed in on an operating system called PenPoint for this new wave of portable devices. By 1991, Campbell had been brought in to help lead the company. That same year, IBM and GO brokered a partnering deal. IBM would manufacture the hardware and GO would provide the software. By 1992, however, the relationship was on shaky ground, and GO was looking for other partners or investment options.

When Dubinsky contacted Campbell, he was excited to hear from her. Campbell's team-building philosophy was unchanged from his days at Apple — bring in the most talented people possible. He tested the waters with Dubinsky to see if she would be interested in exploring opportunities with GO.

## The Fork in the Road

Two exciting options now lay ahead of Dubinsky, one from a leader she knew, respected, and had worked for before, and the other from a new contact with an opportunity to lead a small, unproven startup firm. What was the right career direction? Which option made the most sense?

## QUESTIONS FOR REFLECTION

1. What incidents in Ms. Dubinsky's life do you think shaped her leadership style and approach?

2. How would her early career balance wheel differ from her late career balance wheel?

3. Would you say that Ms. Dubinsky is a success? Why or why not?

4. What challenges do you expect Ms. Dubinsky will face in her next chapter in life?

## EPILOGUE

Ms. Dubinsky's career is well chronicled in the business media.[14] At this point in her life, she felt better about Palm's strategy and accepted the position of CEO. In December 1994, she adopted a 3½-year old Russian girl. Her company was acquired first by US Robotics and then by 3Com. In 1998, she formed Handspring with a long time trusted colleague. In 2000 Ms. Dubinsky was named to *Forbes*' list of the wealthiest Americans, however, shortly thereafter the fortunes of Handspring reversed. In 2003, Palm, going full circle, acquired Handspring and its popular Treo product line for $169 million. By 2005, she was serving on several boards of directors and had started her third venture with her business partner.

[14] See also "The Life and Career of a High Tech Entrepreneur (B)," UVA-OB-0844, Darden School Foundation, for more details.

## REFERENCES

Apple Computer History Weblog. http://apple.computerhistory.org/stories/story Reader$18 (accessed 12 October 2005).

Bricklin, Dan. "The Idea," http://danbricklin.com/history/saiidea.htm (accessed 12 October 2005).

Butter, Andrea and Pogue, David. *Piloting Palm*, New York: John Wiley & Sons, 2002.

Dillon, Pat. "The Next Small Thing," *Fast Company* (June 1998).

Gentile, Mary and Jick, Todd. "Donna Dubinsky and Apple Computer, Inc. (A)." Harvard Business School Publishing. February 21, 1986.

Gergen, David. *Yale and the Frontier of Technology: Donna Dubinsky and the Handheld Computer*, Yale300 Alumni Leadership Convocation. Yale University. April 19–22, 2001, http://www.yale.edu/yale300/aprilweekendvideos (accessed 12 October 2005).

"Graphic indicating Operating Revenues and Net Income for Apple Computers," *USA Today*. 19 September 1985.

Guterl, Fred. "Design Case History: Apple's Macintosh," *IEEE Spectrum* (December 1984).

Hertzfeld, Andy. "The Original Macintosh: Anecdotes About the Development of Apple's Original Macintosh Computer, and the People Who Created It," http://www.folklore.org/index.py (accessed 12 October 2005).

Hixson, Amanda. "The Reshaping of Apple," *Personal Computing* (April 1987).

Jick, Todd. "Interview with Donna Dubinsky," *Harvard Business School Publishing*. December 19, 1986.

Rosen, Benjamin. "Visicalc: Breaking the Personal Computer Software Bottleneck." *Morgan Stanley Electronics Letter*. 11 July 1979. http://danbricklin.com/history/rosenletter.htm (accessed 19 October 2005).

Rudolph, Barbara. "Shaken to the Very Core," *Time* (September 1985).

Tajnai, Carolyn. "Fred Terman, The Father of Silicon Valley" 1985, Paper presented at the Stanford Computer Forum, Stanford, California. See also http://www.netvalley.com/archives/mirrors/terman.html (accessed 12 October 2005).

# 10

# ED NORRIS: THE LIFE AND CAREER OF A POLICE COMMISSIONER

*I worked 14 to 16-hour days in the police business. Only took Sundays off. I buried a lot of good officers. I didn't do what I was accused of in the first place. How could I do anything different? I'm asked that question all the time, and it pisses me off. Would I have saved every single receipt I ever had? I don't know. What can I say? I didn't do what they accused me of doing in the first place. I didn't buy lingerie from the discretionary fund. Nothing. I saved a lot of lives in the city — and proved to people it could be done. I broke my ass for this city, buried seven police officers here, led the nation in crime reduction… why would I do anything different?*

— *Edward T. Norris*
*November 2006*

With a smile as wide as the Mississippi River, former Baltimore Police Department Commissioner Ed Norris[a] had reason to grin in the spring of 2007. A hit CBS radio show in Baltimore (a place he used to love second only to New York City), appearances on CNN and Fox News, an acting role in a popular HBO television series, a clever and devoted wife, a perpetually charming elementary school-age son, and more money than he could ever earn as a cop would make anyone beam. On the inside, though, Norris seethed.

He wanted his life as police commissioner or head of the Maryland State Police back — a hope impossible to attain given that he had agreed to plead guilty in early 2004 to charges of conspiracy to commit fraud and filing a false tax return in exchange for not being prosecuted for lying on a mortgage application. Norris had believed that bargain would prevent him from serving jail time. That did not happen, and Norris spent the next six months in prison, another six months under house arrest, then returned to Baltimore to serve 500 hours of community service in 2006.

Was his life ruined? He was only 46 years old. Were the next 30 or 40 years going to be defined by this? Would those three years really haunt all the subsequent decades of his life? The future he had imagined since he was young was irrevocably changed. From his perspective, the entire country seemed to stand in judgment and condemnation of him. Would he move beyond the worst of his past?

[a] Please view video clips of interviews at https://store.darden.virginia.edu/business-case-study/edward-norris-and-the-baltimore-police-department-a-1266

## Before the Badge

Edward T. Norris came from a family of cops. His father was a butcher who became a police officer at age 32. "He had a military background and saw security in the police department," Norris said. Norris described his childhood as "fun"; he and his younger brother grew up in a racially diverse neighborhood in Brooklyn, New York. Under the watchful eye of their stay-at-home mom, the Norris boys hung out on the fire escape and played hide-and-seek on 13th Street. "There was always someone out there tougher than you," he recalled.

Young Eddie Norris dreamed of one day becoming a doctor or scientist. When he was 10 years old, Norris discovered football — a game he really enjoyed playing. Although he was a good student, being a defensive linebacker in high school was what landed Norris a Division III scholarship to the University of Rochester. By his third year, though, school became less affordable. In August of that year, Norris went to football camp; within a month, he had quit school and was sworn into the police academy on September 2, 1980 — "although I had not planned to stay," he said.

## Becoming a Cop in the New York City Police Department

The elder Norris taught his son that he had to work hard and take care of himself because poverty was only two paychecks away. Determined to meet that challenge, the younger Norris began his police career in one of New York's most difficult districts, Times Square. At the time, 16 officers were assigned to the area, known for its high level of criminal activity. Norris recalled an incident early in his career:

*"Every night you deal with the same people. I was walking 42nd Street in plain clothes and came upon a serious criminal punching a working girl. We ended up in a brawl and serious physical fight. It was a bloody mess, and we both took lumps until my partner helped me arrest this guy.*

*About a year later, I am on the same street when a woman has a seizure. I kneel down to try and help her, and a big crowd gathers. Now, this mob is not exactly full of law-abiding citizens, and I can hear someone saying,*

*'Get his gun! Get his gun!' And then from out there I also hear, 'No, no, man ... leave him alone, he's all right.' Who do you think that was? The guy I had had the tough fight with!*

*Both sides know the rules, the police and the criminals. I never took any cheap shots when I arrested that guy a year before — once he was in cuffs it was over. Being tough doesn't mean being dirty. This is a brutal business, and yet how you treat people out there matters."*

Norris remembered many heart-wrenching stories from his tenure at the NYPD, stories that taught him what he called "lessons in life." Early in his career, he responded to a call from a man who lived in a freezing-cold tenement house. The man's wife of many years had just passed away. She was a double amputee, and her husband had spent the golden years of their lives looking after her basic physical and emotional needs day after day after day. Very upset by her death, the man sobbed as he told Norris, "I have no reason to live now." Norris stayed with him until an ambulance arrived. When it was time for Norris to sign off on the case clearance, he was surprised to learn that the aging couple, living in poverty, were parents to a son — a successful New York City dentist. The poignancy of that story stayed with Norris throughout his career.

## COMMISSIONER EDWARD T. NORRIS OF THE BALTIMORE POLICE DEPARTMENT

As a 20-year veteran of the NYPD, Norris moved up when he took the job as commissioner of the Baltimore Police Department (BPD) in March 2000. Norris had never really considered leaving his hometown, but he decided to run the idea by his wife. Kate Norris had grown up in California and graduated from Stanford University with a master's degree in fine arts. The couple met in a men's shop where she worked on Fifth Avenue. They had a one year old son and had begun to think about where they might like to raise him. After some discussion, the pair decided Norris should explore the opportunity — which, at the very least, offered them a chance to live in a city where they could afford to buy a house, something out of their reach in the high-priced New York real estate market.

Norris's appointment was controversial, and he faced constant and tough critics in the media. His outspokenness often stimulated significant public response in

Baltimore. He subscribed to the "crime reduction" model; he publicly stated that the few hard-core criminals responsible for most violent crimes needed to be identified swiftly and put behind bars and that if BPD did this, criminals would go elsewhere, and violent crimes in the city would drop dramatically. His critics, including the director of the local American Civil Liberties Union, feared his approach would compromise the constitutional rights of citizens and clog the court system. Community leaders who lived in high-crime areas began to meet with Norris to learn more about him and to challenge his philosophy. West Central citizen leader Myrtle Howerton (known widely as "Momma Myrt") remembered her first meeting with Norris:

> "We sat around that boardroom table, and I looked at him and wondered, 'What is that sawed-off shrimp going to do for us?' I remember standing up with my hands on my hips and saying, 'What's all this we've been hearing about zero tolerance?' He said, 'There's no such thing as zero tolerance.' And then he got busy."

Not all community groups were unhappy with Norris's approach. Business leaders on the Greater Baltimore Committee praised Norris and his approach to crime-fighting. The group raised $550,000 to support the reduction of violent crime. Local restaurant entrepreneur Joel Shalowitz believed that Commissioner Norris had immediate credibility among businesspeople. Shalowitz had lived in New York City and had seen firsthand the dramatic reduction in crime under Norris's supervision. He said, "I was really glad to have one of NYPD's strategists on the home team at Baltimore. I just knew he was going to make a difference and had a level of devotion to go beyond protecting only the Inner Harbor."

Norris believed that fighting crime was primarily a numbers game. First, one had to find out the status quo, so his first agenda item was to clarify the numerical crime picture. He wanted to have good measures by which he could gauge progress. He began by poring over a 1999 FBI crime report on Baltimore. He knew that collecting and reporting "solid" police statistics were — like accounting in a business — difficult tasks fraught with subjectivity and a wide variety of approaches. Some systems, for example, keyed off of citizen call-ins. If an automobile theft was called in, it was recorded as such, but if the responding officer discovered the car was actually not stolen, the record was not changed.

This system, in effect, recorded "reported crime" rather than "actual crime." The FBI used a different approach, called Crime Index data collection, in which reports that later proved to be false were deleted from the database.

After studying the FBI report, Norris assigned the deputy commissioner for administration to meet with all unit commanders in the administration bureau to establish and ensure a standardized methodology for defining, measuring, and producing all BPD operational data, specifically crime statistics. Norris believed that unless he could measure the rate of crime in the city, he could not fight it effectively. Norris settled on a dozen or so key measures: annual rates of violent crime, like shootings, forcible rape, robbery, and aggravated assault, as well as burglary, larceny, and auto theft. His strategy was to track those numbers and manage them down.

The commissioner made some critical decisions early on to run the police department like a business by establishing clear measures for data collection and setting goals (e.g., bring the murder rate down to fewer than 300 a year). Reorganizing became an important part of Norris's change plan[1] (for more data see footnote 1).

> The commissioner made some critical decisions early on to run the police department like a business by establishing clear measures for data collection and setting goals

He ended the rotation policy, reduced the police athletic league (PAL) program, made recruitment a priority, decentralized districts and sectors, and shifted command responsibilities to a time-based structure rather than a geographic structure; implanted the COMSTAT system (a database that kept track of everywhere in a specific geographic place crime was committed) and held commanding officers responsible for the statistical results in their districts; decentralized detective services to districts; put two officer patrols into operation; and assigned more officers to the central office to work on clearing up the warrant backlog.

Norris also knew how important it was for police officers to feel proud of their equipment and their department. Police work involves the effective use of many symbols, including uniforms, badges, weapons, vehicles, and even demeanor, all of which can be a significant deterrent to crime. Norris was aware that officers felt

[1] "Edward Norris and the Baltimore Police Department (A)" and "Edward Norris and the Baltimore Police Department (B)" [UVA-OB-0776 and UVA-OB-0777].

183

sheepish about the "soft" colors of their vehicles, so he commissioned a redesign of the paint scheme for police vehicles (including cars, helicopters, and boats) that included a navy blue background with bright luminescent markings. The mayor (facing budget constraints) resisted this request and only allowed enough funds to paint 30 vehicles. Norris used these as "prizes" for the districts that reduced their crime numbers the most. And because the mayor's office had said that he could not repaint all the cars, Norris decided, with a twinkle in his eye, that that did not mean he could not repaint the boats and helicopters, so he did.

The commissioner's solution to changing the culture was to teach by example and establish credibility. Norris believed in being directly involved in law enforcement and never wanted to be viewed as the leader behind the desk. He earned a reputation for being a "cop's cop" (so much so that he was cast as a cop on the HBO television series *The Wire*) by chasing down drug dealers, holding his top commanders accountable for crime in their areas, pressuring City Hall to increase pay for officers, tightening the rules on uniform appearances, replacing old guns, and seeking grants to fund improved technology. Norris built internal relationships through promotion, rewards, and his unwillingness to accept corruption, yet readiness to remove minor complaints from the Internal Affairs Division (IAD). He used fear when necessary and his outsider status to wait, watch, and listen before he got rid of people. Externally, Norris adopted a strategy of transparency — "get the good news out fast and the bad news out faster." Sometimes the press was good, and other times bad. He built trust relationships with the community through frequent radio and television appearances. When he perceived that the local media would not write a fair story on his efforts, Norris contacted the national media in an attempt to get a more balanced hearing. The commissioner talked to numerous business groups and used change agents in the community like Baltimore community activist Momma Myrt to help get his message out.

Norris, by nature, was outspoken and direct in his descriptions of what needed to be done, so his statements often stimulated significant public response. Many found his communication style refreshing; others found it abrupt and insensitive. Norris believed it was better to deal with the facts directly than to beat around the bush. He had opinions and was willing to share them as he saw appropriate.

After losing several colleagues and friends in the second World Trade Center bombings on September 11, 2001, Norris felt compelled to speak out.

He also thought he could make a difference in the fight against terrorism. On October 5, 2001, he testified at the U.S. House of Representatives Committee on Government Reform. He asked the committee, 'Why aren't we all working together to find the people the FBI are looking for? We all need each other if we as a nation are going to successfully counter threats that can come from virtually anywhere, at any time, in any form — including forms that destroy whole cities.' Norris noted that the FBI had not[2] asked for local police help or entrusted local departments with enough information to act on their own. Norris made several points[3]:

- There was a disconnect in information-sharing between federal agencies and local law enforcement.

- Local law enforcement had the manpower to follow up on a high volume of leads (11,533 FBI agents and more than 650,000 local law enforcement officers nationwide).

- Local law enforcement officers were in contact with millions of people daily via interactions including arrests, citations, field interviews, stop-and-frisks, and routine discussions with local populations.

- Local law enforcement agencies had numerous informants and could debrief prisoners about suspicious activities that may be terrorism-related at the same time they debriefed prisoners about traditional crimes.

Norris made three recommendations: (1) federal agents must share all locally relevant information with state and local police officers; (2) police chiefs should receive regular briefings on highly classified information on intelligence and counterterrorist efforts; and (3) implementation of the Communications Assistance for Law Enforcement Act (CALEA), which was passed in 1994 and required telephone companies to update their systems and networks to accommodate federal, state, and local wiretaps.[4]

[2] Edward T. Norris, "Preparedness for Biological Chemical Attacks," Congressional Testimony on "The Silent War: Are Federal, State, and Local Governments Prepared for Biological and Chemical Attacks? *Hearing before the Subcommittee on Government Efficiency, Financial Management, and Intergovernmental Relations Committee on Government Reform, House of Representatives, 107th session, October 5, 2001,* Washington, DC: GAO, pp.107–95, 2002.
[3] Ibid.
[4] Ibid.

## Norris's Philosophy on Police Work

When asked what he hated most, Norris replied quickly: bullies. Bullies (and stereotypes of dumb cops) bothered Norris. His own police academy class was full of lawyers, a chemical engineer, and several individuals with advanced degrees. This fact was also true of the BPD, which had a highly educated work force. Decisiveness, loyalty, and hard work were important virtues in Norris's book. Police work was for Norris a lifelong and noble cause; he said he'd never want to work anywhere but with a police force.

*"I was raised right-wing and lean that way myself, but 23 years of policing made me more compassionate for the underprivileged. Seeing people at their worst — often good people in bad situations — leaves a mark on you. You see terrible diseases, suicides, the worst humanity has to offer — and often the police are the first ones there. Cops aren't exactly in the business for the money, but instead, most of us are trying to make a difference. Looking after those that can't look after themselves."*

Norris's brown eyes held a hint of a twinkle that could quickly turn to sadness when describing the difficulties that many of the less fortunate faced. He rubbed his thumbs when listening to others speak. No matter how many tragic events Norris had witnessed as a police officer over nearly a quarter of a century in the business, the worst were when his fellow officers were killed in the line of duty. Writing eulogies was troubling and a reflective time for Norris. He wondered why he was doing the kind of work he did. But Norris was reminded of his favorite lines from Shakespeare's *Henry V*:

> This story shall the good man teach his son;
> And Crispin Crispian shall ne'er go by,
> From this day to the ending of the world,
> But we in it shall be remember'd,
> We few, we happy few, we band of brothers;
> For he to-day that sheds his blood with me
> Shall be my brother; be he ne'er so vile,
> This day shall gentle his condition:
> And gentlemen in England now a-bed

Shall think themselves accurs'd they were not here
And hold their manhoods cheap while any speaks
That fought with us upon Saint Crispin's day.

## THE BALTIMORE POLICE SUPPLEMENTAL ACCOUNT

By the summer of 2002, Norris was in the media-scrutiny hot seat when he was accused of using an off-the-books account to fund trips to New York and purchase BPD-embossed gifts for visitors. The Baltimore Police Supplemental Account was a discretionary fund established in 1983 through a combination of several previous funds (the Athletic, Christmas Basket, and Unemployed and Emergencies funds). There were no instructions for the use of the funds except for the "benefit of the Baltimore Police Department."[5] Two authorized representatives from the fiscal section of the BPD were required to sign before any funds could be released.[6] Thomas Frazier, one of Norris's predecessors, spent approximately $300,000 from that account during a five-year span in the 1990s.[7] When the authors of earlier Darden case studies on Norris asked him about the fund in November 2002, Norris said:

*"We had people dying on the streets, I had just lost an officer in the line of duty, and I was being dragged through the dirt with accusations of theft for money spent from a discretionary fund for business trips and honorary gifts. Okay, so I'm rotten at saving receipts, but I can save lives."*

Norris described a typical outing to the Baltimore Orioles baseball games:

*"We spent something like one thousand bucks a game. When I took staff members to ball games, I was told, 'All right commissioner, you're showing up tonight. We're taking the warrant unit command staff.' We would go to the game and I would talk to the people who worked for me, we'd buy beer and crab cakes, hot dogs, whatever else. And we'd have a great night."*

[5] *United States of America v. Edward T. Norris, John Stendrini* 2003R00390: 4.
[6] Ibid: 6.
[7] Wilber Del Quentin, "Norris, Police Spend Off-the-Books Funds on Trips, Gifts, Meals," *Baltimore Sun,* 14 August 2002.

Norris was not the one who paid the bill. Instead, members of his staff were to submit the receipts and list who was in attendance. Sometimes he included visitors from his former employer, the NYPD, if he had extra tickets. He also used the account for business dinners, to buy combat boots (described as "dress shoes for personal use" on the indictment), police shirts (labeled "custom dress shirts for personal use") for which Norris paid half from his own checking account, and police rescue tools (called a "personal gift for himself").

Admittedly, Norris was a poor bookkeeper. For example, he was invited to speak at a graduate school class on leadership at a state school in Virginia in 2003. When asked if he had receipts to submit for reimbursement, he hesitated, and then agreed that repayment for gas would be appropriate. He never did submit the receipts for repayment, "I just got busy and forgot," he said. Several administrators within his department were in charge of the discretionary account, yet even with the heightened media interest, few of them had paid attention to the details of submitting accurate receipts.

## STEPPING UP TO MARYLAND STATE POLICE SUPERINTENDENT

Early in 2003, Norris left BPD in hopes of developing a new vision for the state police — to be the national model for homeland security organization and effectiveness. He accepted the Maryland governor's invitation to be superintendent of state police. Making the move to the Maryland Department of State Police proved to be a contentious one. Mayor Martin O'Malley and other members of Baltimore City Council were upset over losing their top crime fighter — especially after working out a deal that would have entitled Norris to a $100,000 bonus if he remained commissioner until January 2004. The *Baltimore Sun*'s allegation of excessive spending from a discretionary fund remained a hot topic and was mentioned in several media descriptions of Norris's move to the Maryland State Police.

Although Maryland Governor Robert Ehrlich appointed Norris superintendent of the state police, he was required to obtain consent from the Maryland Senate to allow Norris to serve. The hearings were controversial and, according to Norris, "I was kicked around like a beach ball." Momma Myrt appeared before the state senate, told them how changes to the city police had improved her life, and

scolded the governing body for trying to block Norris's appointment. With a vote of 41 for and 3 against, Norris was appointed superintendent.

Norris worked on his plans to combat terrorism and his voice garnered national attention. On ABC News *Nightline* on March 3, 2003, he said:

*"We are the homeland security defense.... There's 650,000 cops in this country. Local police officers, sheriffs, state troopers who are at the front of this fight. They're going to be the ones to confront these terrorists, either in a car stop, an arrest, a car accident. There's a million ways that people come in contact with the police. We've gotta be prepared. If a sheriff's deputy in a town in Maryland stops somebody, they should have a place to call to run a name at three o'clock in the morning on a weekend. And that's what we try to provide."[8]*

The continuing controversy over Norris's use of the discretionary fund marred his first few months as colonel. The city paid Ernst & Young for an independent audit of the account and found a $61.85 purchase of clothing.[9] Peggy Watson, Baltimore's finance director, conducted her own investigation and asked Norris to repay $7,663 for items she believed were questionably charged to the fund.[10] Rumors of the federal investigation led by U.S. Attorney Thomas M. DiBiagio and an impending indictment grew louder.

## STEPPING DOWN

On December 10, 2003, only 10 months into the job, Edward Norris resigned his position at the Maryland Department of State Police — one day before Maryland's U.S. Attorney DiBiagio held a news conference announcing Norris's indictment on one count of misappropriation of funds and one count of conspiring to misapply funds. Norris was also charged with "lying on a mortgage applica-tion." He listed $9,000 of his father's money as a "gift" when he actually paid his

---

[8] ABC News *Nightline,* 3 March 2003.
[9] Tom Pelton, "2002 Independent Audit Found Little Misspending," *Baltimore Sun,* 12 December 2003 http://www.sunspot.net/news/local/crime/bal-temd.audit12dec12,0,3801377 (accessed 12 December 2003).
[10] Ibid.

father the money back. "Lying on a mortgage application is a federal crime," said Joseph Falk of the National Association of Mortgage Brokers. "It includes bank fraud, wire fraud, and mail fraud, and potentially a host of state offenses. This can result in jail time."[11] That charge proved to be the "head shot," as one attorney told Norris, because it carried a 30-year sentence. The grand jury charged Norris with diverting $20,000 from the discretionary fund for inappropriate purchases and overtime payments to aides and drivers, and lying on a mortgage application. On March 3, 2004, three more charges were levied against Norris, alleging he falsely filed tax returns between 2000 and 2002. The false tax returns were apparently meant to cover the money Norris allegedly received from the discretionary fund which he failed to pay taxes on it.

On March 8, 2004, Norris pleaded guilty to the charge of conspiracy to commit fraud. In exchange for his guilty plea of misusing a police discretionary fund, DiBiagio's office agreed not to prosecute him on the mortgage application lie charge — one act Norris had admitted to and that would certainly have meant incarceration.

The mention of a few women, identified only as "Females One through Eight," in the federal indictment, became a sensation that kept newspapers selling and rumors flying. Personally, it was the most hurtful part of the ordeal to the Norris family. Norris struggled to keep his composure three years later when he described some of the vulgar questions federal investigators asked his wife Kate Norris about their personal life.

Waiting for his sentencing, the family moved to Tampa, Florida, and created a new life. Norris got a tattoo of a phoenix rising (the mythical bird that never dies) on his shoulder. Rides on his used Harley-Davidson motorcycle provided more than enough time to think about his future. In Florida's climate, "you could ride a bike 365 — I loved that," he recalled. They bought a modest house and made friends with the neighbors. Kate Norris started her career in real estate, and their son Jack played soccer and attended the local school. His elementary school was just on the other side of their backyard fence. By then, Norris's son was five years old, and for Norris the thought of leaving Jack and Kate for jail was devastating.

---

[11] Noelle Knox, "10 Mistakes that Made a Flipping Flop," *USA Today*, 22 October 2006 http://www.usatoday.com/money/economy/housing/2006-10-22-young-flipper-usat_x.htm (accessed 8 June 2007).

Brought into court in handcuffs, Norris was sentenced on June 21, 2004, to six months' incarceration followed by six months of home detention. The judge also ordered that Norris pay a $10,000 fine, and perform 500 hours of community service in Baltimore. The community service penalty was 10 hours more than the maximum usually given. "Intentionally punitive," was how Norris described it. The plan to plead guilty on the discretionary account charges to avoid spending time in jail had failed. The couple decided not to tell Jack where his father was headed. Instead, Jack believed his dad was going "away to work." To help keep in touch, Norris had pre-arranged 26 different mail packages containing a card and toy for Kate Norris to give their son from him every month.

## Being on the Inside

Getting into a first-rate prison camp was, it seemed, as tricky as getting into an Ivy League school. Typically, the U.S. Bureau of Prisons used various criteria to assign inmates to particular correctional facilities — what crime they committed, what their career backgrounds were, and where their families lived. In contrast, however, Norris's incarceration was almost surreal. Trying to disguise his looks, the formerly clean-shaven ex-police commissioner grew a beard and mustache and shaved his head (called the "Murder One" haircut in prison). Although a couple of retired NYPD cop friends escorted Norris to jail at Eglin Air Force Base Federal Prison Camp — romping a bit along the way grabbing that last taste of bourbon and good steak — they arrived at the wrong entrance. Norris called prison officials who sent a van and a guard to pick him up. The dormitory-style accommodations, relative scarcity of guards compared with the number of inmates, and limited fences helped Elgin earn the nickname "Club Fed." Once inside prison walls, Norris tried to disguise himself as a drug dealer. Finally, the former CEO of Rite Aid, Martin Grass, told him, "Look, everybody knows who you are so forget it."

Six weeks into his prison term, Hurricane Ivan headed toward the East Coast, and the prison camp was evacuated. Prison officials herded inmates into the visiting room and told them they were being moved. The only things prisoners were allowed to bring with them were a change of underwear, toothbrush, and a single book. Fearing trouble, none of the inmates was allowed to call family or friends to let them know what was going on. "I was shipped around the Southeast taking a tour of the prison system," Norris said. Their first stop was supposed to be a place similar to Eglin at Pensacola, Florida. Instead, "I spent six weeks in a high-security prison in Yazoo City, Mississippi," Norris said, "where we had to sleep on bare mattresses on cell floors and locked in 20 hours a day." Yazoo City was a new facility that was unprepared for inmates; it had no bedding, laundry, food service, or other necessities, yet it was home to Norris and his fellow inmates for two months. None of the prisoners knew what was going on outside the walls because they had no mail, telephone calls, or visitors. It was almost as if few people in the prison system knew what was going on with these evacuees either. The author of this case sent Norris a letter at Eglin that was forwarded through the system to Lakewood Station in Atlanta before being returned to sender as "unknown." Finally, one mail delivery brought him letters and eight books, so Norris was able to read and catch up on events happening outside the prison walls.

## One of the news items Norris learned about was that the U.S Attorney who led the indictment against him was reprimanded by the U.S. Department of Justice

One of the news items Norris learned about was that the U.S Attorney who led the indictment against him was reprimanded by the U.S. Department of Justice for sending e-mails to his staff asking for "front page" public corruption indictments by November 2004 (just before the election). The Justice Department responded with a letter saying that any public corruption indictments by DiBiagio's office would require its approval. DiBiagio resigned on January 3, 2005.

Following his stay at Yazoo City, Norris was sent to a federal prison in Atlanta called USP Atlanta that housed high-security male inmates. On the bus ride, Norris was nervous that his cop background would cause him trouble as that jail had a bad reputation. He told another inmate he had befriended at Eglin about his concern. This inmate stood up on the bus and told the other 20-some prisoners, "Look, nobody gives up Eddie's profession when we get there." And to their credit, Norris's identity was safeguarded — he became the "drug dealer" he first described himself as. Just like on the outside, loyalty was a virtue that Norris highly regarded.

This move was the low point of Norris's whole ordeal. Arriving at night and then being stripped and body-cavity-searched, handed the orange pants and shirt, and given shoes of two different colors took the last bit of dignity from Norris. "My life had become so absurd," he said. Inmates were given Kraft Lunchables with Spiderman on the package to eat, which hit him hard. Spiderman was his son's favorite cartoon, and the pair had watched a Spiderman cartoon movie the night before Norris went to prison.

"I got to spend a night in the hole," Norris said. In one of the most notorious prisons in the federal system (Al Capone spent time there before being sent to Alcatraz, as did crime boss John Gotti), Norris was again sleeping on a floor, "under a sink, keeping the rats out by stuffing the bottom of the cell door with a rolled-up newspaper," he recalled. Eventually, he made his way to the federal prison camp next door called USP Atlanta.

## BEING ON THE OUTSIDE

After serving six months in various prisons and camps around the Southeast, Norris was sent home under house arrest on January 17, 2005. Wearing an electronic sensor bracelet that tracked his movements, Norris rejoined his family and started life again, looking for employment as a convicted felon. Finding a job was difficult and demeaning. Norris was able to find work as a clerk at a shop until someone called the company's corporate office to complain about his being employed there. He was let go immediately.

The former commissioner remained a popular Baltimore figure, however, and even the *Baltimore Sun* wrote favorably about him on February 28, 2005: "So it goes these days for the man some believe is the best police commissioner in the history of Baltimore, a third-generation New York officer. This is the man who did what his predecessors couldn't — and his successors haven't. He reduced the killing."[12]

When the case authors asked that same journalist, Ryan Davis, who first met and wrote about Norris during his trial, about Norris's conviction, he said he was disappointed and "wished he hadn't done it — we wanted him to be commissioner." Davis believed that as a public figure, Norris should have been held

---

[12] Ryan Davis, "Jobless Norris is Back—On the Radio," *Baltimore Sun,* 28 February 2005.

to a higher standard of personal behavior than the rest of society. His role as a reporter, Davis said, was to write about issues to generate change. For example, as a reporter in Florida he wrote a story about the sheriff's department's purchasing process. Within a week, the sheriff's office altered the purchasing policy to include bids — making it more competitive. In Baltimore, however, Davis said it was a different story:

> "In Baltimore, it was a hopeless feeling beyond the expectation that you could write a story and get it fixed. I wrote about a 15-year old being arrested 10 times in 12 months. He never got services or was retained, and then got shot in the head. I wrote about his killing, too, but nothing changed.
>
> The system pieces in Baltimore don't work. They don't fit well together. There is no common strategy between the police, prosecutors, courts, and jail. The state runs the jail. The city focuses on the police department as if BPD is solely responsible."

With local interest in Norris still high, a local Baltimore radio station, FM 105.7, called Norris one day in Florida:

> "I was living in Tampa and the general manager of the station, who knew who I was but didn't know me called. Because of my style, being kinda blunt, controversial, outspoken, he wanted to know if I would be interested in doing a radio show. When he first called I said, "Naw." I wasn't going to talk to anyone from Baltimore, you know. I really wasn't interested in doing anything in Baltimore because of what happened. And then I thought about it. And I'm not doing anything else. So he convinced me to do it for an hour a day. They sent me a box, a Zephyr (an instant messaging device), a piece of equipment to my house, and sent people from the CBS affiliate in Florida to install it. Every day at noon I'd go on a show called Out to Lunch. Big O and Dukes were the guys on the show at the time. I was just from 12 to 1 every day on the radio answering questions talking about issues. They sent me a check every week with an hourly wage."

Norris was comfortable on the radio from his time as commissioner, and many people tuned in to hear the former top cop. From the moment Norris was put

on the air, calls flowed in from listeners with positive words and thoughts for Norris. "People called in wishing none of this had happened, and they were glad that

**From the moment Norris was put on the air, calls flowed in from listeners with positive words and thoughts for Norris.**

I was back," Norris said. "Cops called in anonymously." Eventually, attempting to make the program more entertaining, one of the program executives called in with something negative to say.

Following completion of his house arrest, Norris returned to Baltimore in August 2005 to fulfill his community service requirement. "That I was not allowed to fulfill my community service hours in my hometown was unheard of," Norris said. "Bringing me back to Baltimore was ridiculous." Beyond that, it was dangerous. As a convicted felon, Norris was unable to carry a weapon. "I was a former police commissioner who put a lot of violent criminals and drug dealers away," Norris explained, "and now, I have no way of protecting myself. I'm a target."

Upon his return, Norris planned a party to see his old pals in uniform. Yet the culture of vengeance Norris was all too aware of as police commissioner remained intact. All BPD officers were warned that if they had contact with Norris, their positions would be in jeopardy. "The guys were going to come anyway — they didn't care about threats," Norris said. "I canceled the party because I don't want to cause problems for anyone else."

The Saturday evening before his first Monday morning studio appearance on FM 105.7 in Baltimore, Norris took a stroll around downtown. He was walking with Bob Philips, the general manager at CBS radio and FM 105.7. "When I got here," Norris recalled, "I was pretty bitter." As he walked, people stopped and gave him hugs. When he went into a restaurant, many embraced Norris and welcomed him back. A lot of people apologized to Norris for his troubles. That was the beginning of his new career in Baltimore.

When his job at the radio station ended, Norris headed to the League for People with Disabilities, Inc., to work off his community service hours. "I drove past this place when I was police chief and never gave it a thought," Norris said. "A friend suggested this place and it seemed like a good fit." He checked into a computer that logged his time and kept his parole officer informed of his work and whereabouts. At the league, Norris helped people with disabilities put on and take off their gym clothes, get out of their wheelchairs, and lift weights. He taught people from all walks of life about weights, weight training, diet, and nutrition. His presence lifted their spirits, too. The common bond they shared was that they had all faced difficulties in their lives and were trying to work through them. Norris had been serving communities all his life, and he welcomed the opportunity to serve in a different way. On the other hand, it was a constant reminder of the Justice Department investigation and his prison sentence.

Norris commuted on weekends back to Florida, arriving Friday nights and returning to Baltimore every Sunday evening. The commute, and being away from his family, was difficult. "We were happy in Florida," Norris said. "We had a nice place, good schools, and plenty of friends — friends who stuck by us. We were ready to give it a year and decided we didn't want to live like this. So I told the station I couldn't do this anymore."

With his popularity soaring, the general manager invited Norris to be on the radio four hours a day — "as a real job with a salary," Norris said. They changed the name of the talk show to *Ed Norris with the Big O and Dukes*. A few months later the radio show became *The Ed Norris Show*. He was on the air Monday through Friday from 10 am to 2 pm. The show targeted 25- to 54-year old men. Norris's appeal, however, extended to a much broader audience. The listenership became more ethnically diverse, and telephone calls increased 25 percent. The show's female audience grew as well.

Norris was awarded *City Beat*'s "best talk-show host" and won second place in *Baltimore* magazine's listings. FM 105.7 continued its growth strategy extending its local base and canceling syndicated programs. "We beat [syndicated radio host] Rush [Limbaugh] for listeners," Norris remarked with that old twinkle in his eye. In 2006, the Norris family reunited when his wife and son moved back to join him in the Baltimore area.

## BEING A RADIO TALK-SHOW HOST

With an open mike, Norris spent four hours each weekday talking, answering questions, stirring up controversy, and playing Baltimore's de facto mayor. During the general election of 2006, there were bumper stickers that read, "Eddie for Mayor," and the city received three pages of write-ins with Norris for sheriff of

Baltimore County — a position he never sought and was unable to ever hold given his criminal record.

Although Norris had always paid attention to the news, his new position meant paying even more attention to current events. "I watch the news and read whatever I can," He said. Prep for the next day's show was done the preceding evenings (deciding on topics, questions, researching facts, looking for guests). Norris's daily routine meant waking up between 5 am and 6 am, working out. He then drove 35 miles to the radio station — preferably on his motorcycle — arriving close to 8 am. Collaborating with the general manager and others at the station for show topics and ideas kept Norris busy until the show started at 10 am. Norris described his approach to his program:

*"Whatever pisses me off the most is what I lead with usually. I read something and try to tell people what's going on — given my experience. I try to give the real story. Other talk-show hosts can talk about their opinions but they don't have that kind of experience. I truly know both sides of the fence. This is my public service — I talk about stuff I'm familiar with... terrorism, the War on Terror, the war in Iraq, the Baltimore Police Department."*

> I try to give the real story. Other talk-show hosts can talk about their opinions but they don't have that kind of experience. I truly know both sides of the fence.

After the show, Norris cut commercials and taped product endorsements. Several companies were eager to be associated with the sharp-mouthed entertainer. Although he was unable to help others as a police officer anymore, Norris continued to positively influence people and improve their lives — something he seemed not to notice. For example, Norris had his own "get out the vote" campaign:

*"One of the biggest compliments I've gotten from people was when I was in Ocean City at Bike Week ... we were broadcasting there for Bike Week. A woman came up with her husband, they were Harley riders, and she said, "You know I haven't voted since I was 18. This is the first year I did, and it was because of you."*

When one of the case authors interviewed Norris in November 2006, they walked into a restaurant and two young adults, both MBA students, immediately recognized Norris. One student, an African American, promptly introduced himself and said, "I listen to you every day." He then said he had read the book about race relations Norris had recommended on the radio.

## TURNING LIFE AROUND

By June 2007, Eddie, Kate, and Jack Norris lived together in a suburb of Baltimore, and were moving past the challenges. Eddie Norris had worked off his public service at the League for People with Disabilities, Inc., while Kate Norris worked on her art. His character in the HBO series *The Wire* continued to be developed, and Norris enjoyed the opportunity to at least play a cop on TV. When weather permitted, he rode his motorcycle to work at CBS Radio. Otherwise, he jumped into his sporty candy-apple-red BMW for the commute. As the host of a popular talk show renamed *The Ed Norris Show, Locked and Loaded,* Norris lived the life of a public figure once more. There was even talk of syndicating the show.

That Norris would become host of a talk show and be included as a member of the news media was ironic. The media had played an important, and at times hurtful, role in Norris's life as a police officer, during his rise to commissioner and state superintendent, throughout his indictment, and again after his incarceration.

As a convicted felon, Norris not only lost his right to vote, hold public office, or possess a firearm or ammunition, but worst of all, he would never be a cop again:

*"I still believe the move I made to Baltimore was the right one, many lives were saved, and it didn't happen by accident. It took a lot of hard work, profound courage, and relentless drive on the part of many including the seven officers who gave their lives in those three years. It was a truly worthwhile endeavor.*

*General Barry McCaffery told me it was my duty to testify at the House committee on terrorism in 2001. So I did. And as I left, I was told they would make sure I lost my job. Well, I did. They did everything they could. I'm no thief. And I never took nothing from nobody ever. Not ever in my life. I was sent to prison for taking my staff to Orioles games."*

## QUESTIONS FOR REFLECTION

1. Should people in positions of visibility be allowed to have a private life? Why or why not?

2. What kinds of secrets should people be allowed to have?

3. What kinds of secrets do you have? How do these affect your behavior?

4. How many people do you have in life with whom you can talk about anything — no holds barred? Politics, religion, money, marriage, parenting, sex, etc.? That is how many people in life know who you are completely? How valuable to you are these people? List their names here.

5. What is your definition of "good character?"

6. Steve Covey once told my management class that if a person would cheat on his wife, he'd cheat in business. The founder of a billion dollar business once told me that that was not true, that he knew lots of chief executives who "cheated" on their wives regularly and he'd trust them any day in a business deal. What's your view and why?

## REFERENCES

ABC News *Nightline,* 3 March 2003.

Davis, Ryan. "Jobless Norris is Back—On the Radio," *Baltimore Sun,* 28 February 2005.

Knox, Noelle. "10 Mistakes that Made a Flipping Flop," *USA Today,* 22 October 2006 http://www.usatoday.com/money/economy/housing/2006-10-22-young-flipper-usat_x.htm (accessed 8 June 2007).

Norris, Edward T. "Preparedness for Biological Chemical Attacks," Congressional Testimony on "The Silent War: Are Federal, State, and Local Governments Prepared for Biological and Chemical Attacks? *Hearing before the Subcommittee on Government Efficiency, Financial Management, and Intergovernmental Relations Committee on Government Reform, House of Representatives, 107th session, October 5, 2001,* Washington, DC: GAO 107–95, 2002.

Pelton, Tom. "2002 Independent Audit Found Little Misspending," *Baltimore Sun,* 12 December 2003 http://www.sunspot.net/news/local/crime/bal-temd.audit12dec12,0,3801377 (accessed 12 December 2003).

Quentin, Wilber Del. "Norris, Police Spend Off-the-Books Funds on Trips, Gifts, Meals," *Baltimore Sun,* 14 August 2002.

*United States of America v. Edward T. Norris, John Stendrini* 2003R00390.

11

# Walt Shill: The Life and Career of a Senior Consultant

*"I think the idea of the sabbatical came to me even before the bicycle trip did. I read a book by Lamar Alexander — who later became a United States Senator — called 'Six Months Off'. He described his six years as governor of Tennessee and how during that time he gradually got more and more distant from his family without even being aware of it. He wrote that it finally hit him one day when he was sitting at dinner with his family and realized that all the children were facing his wife. He was a visitor at his own table. He decided right then that it was time to take a break, to reflect, to get reacquainted with his family."*

When Walt Shill[a] read Alexander's book in 1993, he was in the process of being elected partner at the Tokyo office of a leading global consulting firm, the first American to do so. Shill was only 33 years old, yet the awareness of being disconnected from his family and his own health had begun to bother him. As a hardworking, energetic graduate of both Virginia Tech and the University of Virginia, his career in consulting in Japan and the Far East together with his impending appointment as partner had seemed like a dream come true. But Alexander's book and Shill's growing awareness of his own situation worried him. Since graduating with his MBA eight years earlier, he'd gained 70 pounds and become increasingly married to his travel schedule. Now, on the verge of a career milestone that most viewed with eagerness, Shill was beginning to wonder if making partner was all there was in life.

> Since graduating with his MBA eight years earlier, he'd gained 70 pounds and become increasingly married to his travel schedule. Now, on the verge of a career milestone that most viewed with eagerness, Shill was beginning to wonder if making partner was all there was in life.

## BACKGROUND

Shill's parents met on a train; his father was a Navy recruit from a poor Mississippi family, and his mother was the daughter of a well-to-do family from Connecticut. They moved to Mississippi eventually, and Walter Shill was born in 1960 — the eldest of what were to be six children. Shill's father was

[a] Please view video clips of interviews at https://store.darden.virginia.edu/business-case-study/odyssey-the-life-and-career-of-a-senior-consultant-1273

"very task-oriented," and created a household atmosphere that Shill saw as the source of his own industrious character.

While attending college at Virginia Polytechnic Institute and State University (Virginia Tech), Shill made the football team as a walk-on. By November of his first semester, though, the demands of athletics were wreaking havoc on his grades, and since he wasn't doing terribly well at football either, he decided to quit the team. The values Shill had developed in his youth made this a difficult decision:

*"I think that's been in the back of my mind a long time. I... thought it was a smart thing to do... but it was very, very tough. I had somehow defined myself as 'not being a quitter.'"*

Shill also met his future wife during his first year at Virginia Tech. They married four years later in 1979, and moved to Tennessee so that Shill could take a mill job with Alcoa as a mechanical engineer. His experience upon arrival typified in his own mind how he viewed and handled new undertakings and unfamiliar assignments throughout his career:

*"I was sure they'd made a hiring mistake. I was terrified that I was going to screw up and get fired. So, I went in with this fear, and just applied myself. We had three or four shutdowns a year and you'd prepare for them endlessly. And then for one week, they'd stop all the equipment and you'd go in and do all the maintenance. It was a very intense 24-hour effort, like an exam. And I found that if I applied myself I could get it all done. I got promoted relatively quickly, and after a couple years I started thinking, 'Is this all there is?'"*

An assignment at Alcoa also introduced Shill to Asia Pacific. Shill was working with the main union in the plant, the United Steel Workers, to develop five year targets for quality, cost, and other measures — only to find out three months later that a Japanese competitor had already beat those targets. This experience planted a strong desire in Shill to visit Japan and to figure out how they were able to do what they were doing. Soon after, Shill left Alcoa to get an MBA. He applied at several schools and decided to attend the Darden Graduate School of Business at the University of Virginia.

## THE DARDEN MBA PROGRAM

During the fall of 1983, Shill arrived at the Darden School to a familiar, creeping sense of dread:

*"Once again, I thought they'd made a mistake. I'll never forget the first day, sitting in an auditorium, and I asked the woman next to me where she went to earn her undergraduate degree. 'Princeton,' she said, 'How about you?' 'Uh, Virginia Tech,' I said, and quickly asked her where she'd worked. It was Goldman Sachs, on Wall Street. And I said, 'Who's that?' I'd never heard of them, didn't know what an investment bank was or what an income statement even was. When she asked me where I'd been, I told her it was a factory in Tennessee, and I began to think, 'I'm in deep, deep trouble.'"*

To manage his concern, in a now typical pattern, Shill began working 80-plus hour weeks. He earned excellent grades, including a scholarship, and managed to get a summer fellowship in Japan. This was his first trip outside the United States, and it left a deep mark on him:

*"That was a life-changing experience. I don't think I slept that whole summer. I did everything you could possibly do in those 10 weeks. And I just loved it; I was so enthralled with something that was so unique and so different."*

As a result of his visit to Japan, Shill decided to enter the joint degree program in Asian Studies. This three-year program would give him two degrees, the MBA and an MA in Asian Studies and require him to spend six months in Japan doing research and working for a Japanese host company. This second, lengthier experience reinforced Shill's fascination with Japan and Asia. When it was time to find a permanent job after graduation, he knew that getting back to Japan would be part of his job-search strategy.

### Japan: Career and Family

After graduation, Shill took a consulting job with McKinsey and Company, who promised him a position in Tokyo if he performed well at their Cleveland office. When Shill arrived in Cleveland, he felt the familiar pattern — a panicked sensation of being in over his head, followed by hard work, and good reviews. His two years in Cleveland also saw the birth of his first son. Holding to their commitment, McKinsey transferred Shill to Japan, and he and his family moved to Tokyo in 1989. About this time, Shill's wife began to voice her concerns about his compulsive need to achieve:

> *"She was getting sort of sick of this pattern of reaching for the stars, getting there and then having to prove that I belonged there. My first three or four years in Japan I was working 70, 80, 100-hour weeks. I worked at least one day during the weekend, and it was almost a vacation to go into the office in blue jeans and do what I wanted to do. There was always this idea of being partner versus not being partner... I can't say that I wanted to be a partner so much as to prove that I could be."*

As Shill's position in the company grew, so did his family when a second son was born in Japan. Despite the new arrival, Shill's weekly schedule left little time for family, exercise, and vacations. He was working hard, traveling frequently, and his lifestyle was taking a toll on his health. Shill gained 70 pounds over that four-year period and began to notice that he felt constantly fatigued and even faintly ill on a regular basis. He also started to feel increasingly dissociated from his family. Work and family were becoming ever more difficult to juggle.

Other events in Shill's family life also had begun to cause him to think about "what's really important in life," as he put it. Shill and his wife had always wanted a girl, so they initiated a long series of events that would allow them to adopt a Japanese child. The stringency of the adoption screening process was, in Shill's words, humbling and oddly revelatory. While working through the adoption process, he wondered more about his status in life and his condition and the role that family played. Then in the midst of this process, Shill's mother passed away at the age of 65. His father had died prematurely at age 48 from cancer, so his mother's passing was an event which prompted Shill to reflect further. In addition, serving as executor to his mother's will, he was immersed in family management details and memories. Amazingly, their new infant daughter joined the Shill family about a week after his mother passed away:

*"Being the executor of the will forced me to deal with a lot of details in life that I don't normally deal with. I'm used to multibillion-dollar mergers, not to keeping track of who gets the refrigerator. And the adoption process was very humbling. People come to your home and start asking questions: "Have you ever hit your wife? Do you hate your kids?" And again, I'm used to big business deals and I'm thinking, "None of your business." But sorry, if you want to adopt, this is what you have to do. Those two experiences sort of foreshadowed the bike trip, making me say to myself, 'You aren't as important as you think.'"*

In the end, Shill's hard work paid off: in the summer of 1993 when he became the first American to be elected partner at the McKinsey's Tokyo office. He finally paid a visit to the family doctor:

*"I was 34 or 35, and the doctor said I was right on track: if I kept living this way I'd be dead in twenty years, if not sooner. I'd gained 70 pounds since I'd started at Darden, my resting heart rate was 85, my blood pressure was almost 260. Over the next months, something changed in me. My wife was a big part of it: she decided I should get a bicycle for Christmas. She said, 'Look: now that you've made partner, I'm not going to hear any more about what you need to be. You need to do something other than work.'"*

As his wife's words and his doctor's warning sank in, Shill began to realize that "the allure of being an achiever at McKinsey was gone." As he began to think about what he wanted to do with his life, the goal of getting fit came to the fore. Typically, he attacked this new goal with the same vigor he had every other objective in his life. He began getting up at 5:00 am to squeeze two hours of intense exercise into his daily routine. At first he rode an exercise bicycle, in part because he could do it without stressing his joints and also because he could monitor his heart rate. He bought a heart rate monitor and began reading intensively about heart rate, marathon training, diet, and recent scientific findings about the connection among all three. He was determined to utilize his exercise time to the best advantage by regulating his heart rate with research on the most benefit to be gained. Shill started riding the bicycle 10 miles in the beginning and over two years worked up to 60 or 70 miles.

On occasion, he postponed early morning meetings in order to complete his exercise; it had become a top priority.

The added time pressure of his new exercise regimen meant that on many nights he had only four hours of sleep. Yet he felt more productive on the job than he could ever remember. His resting heart rate fell; his performance ratings at McKinsey went up. In the meantime, Shill's wife was eager to return to the United States so he began investigating the possibilities of moving back. At some point during this period — the summer of 1995 — the idea of riding a bicycle across the United States began to take shape in his mind. Shill created a two-part challenge for himself: first to test his growing physical fitness, and second to sort out what he wanted to do with the rest of his life. In the end, the central activity he chose served both purposes. Shill decided to undertake a personal odyssey, alone, in the form of a coast-to-coast bicycle trip — a journey which Shill knew would require a vast improvement in his physical conditioning. To prepare, he planned a series of increasingly difficult training exercises for the summer of 1997. He ran a half-marathon, climbed Mt. Fuji, and rode his bike to the top of South Carolina's Mount Mitchell and Maui's 10,000-foot Mt. Haleakala.

During this time, Shill's 18-year marriage, what he described as a strong union between two very different people, began to take on a new dynamic:

*"I often think of myself as a kite, and her as the tension to hold me back. If she lets go, I'm gone, I crash. But I can climb higher and higher as long as there's some tension there. For her, I'm a sort of her alter ego: I'm able to get her to do things, like go to Japan that she would never have done otherwise. The problem is that I'm very disruptive to the home life she wants to create. And in a way I think moving back to the United States was a way to make amends for that. I was ready for more adventure, and for me it was really a struggle to move back to suburban America."*

But in June of 1997, the Shills did just that. Shill took a position at McKinsey's Washington, D.C., office, and the family moved into a home in Reston, Virginia. Smiling, he described the scene — a tidy suburban house with a minivan, 10 minutes from his in-laws — and admitted, "It's the antithesis of everything I would have wanted to do."

## THE SABBATICAL

Although Shill and his family moved to Virginia in June of 1997, he had nego-
tiated delaying going back to work until January of 1998. Shill was no longer as
certain of his plans for the future as he had been in earlier days, when a series
of stepping-stones — get the first job, get the MBA, get the consulting position in
Japan — had been clearly visible in front of him:

*"In the past, it was easy to just put another target out there and go after it.
But after becoming partner it wasn't so clear what that next target should
be. That's where the sabbatical idea came from — and I didn't call it a vacation. I felt like it should be some type of challenge."*

As the summer of 1997 approached, Shill worked out the details of his bike trip
with typical thoroughness. He had maps laid out county by county for the entire
trip. He read voraciously accounts of other similar journeys. He planned to ride
solo, both to eliminate dependence on others and, in hopes of meeting people
along the way more easily, yet also to be alone with his thoughts about his life
and his future. He planned to bring a tent and sleeping bag — so that he wouldn't
have to rely on roadside accommodations — a credit card for food purchases,
some simple tools and not much else. On August 23, 1997, two and a half months
after moving to Virginia from Japan, Shill said goodbye to his family and boarded
a plane for Seattle, feeling a deep ambivalence:

*"In the airport when my family saw me off, I remember turning, and walk-
ing away, and it felt like shit. I thought, 'This is an incredibly selfish thing.'
On the other hand, I was feeling free and physically light, almost naked.
I had this little backpack on — I didn't have my briefcase, no documents
to prepare, no meeting to present at, no real schedule. It was an incredible
feeling of independence and lightness."*

## THE TRANSCONTINENTAL ODYSSEY

After arriving in Seattle, Shill hitched a ride northwest to the Olympic Peninsula
in a dilapidated pickup with a seemingly "very unprofessional" bike mechanic
named Steve. Shill, in his self-proclaimed "purist" thinking, wanted to make it

truly transcontinental, so rather than starting from Seattle, he determined to begin at water's edge as far west as the land stretched. He decided to keep a journal during the trip, from which we are able to quote. (All excerpts will be shown in italics.) His first entry taught Shill a lesson about apparent status in life that was to be repeated in various ways across the country:

*Steve treats me to an exceptionally detailed tour and gives in-depth answers to everything from the history of the area to logging and salmon-fishing. I am impressed to learn that Steve reads 1–2 books a week and watches the Discovery Channel almost every night... I was very impressed with his knowledge and the breadth of his life. My earlier judgment fades and I chastise myself for my initial estimation of him as a person by the profession or job he has... I'm ashamed of how distorted my values have become over the years.*

Steve dropped Shill off in a village called Neah Bay on the Olympic Peninsula, near the extreme northwestern tip of the Lower 48 states. That night Shill pitched his tent and climbed into his sleeping bag, but sleep would not come. He tossed and turned nervously until 4:30 in the morning. Finally he got up, ate, packed, and in order to start his journey "the right way," began to ride west — toward Cape Flattery, seven miles away by dirt road, the *very* westernmost point on the peninsula. At that moment the skies opened up in a downpour. It was not an auspicious beginning.

*I start pedaling but something is wrong... very wrong... it's like I have no air in the tires... but I checked that... I feel like I'm pulling a 25-foot motor home... The dirt road is as bad as I could imagine: washboard, rocks, deep puddles and cars driving by... When I reach the platform looking west I get a picture taken and I am by myself... I look west and think of Japan... I have said hundreds of goodbyes, but somehow this one touches deeper... perhaps lack of sleep or perhaps an anticipation that this journey will somehow take me much farther from Japan.*

As Shill turned and headed east, he began to cry. The emotion surprised him, he did not think of himself as an emotional person, and he was glad there was rain falling to disguise his tears from passersby.

And then, another, more ominous surprise: his heart was racing. From a training rate of 120 it had shot up to 160, which terrified him. For the first two days he could ride only 80 miles a day instead of the 100 he had planned on. On top of that, a phantom left-shoulder pain which had plagued him during training had returned with a vengeance. The fatigue, at least, was a symptom of nerves and sleeplessness, but soon he felt calmer and stronger, though the shoulder pain continued. His odyssey had begun:

*The scenery is astounding. Huge cedar trees line the road, six feet around, moss hanging from the trees and growing on the cedar roofs of the houses and even on the road. I am afraid to stop for fear of the moss growing on me.*

On day three, Shill hit an apparent obstacle in the town of Burlington, Washington, with the Cascade Mountains looming ahead. In the pouring rain, a tire went flat. The tire itself was badly gashed, and Shill had spare tubes but no spare tire. The one bike shop he could find was not an encouraging sight: a few old bicycles, no accessories on display, the shop empty, save for the proprietor and his son:

*He begins looking at the tire but has no Presta valve adapter, patch kit, or Tuffy liner... a bad sign... I silently criticize him and his workshop and wonder if he is even competent. We put a patch on the inside of the tire and then I ask him if he knows how to adjust the front derailleur so I don't drop the chain. He tries to adjust it and gets nowhere... then he says, "Whoa! Look at this..." I see that my right bottom bracket is screwed out 3/8 of an inch. For those who don't cycle, this is the same as getting a flat fixed and someone finding that your transmission is falling out. I see him completely disassemble and reassemble the bottom bracket and I realize that this man is a first-rate machinist. He then explains, "You may have been having some problems with your shoulder or hips because of this, and it looks like it has been this way for at least six months." At least three other mechanics looked at my bike before the trip and none saw it... I feel that my initial judgment of him was all wrong, and I am ashamed as he charges me $20. I head out, thankful for my flat.*

Reflecting on the experience months later, Shill said, "That was the first time that the trip took on a different meaning. I was meeting someone for a purpose." It was a realization that would strike him several times:

> *At a grocery store in Keller, Washington, I casually ask the cashier if there's a place to camp nearby... At that moment a mountain of a man walks in with bib overalls, no shirt and numerous tattoos. She yells, "Hey Bob, where can this bike rider camp for the night?" My bowels loosen. He comes to the cash register with an 18-pack of beer and a bag of ice. He says, "I know just the spot — throw your bike in my truck and I'll take you there."*

Riding out in the pickup with Bob, Shill began to worry about his safety and to wonder if he had been set up. When Bob dropped him at a beautiful campsite along his intended path and wished him well, Shill added another reassessment to his view of the world and the people in it.

The further Shill rode, the more he became convinced that the people he was meeting along the way were the real focus of his journey. Virtually every day, he said, someone told him or showed him something which seemed directly relevant to his own life. No one knew who he was or where he was from, and no one cared how much money he made. Gliding along the periphery of other people's lives made him feel strangely anonymous. When he scaled the first of the mountain ranges it became clear that the trip he had envisioned — six weeks of single-handedly conquering the continent — had become something else entirely.

When I got to the top I didn't feel like holding my hands up and saying, "Okay, I've done Logan Pass. Check it off the list. Now what's next?" I didn't feel that way about the mountains or where I was going, the way I have so many times in my life. It was a sense of *accomplishment*, but not of achievement or distinction.

> *I have never experienced such vast emptiness and open space. At times I can feel my mind being washed and cleansed by the space and wind... When I start early enough the silent stillness is so different from life in Tokyo that I cannot even imagine I was there... Did it happen?*

From the Olympic Peninsula, Shill biked over the mountains and crossed the deserts of Washington State, cut across the Idaho panhandle into Montana, and crossed the Missouri River. Still worming his way through the eastern slopes of the Rocky Mountains, Shill found himself in the rugged hills of Belt Creek Canyon, a landscape of grueling climbs which left him parched. He stopped at a bar in a tiny town to slack his thirst:

*I walk inside and it is so dark I cannot tell if anyone is there. The bartender is a worn-out man with tired eyes and gray matted hair and a deeply rutted face. He gives me a long stare and raises his eyebrows but says nothing. I ask for water and he fills a glass with ice and squirts water in. I watch the TV in silence, and he fills the glass again when it is empty. As I finish I ask him how much, and he raises his hand palm up, looks down and shakes his head ever so slightly. I leave a dollar on the counter and walk out.*

Belt Creek rushes through the old mining town of Monarch, Montana. Shill found himself there one evening, in front of an old shack where two young shirtless men sat drinking beer. A mongrel dog was chained to the porch. When Shill tried to skulk by, one of the men called out to him, and he readied himself for a confrontation. Instead, the two men greeted him with handshakes, asked him how far he'd gone that day and directed him to a rental cabin by the creek. "If you need anything, just call me," one of them said, leaving Shill deeply touched and again, inwardly repentant.

*It is early Sunday morning and I have the road to myself as I climb up Kings Pass (7,393 ft). I have two hours where I hear nothing but Belt Creek rushing down the mountain, my own breathing, and the tires on the road. I cannot count myself as a religious person but I will long remember this time as the closest I have ever been to a worship service.*

At the top of the pass, Shill met another cyclist and his wife, who turned out to be wheat farmers from Great Falls. Almost automatically, Shill found himself asking if they were able to make a good living through farming wheat. "I am doing what I love to do," the husband replied. "I am not wealthy, but we consider ourselves very rich: a good family, time to bike and ski, and a great place to live. What else do I need?" Shill was unable to answer.

After the Rocky Mountains, Shill was surrounded by the flatlands of eastern Colorado. He needed a bike tube desperately — he was down to his last tube and it was patched in several places. Like a bicycler's mirage, in a one-stoplight town, a bike shop suddenly appeared. Shill wondered if he could get real help in this isolated place, and he thought as he entered, "Why a bike shop in the middle of nowhere? How could they make a living here?" He was more surprised to see the proprietor was a middle-aged woman named Debbie:

> It turned out she'd opened the bike shop six months before, and business was going quite well — and my consultant mind kicked in: How do you get enough throughput here, in this tiny town? She started telling me about the tourists, and I was sort of enjoying the whole thing. Finally I said, "What in the world prompted you to open a bike shop in this town?" And very matter-of-factly she said, "Well, eight months ago my eight- and eleven-year old sons were killed by a drunk driver, and this is my healing place." It was like a sledgehammer. I don't remember anything else she said. I don't remember buying the tube or getting on my bike.

For the next six hours of empty highway, Shill had nothing to do but think about her words, and he credits that solitude for etching the experience so deeply in his memory. He rode on, weeping, deeply thankful for everything he had, but mostly for his own wife and family awaiting him in Virginia. The solitude, though had another side:

> There seems to be no sound lonelier than that of a passing car going the same way as I. It is strange. A car going the opposite way does not have the same effect. Perhaps it has something to do with the Doppler effect. Perhaps it is the feeling of being passed by, a conversation that could not happen or someone going home and getting there weeks before you get to yours. I get bored and lonely enough at times to wave at all oncoming cars just so they will wave back.

More conversations did happen as Shill neared the eastern border of Colorado, and by now he knew better than to try to judge the stranger in advance or to predict what would transpire:

> An old man in his late 60s or early 70s comes up to me. His face has been deeply etched by the weather and he has a growth of some kind over his

*left eye. His hat is a faded, frayed, and dirty white cowboy hat. His orange windbreaker has not seen a washer in years and his jeans should have been in the Levis' museum. He comes up to me close and says in a loud voice, "I've been listening to you talk about this trip… call it what it is, son!" What do you mean? "This trip of yours — call it what it is! All this talk of living in Japan — call it what it is! Pure damn foolishness!" I am not quite sure what to say, and I am growing afraid of what might happen next. There is a long pause and then he says, "Make sure you enjoy it and be careful." He leaves. A few minutes later I get up and as I start to pay my bill the waitress says, "Hank's done taken care of it."*

As the Rocky Mountains disappeared beneath the western horizon, the completion of the trip — a goal he'd harbored for several years — took on the feel of certainty. With it came an older and more unwelcome thought: "What do I do next?" Shill felt a wave of confusion and guilt and anger as his old mind-set returned, his natural tendency for looking automatically ahead for the next mountain to climb.

The cornfields of the Midwest provided an unlikely respite. With nothing to do for three weeks but pedal across a table-flat landscape, Shill got to thinking:

*I decided that maybe there is not another mountain. And maybe there shouldn't be another mountain in life. And I could smell the corn and the cows, and meet more people, and somehow shift my focus away from getting over the mountain to what was going on around me, which was nice.*

*The generosity continues to shock me. Nina offers for me to take her car so I can get a decent dinner. Jim stops and buys me a cup of coffee to drink while I clean and adjust my bike. I am afraid either I have been too busy to experience such generosity or I have been in the wrong places.*

At one point, Shill lost his wallet. He had just checked into his occasional motel stay and realized that he didn't have it with him. He thought immediately of the hassle with trying to make the calls to cancel the credit cards, of trying to figure out how to get food, of how disconnected and vulnerable the loss would make him and of the loss of his journal. The office then called him and informed him that someone had found the wallet in the parking lot and had turned it in. Shill was exhausted and must have dropped it while walking his bike to his room:

> ... I have just returned from the motel office to pick up my wallet. My wallet was turned in to the front office 15 minutes before by Phil... it contains everything — money, credit cards, ID. I could not even buy dinner without it... but much more importantly it contains my journal... irreplaceable. As I walk back to my room, this big guy walks straight toward me in the parking lot. I get nervous and he introduces himself as Phil. If you saw Phil walking down the street in D.C., New York, or Chicago you would lock your car door. He is easily 300 pounds, a face not even his mother could love and clothes that suggest the Salvation Army is running low on donations. I reach out to give him a twenty and he indignantly refuses. He speaks quickly and confidently... "You reap what you sow; I just hope that someone would do the same for me someday."

## WINDING DOWN

Shill had long since convinced himself that finishing would not be a problem, and as he worked his way through the boredom of doing what he knew he could, he found he was able to focus more and more completely on the journey itself. Physically, he recalls, he "turned into a machine," upping his pace to 120 miles a day, and even managing two consecutive days of 150 miles — the equivalent, in calorie expenditure, of back-to-back marathons. His immersion in the task at hand reached frightening depths: at one point, he literally woke up pedaling, with no idea where he was or where the last four hours had gone.

With 3,800 miles of road and six weeks of time behind him, Shill was now on familiar territory: a 50-mile trail leading into Washington which he'd ridden numerous times the previous summer during his training. Surrounded by weekend cyclists, he fit right in. His eldest son even rode out to meet him, and they covered the last five miles together. Shill recalls the unexpected emotions he felt at the end of the road:

*I'd always felt that I would get to the end and feel this triumphant feeling: "It's over." I didn't feel that way at all. It wasn't a letdown, but there wasn't this sense of accomplishment — it was like the journey was continuing, and this was another stop. It's almost as if I'm still on it. I'm not pedaling any more, but I'm still on a journey.*

## WHERE NEXT?

Shill was still deciding where that journey would take him next. For the time being, at least, he was on familiar ground: consulting at McKinsey's Washington, D.C., office. As he was about to begin his new assignment, Shill thought about many things. With his new job came the danger — underscored by the thoughts he fought off near the end of the bike trip — that he would lapse back into the workaholic mindset which had jeopardized his health. Given his pattern of feeling overwhelmed with new assignments and his method of dealing with it by working harder than most, Shill was well aware of this possibility. A few days before the start of his new job, thinking by analogy of his training regimen from the year before, he mused on a possible solution:

*"When I was training, I often would watch my heart-rate monitor, and push myself to get so many minutes in certain heart-rate zones. Then, there were other times when I wouldn't watch it, and I'd tell myself I was going to work at 90 percent instead. I wouldn't push myself to the limit. And afterwards I'd find out I'd actually spent more time in the higher zones, when I thought I was doing 90 percent. So there seems to be this area where I can accomplish more with far less pain and sacrifice, and that's what I want to do. Can I do it? I don't know."*

With the memory of Debbie, the bereaved Colorado bike-shop owner ingrained in his mind, Shill put a face on the sacrifice that pushing himself to the limit entailed: less time spent with his family. He said he was determined to rearrange those priorities. Part of his new work as a partner at McKinsey involved mentoring younger coworkers, and Shill found himself including this newfound perspective in his advice to them:

*"I tell them that the partner track at McKinsey is like a pie-eating contest. And if you win, the prize is more pie. So it's not what you think it is. I try to tell them, "Find something like bicycling that you really love and see if you can share it with your family somehow."*

Shill said he was more able to see the symptoms of a workaholic in others because he had come to see them in himself and that perhaps also he had become more able to perceive his career through the eyes of his wife. To her, his professional achievements to date had been like a series of hurdles, and not all of them had been worth jumping over. Yet, Shill had no regrets: he believed that only by enduring all the pain of their dislocations and family-life strain had he grown sufficiently as a person to fully understand and embrace her point of view.

Shill continued to wonder about what the future might hold, and while he acknowledged that the immediate days ahead would be spent at McKinsey, the years ahead were less easily discerned. He borrowed his wife's favorite metaphor in talking about the future course of his career and revealed the influence of her values too:

*"Two to three years from now at McKinsey there's yet another hurdle, of being a director or not being a director. And I'll either make that or not make it. Maybe I can prove this wrong, but I think it's going to require a level of effort and a level of time that I don't think I want to commit to. What I've decided to do is try McKinsey on my terms. If they keep me, great — because McKinsey would be a great place to stay — and if they don't keep me, then I shouldn't be there."*

Shill saw a number of diverging career paths. The dream of owning his own business, which he had harbored since his Darden days, still held a certain appeal. He thought of combining teaching and consulting in some way, and the notion of starting his own consulting company also occurred to him. But here the central — and unexpected — revelation of his bicycle journey made its presence felt, as Shill frankly admitted that he no longer felt the way he once did about the consulting business.

> "I worry a little bit about the values of consulting. Most people in most businesses, in fact, take on a set of values that they judge other people by, and I don't agree with them any more. I think that's probably the biggest change of the trip. Maybe you're required to do it to be successful, because you do have to judge people and make quick decisions and relatively rash judgments with little information. What I've realized is that that may work in business, but for individuals, it's a big mistake."

At the end of his bicycle odyssey, Shill still wondered about where his path would take him next:

> I worry that I will fit right back in...that the lessons learned and the experiences gained will be shoved aside by the rush and pace of suburban life and professional imperative. How can I preserve this sense of journey — of exploring, seeing, smelling, and sensing the world around me? Can I remember how useless the stereotypes were and how ashamed of my judgments I was? Can I continue to smell the corn and cows? Can I taste again that pure, sweet air of the high Rockies? Can I ride in my mind once again up Belt Creek on that serene Sunday morning? Can I remember and feel for Debbie and her courage and healing?

## QUESTIONS FOR REFLECTION

1. What does it take for a person to lose 100 pounds and become fit?

2. What lessons do you think Mr. Shill learned from his bicycle odyssey?

3. What do you suppose his next chapter in life will be?

4. Would you say that Mr. Shill is successful? Why or why not?

5. How would you draw Mr. Shill's balance wheel?

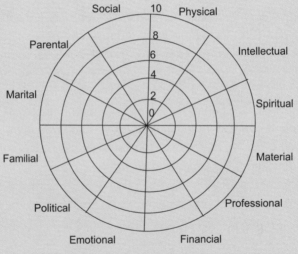

A Personal Developmental Balance Wheel.

## EPILOGUE

Subsequent to the case, Mr. Shill invested in and became the CEO of a small company. After several years, the company went bankrupt. Mr. Shill said it was

a very difficult time as he tried to save the company and provide for his employees but that he'd learned a lot from doing as opposed to advising. After that, Mr. Shill was offered a position to start a new strategic consulting practice for a major consulting firm. He worried that this job, one he knew he could do, would cause him to revert to his old lifestyle. In the end, he took the job because he liked the challenge. In his new role, the stress level went up and he regained the weight he'd lost earlier. He also began serving on the board of trustees for his alma mater.

# 12

## TOM CURREN: THE LIFE AND CAREER OF A SENIOR EXECUTIVE OFFICER

*He tried to calculate it. He would drop 10 feet if the pin held, and he could extricate himself easily enough. But if it didn't, he'd go 40 feet, hit the ledge 20 feet below John and probably be killed. Perhaps 15 minutes had gone by and he hadn't moved. Years of rock climbing were working in his head — he just didn't know if he could make this last section or not.*

*There seemed to be a tiny flake at knee level on the steep wall. Was that another six feet above it? Eyes inches from the rock, the hand caresses over it. Yes! A ripple perhaps 1/32 of an inch... but a ripple. Somewhere inside him the move is being weighed: "You've stood on as small things before... I know, but that was on boulder problems four feet off the ground. Why do I come up here any way?"*

*He stood on tiptoe feeling very secure on the half inch ledge. Strange, when he'd first reached it he was apprehensive about stepping on to it. Now, 20 minutes later, it felt like a truckstop.*

*He was clothed only in shorts, thin socks and EB climbing shoes. He dipped his hand into the bag of gymnastic chalk hanging from his waist, dried the moisture off his finger tips and dusted off the little hold.*

*Far down in the valley, a crow glided. Eight hundred feet below, little toy cars wove their way through the valley floor. Without a conscious decision to start, but rather attracted as a magnet, the left foot went up, weight shifting carefully to the tiny hold. As he straightened his left leg, the right foot moved up, tapping the smooth granite. Now 10 inches from the truck stop... 15 inches. Don't come off now left foot! Please don't come off now. Warnings exploding in his head and he knows, absolutely, that the piton will not hold the fall. You're committed, it's only 15 inches to the truckstop, but there is no going back.*

Tom Curren's mind snapped back, his eyes refocusing on the picture in front of him on his desk. That was six years ago. Today, he was sitting in his office in Marriott World Headquarters, talking about his life and background.

## TOM CURREN'S EARLY LIFE

"I am basically an only child, in that my mother didn't remarry till I was about 10. Mom was married during the war. My father went off, and then they separated when he came back, so I never lived with my father and never really developed a close relationship with him. So, I was raised by my mother and my grandmother.

"My mother remarried when I was 10, and had three more children. There was also a daughter by my step-father's first marriage, so there were five of us in all. With all the other half brothers and step-brothers, there was quite a family.

# T  O  M

"I think I was a pretty quiet kid, serious, fairly introverted, and probably ... you know, I would characterize (myself) as a late bloomer. I never did particularly well in school; my grades were always middle of the class at best, and I never participated in a lot of extracurricular activities, never did much in the way of athletics. I had a few friends but was basically sort of floating through life.

"I went to private school up in Connecticut at a boarding school called Hotchkiss. Then I went directly into Trinity College in Hartford. I wanted to take some pictures in college, and so this other guy and I, we shot pictures all year and did our own darkroom work and published our own yearbook. I built an underwater camera case for my camera. I dated a model; I thought that was a big deal, she was on the cover of everything. I was pretty active socially.

"I graduated in 1965 with a degree in economics, went directly to Wharton, got my MBA in 1967, then went into the military in 1968 as a supply officer in the Navy. I got married in 1970, got out of the Navy in 1971, went to New York, lived and worked in Manhattan for eight years — first working for an advertising agency from 1971–73, then for McKinsey's New York office, from 1973–77, and in 1977 came to Marriott where I have been for the last 11 years.

"I can't think of a setback I had other than being fairly withdrawn in the early part of my life. In the early part of college, things just sort of began opening up for me. I began doing and accomplishing more and more. I went through the beginning part of college, like, middle of the class and then shifted majors from math to economics. Towards the end of my senior year, I became more active. I became president of my fraternity, my grades picked up, and I decided to go on to graduate school.

"I went to Wharton. I was in the top 10 percent of my class there. I started a company when I was there, a little venture company, Allen-Curren Electronics. For some reason, I became interested in business. It was more of an intrinsic interest in the problems and the problem-solving, and I just pursued that interest.

"Then, I did a stint in the military, which was tremendously helpful. I was 24 when I came out of that. Although I felt like I'd 'lost' three years in the military, it was a great experience. I was at sea for nine months, an officer on a ship, one of 12 officers with 300 crew. I stood watches at night, ran a ship. I loved the ocean, loved being at sea, loved operating in the Philippines and Japan and Vietnam. Its was just a tremendous experience. It was an oiler; we refueled surface ships."

## BUSINESS EXPERIENCE

"I was interested in marketing, and I was trying to find a way to learn marketing, package-goods marketing, as fast as I could. The choice came down to either learning from the brand-management side at Procter & Gamble, General Foods or from the agency side working on a Procter or General Foods account. I went the agency route and went to work for an advertising agency in New York, working on Procter business. Again, it wasn't the agency I was picking, it was the account, because there was another agency, whom I thought was a better agency, but they wouldn't guarantee what account I would be on. I might have been on Camel cigarettes, and I wouldn't work on cigarette advertising.

"So I worked on Procter soap and detergent business for 20 months and was very successful. I was promoted from assistant account executive to account executive, working on Cascade, which is a dishwashing detergent that 'Fights drops and spots. Leaves glasses virtually spotless!' That was a terrific experience. Cascade was a great learning brand; Procter had 33 sales districts, and something was going on in every one of them. We were defending against Palmolive in six districts, running a copy test in three districts, competing in low-phosphate districts, rolling out a 65-ounce size in some districts, lemon fresh in other districts, testing a 'media heavy up' in one district, and two more districts as controls. *All* of this stuff going on. It was just *tremendous* learning.

"I took the brand through a budget cycle (this was 1971–73), but I knew that I wasn't interested in the agency business *per se*. I didn't like selling advertising, although I liked the business itself. I really identified more with the Procter people than I did with the agency people; I viewed myself as their partners and got involved in a lot of aspects of their business and was pretty highly regarded by them.

"Anyway, after about 20 months, McKinsey called me up and said they were following up on a Wharton campus interview from several years earlier. I had my military commitment then, but they were interested in me and had put me in a 'look up' file for later. So they tracked me down (this was all in New York; I was living in Manhattan), and they said, 'Why don't you come to our New York office in the marketing practice?' So I did and spent four years there.

"I guess the summary of all the career decisions I made early on was, in retrospect, really looking at what job I could learn the most at. Certainly that was true with the first two jobs. With the Marriott job offer, I said I've learned a bunch of stuff and here's a place I think I can apply it, and I found it was *time* to apply it. But everything else was not driven by money or any long-term view of where I was going to be. It was more 'what can I get out of the next two or three years here?' Now, I never went to those places knowing I was going to leave, but I was not making a long-term commitment to advertising or to consulting; I was saying, 'Yeah, that's open-ended, but what I am sure I can get out of the next three years is a lot of learning experience.'"

## WORKING AT MARRIOTT

"Between my third and fourth years at McKinsey, my learning was peaking out: I knew I did not want to be a consultant long-term for all the usual reasons: travel, lack of continuity in studies, lack of continuity in people, and so forth. So it was a two-step process: I decided to leave, and then I had this typical systematic search and screened all these companies. Marriott missed the screens totally, but they were searching for somebody, and when I began to find out about the situation, it fit perfectly.

"Gary Wilson, who was Chief Financial Officer here at the time, had planning responsibility for the company which consisted of senior management getting together once a quarter or every six months to talk about the issues. Somehow, he knew a McKinsey person could do planning, so Marriott retained a search firm and recruited several senior McKinsey people, but they weren't interested. They thought it was, I don't know, too risky because the function had never been done at Marriott, but I thought it was terrific, 'cause I thought this was a great company and I've got what they need — which was basically a very disciplined approach to thinking. I knew I didn't have a lot of operational experience, but they didn't need that. The company was full of operators and strong finance people, but they really lacked 'planning,' particularly a marketing approach to planning. I don't think Bill Marriott knew what he was hiring. I think he thought I was going to be some sort of corporate marketing officer; I don't think Gary knew either. He wanted me to take minutes at these (quarterly or semi-annual planning) meetings, but *I* knew.

"I was there a couple of months, and Bill Marriott finally called me and said, 'We've got a problem with this business. It's got a new general manager, and

I want you and the general manager to go figure it out.' That was in early 1978, and I sort of ushered in the era of very 'issue-based planning' as opposed to a planning process. Even to this day, we spend less than 20 percent of our time on process; 80 percent of our planning time is issue-driven. Some of the issues are acquisition-related, some are business start-up, and some are existing business strategy.

"So I started in July 1977. I was hired in as Director of Corporate Planning with no staff (which is why some of the most senior McKinsey people turned it down), a new function, and no structure as to what it's going to be. I guess I never looked toward the risks, just saw the possibilities. It was great because I knew they had gone after more senior people, so I could negotiate a big step up in salary. So I got a bump (up in salary). After about a year, I hired somebody, a young consultant out of Booz-Allen. So we had a two-man department, and then a three-man department. We did basic strategy diagnostics in many of our major businesses. I just stayed doing the same job, and it became more senior and influential within the company. Finally, the job was regraded up to Vice President.

"Around 1981, I got in the new-business start-up game. Then, we started developing other products. We wanted to get into the whole elderly area. Bill Marriott had an interest in that, but it wasn't well defined. We hit on 'life care' early on, but we weren't sure about it, so we said, 'Okay, let's survey the whole category ranging from hospital management to psychiatric hospitals to day care to life care,' etc. So we did what we would call 'a category assessment.' We did it inside our planning department and used a hospital management consultant firm up in New York to give us some industry expertise. We did the category overview and said 'life care' is what we want and created what we now call our Senior Living Services Division. We worked similarly with time-sharing and some other products that segmented the lodging market. We did that all up here in Corporate Planning.

"So my job began to take on a new-business-development component. Then it began to take on an acquisition aspect when we acquired about a half dozen companies, the largest of which was Saga (a large food services company). Most of these deals were closely related; they were businesses that we were in, so our work wasn't entering a new category so much as it was me and my department being the strategic conscience of the company — basically, saying, 'Does this business make sense? Are we over valuing it?' So the job brought me into the new-acquisition-strategy business.

"The next evolution was I began decentralized strategy development. When a division becomes large enough to support the caliber of strategic resources that we sustain at corporate, we set up strategic planning in the division. We have a group in hotels, we have a group in food service management, and we have a group out at Host. Those are dotted-line relationships to me and solid lines to a senior operating person.

"Today [1988], I've got a Corporate Planning Department of about a dozen people. I have the Central Market Research group, which has about 40 people in it (we do about six million dollars worth of consumer research), and then I have a dotted-line relationship to three division-level planners.

"In terms of influence, stature, and compensation and so forth, I think I am among the top 10 people in the company. I am one of the six voting members of the Finance Committee that approves projects over a million dollars or any change in strategy. My influence varies depending upon the decision. If it is how a financial deal is structured, I have no say and don't pretend to have any say. If it's a strategic decision (Should we be in this business? Is it correctly positioned? Is the pricing right? Do we understand what the customers want? How much should we pay for this company?), I am one of those handful of votes."

## ON STRATEGIC PLANNING SKILLS

"When I hire people, I look for three qualities, and I think this has accounted for a large part of my success. First, I look for people that can do what we call 'integrated business analysis.' That is, they can take complex business problems, break them down, and solve them. We look for people that can do that fundamentally from a marketing standpoint as opposed to a financial standpoint. They have to be comfortable in all the disciplines, but their depth has to be marketing. When I say 'marketing,' I don't mean tactical marketing. They don't have to have worked at Procter & Gamble and know all about in-ad coupons and all that. They have to fundamentally think of business problems in terms of segmentation, targeting, and positioning, understand how to use consumer research, and basically approach problems in their stomach from a marketing standpoint.

"In junior people coming right out of school, we look at their resume, but more, we ask the case questions (and we team-interview), we draw out that ability.

We also hire people at a more senior level, and we look at their resume and see if, in fact, they have being doing that for the last five years. We also ask them case questions. So we look for problem solvers.

"Secondly, as I said, they have to do it from a marketing perspective, because our finance people are so strong, and we are very team-oriented here within the company.

"Thirdly, I look for a set of personality traits that are very pragmatic, not elitist, not overly academic. We're not interested in anybody that can really, really get excited by correlation analysis and r-squares and plotting little things, you know. We want people to have a line aptitude, an action aptitude, toward their work, people that have values that fit in with the values and style of the company. This is this clean living and hard working, almost, Midwestern type of work ethic; it's cultural. And we need people that are aggressive and yet are team-oriented at the same time. So it's a difficult blend we all struggle with. We want a little bit of perfectionism, but we also want a tolerance in people — to know how far they can push and how to build consensus. We really are looking for champions, for people that can take a point of view, drive things through and, you know, make things happen.

"There is a spectrum of things I don't like in subordinates. I've had people that were strong but couldn't recognize anybody's priorities but their own. They were too narrow. And then I have had another person that was so nice and friendly and empathetic that that person really couldn't push through their own agenda. Again, it's that middle ground of aggressiveness — you know, being a team player, knowing how to make things happen."

## TOM CURREN, THE PERSON

"I am a pretty serious person. I mean I am pretty interested in getting results. I'm becoming more and more interested in people. I have always been interested in developing people. One of the things I am proudest about is the people I have brought into this company and what they have done. One of my objectives is to have sponsored or brought in a substantial proportion of the top 100 people in this company. That's personally rewarding. Also, I think I reflect a point of view and an emphasis that's complementary to what is the natural inclination of some of the other people.

"I think I am a caring person; I think I am a sensitive person. I think I am aggressive. I am very strong in conceptual integration; the way my mind works, I can synthesize concepts very easily. I am always looking at concepts. I am primarily a visual person, so I am a concept synthesizer. I am less interested in the details.

"I am interested fundamentally in being on the leading edge of whatever we are doing. I think we've now developed our ability to develop new businesses fairly well. I think the edge at this point is the culture of the company and the human resource management of the company. So I find myself working more closely with human resource people and line people on human resource issues. And more and more of the work we are doing is taking all the strategy and marketing work we've worked on and applying it to the human resource side. We have done that in several businesses, and now we are looking to do that at corporate level."

## TOM CURREN'S PHILOSOPHY OF LIFE

"I am looking for balance between my objectives at work, in my family life, in my intimate relationships, and for myself and the things I do for myself. Work can be all-consuming, particularly my position in a company that is aggressive in its growth goals and requires as much as this one. I have objectives in all those areas and am constantly working on all of those. I live my life out of intensity and learning. I think if you had to distill it down to the one thing I am about it is 'commitment.' Commitment and excellence.

"I think if you want to accomplish anything, you need the commitment and to find a coach, as well as a series of resources from which you could learn. To me, it doesn't matter what you are committed to, so long as you make that statement and you live your life out of that commitment. I am constantly working on the balance between commitments to myself, to my relationships, and to my work. Obviously, they all overlap, and the more you can integrate them, the more effective you are in all of those areas. I *work* on that balance.

"My mother and grandmother were middle-class. They were not wealthy. I think a lot of the values I learned are from my grandmother: thrift and hard work, save your pennies and learn your multiplication tables and ... the *basics* seem to be there."

## ON MARRIAGE

"I've been married twice. I met my first wife while I was down in Supply Course School in Athens, Georgia. We had two children, two girls that are in New York whom I see quite frequently. They are terrific, both teenagers now.

"I think in my first marriage I never developed the depth of the relationship or the commitment that I have with my current wife or, in fact, many of my current relationships. There were reasons that weren't necessarily good, but we got married, and we sort of drifted along. I had my job, we had some children, and we were committed to our children. In terms of *our* relationship, there really wasn't anything there. We began to drift apart; there just wasn't much of an investment. We finally said, 'This isn't working.'

"Work provided a smoke-screen almost for what was going on at home. I became more aware in the later years of how little we had in the marriage, but I didn't invest in saving it. Knowing what I know today, I would keep the investment in *any* person I was with. I would not say, 'This person has all these faults, and I am going to find a better person.' I would say 'Am I committed to this person?' And I would just make the commitment, and I would make it work.

> Work provided a smoke-screen almost for what was going on at home. I became more aware in the later years of how little we had in the marriage, but I didn't invest in saving it.

"It isn't so much a matter of finding the ideal person. But I did, in fact, find somebody that, as I said, I have this visceral attraction to and who also is very interested in learning and growing together. We are both pretty high-strung people and not the easiest people to be around, but we are forging something that is really strong, and I am very committed to that.

"I don't know what criteria it takes to make a commitment to another person, and that doesn't matter. All that matters is the commitment. You are either in a state of commitment or you're not. The reason it doesn't matter is because, once you commit, you're committing in the face of any circumstance and any reason. You're *not* 'well I am committing to this relationship as long as it works out,' or 'I am committing to this job as long as it is not a problem.' *You commit!* Who knows how you commit? Now, it's important that you choose your commitments carefully. When you commit, that's it, you do it. I don't mean you should live so rigidly that you've got all these commitments and when you break them you feel bad, but you take those things seriously.

"Now the area of commitment that I am struggling with is, psychologically, my concept of myself within the concept of a relationship. The more intimate a relationship is, the more joyful and also the more potential for pain with a sepa-ration. I have been learning not to run when the going gets rough. When I run, I don't mean leave the house in the middle of an argument, but I mean 'shut down,' withdraw. Just to stay in there and battle it out. To me, that is commitment.

"I came to Washington in 1977 and met Judy six months later. We dated for about three years, then she went off to Stanford Business School and got her MBA out there, and I went out and visited her every six weeks for two years. She's a native Californian, and we had a great time engaging in outdoor and active things that we like to do. She came back East in 1982, and we were married in 1984.

"We have no children from that marriage. We live with her children from her first marriage, a son that is just going off to Stanford this fall and a daughter that will be a sophomore in high school. Then my two children, a sophomore in high school and one entering eighth grade. Four children total. Two children in the house full time and four children every fourth weekend or week together at the shore or whatever. My children are in New York most of the time."

## ON PARENTING

"I think, first of all, that when I came down here and my wife and children stayed in New York, I wanted to make sure that they didn't have the same experience I had when my father left me and my mother. He rarely visited me. I am estranged from my father.

"I am very careful about that (not giving his daughters the same kind of experience), so I continued to go up to New York every third weekend and see them and have them down here for a month at a time for the summer and so forth. Basically, we have kept up that pattern for about 11 years. They come down once a month now rather than every third weekend. So I stayed close enough to them so that I knew what was going on. It wasn't one of these relationships where you take them to the circus, and you don't really have any feel for them.

"They were two and four when Cathy and I split. So they were pretty young. I have had to accept that I am not the primary parent, but I kept involved and feel comfortable with that. I don't know how, it's been on the kids psychologically.

"I have tried to teach them a sense of humor and a love of the outdoors. I had the kids learning rock climbing when they were four, in Central Park. They know my 'three rules' of rock climbing: Use your hands, no knees, and little steps. They scramble over those rocks. I took them around on the back of my bike. I taught them a sense of humor, sensitivity towards people, and I think also a seriousness of purpose, although I don't know if they have gotten that yet; it is hard to tell when they are teenagers. I think they are very clear about my love for them and my interest in their well-being and development."

## A TYPICAL WORK WEEK

"I am generally up before 6:00 every morning, either to run or work out early in the morning or get to work early. I make fresh orange juice for the whole family. We have a big commercial juicer, and we buy oranges by the carton. I get breakfast set for everybody. I am generally at work by, it varies, between 7:00 and 8:30, although what I am trying to do is block two days a week where I have open time in the morning till 10:00. I find that I need that, because my work, the rest of my life, is so heavily scheduled.

"So I am managing to put in those blocks of time. I am generally at work here till 6:30 pm, not through any specific intent, but usually there's so much to do, and I get involved and look up, and it's 6:00 and 6:30 by the time I wrap things up. Occasionally I work weekends but not that often. I think the last time I calculated, I put 50 hours a week directly into work. My travel schedule is fairly light; on average three or four overnights a month. It really is what I want to make it to be.

"I read at night, between 11:00 and 12:00 in bed. I read a little on the weekend. It takes me a long time to read a book. It took me six months to read *Chesapeake*. I just don't put that much time into reading. When I read something (non-fiction), I'll read it, I'll underline it, I'll re-read it, I'll read sections, re-read, I'll underline it, and then I'll take notes on it. So I have summarized on maybe four pages the key things I got out of a book. And then I'll go back periodically and read it and underline it. I think what I've got is some pretty good study habits. I don't know where I developed them. I noticed that in graduate school I would be very thorough about studying things, and I would then retain things that way.

"I put a fair amount of time into exercise. I exercise five or six times a week — running, racquetball, and weights. I put a lot of time into personal development. I would say I spend at least five hours a week doing some forum or course on leadership, seeing a consultant or applying something.

"Weekend activities are either doing projects around the house, doing things with my wife or the kids, doing active things. I got into rock climbing for about five or seven years, then I stopped that. The thing I am particularly interested in now is windsurfing. I have a board, and Judy has a board, and we have a place down on the Eastern Shore on the water. I am learning that. As with anything, if you want to get good at it, you get a coach and be committed. I found an instructor in the D.C. area, and he is giving me some lessons. I am just learning to do it. It is tremendously exhilarating."

## THE EMOTIONAL SIDE OF TOM CURREN

"For a long while, I had a tremendous lack of self-confidence and self-awareness. I viewed myself as this kid who was lonely and who really, in many ways, wasn't encouraged to express his feelings, to express anger, or to be in a lot of activities. I got a lot of things, I developed a lot of good core values, but I think I didn't really... it was something in my early life that really seemed to me that I was within this box, and it created a very limited view of myself. I developed this view that I was different, primarily in a negative way.

"Most people would say, 'Oh, you're pretty good! You succeed at this, you succeed at that, you do this, you take up rock climbing, you're a 5.8 lead climber, you take up this sport and that activity.' People tell you how good you are, and

you get all this money and stuff. Yet I had this Mr. Magoo type of view, that I was just bumping through life.

"Finally, after about 20 years of this (I am 45 now), when I was 40, I began to look at the last 20 years and say, 'There isn't much evidence for this view of myself as sort of a wimpy loser.' Psychologically, I had to develop the self-confidence and a sense of being and awareness.

"Early on I was very careful not to compete head-on. I think that that's accounted for a lot of my success, because I've chosen areas that others didn't stake out. I chose a niche in Marriott, for example. Nobody had this area staked out, and I just did it and sort of expanded it. Now, if you talk to people here, the senior executives that have worked for me will cite as a strength that I get along with everybody. I am clearly a team player, because I don't have line-management ambitions. I'm not jockeying for their jobs or involved in the politics of that. So, by being different I am sort of in a different game. It's almost an internal game.

"All this money and stature — I didn't seek this. It was a by-product of what I intrinsically wanted to do. And for a long time, I was naive about what I had. Now I am a little more responsible

> "All this money and stature — I didn't seek this. It was a by-product of what I intrinsically wanted to do.

in terms of recognizing my position and the obligations it entails. I have to be careful of what I say. You can say something to a junior person, and they take it to heart. I didn't understand that at first, but evolved into that.

"I think psychologically one of the things that I have been working a great deal on is anger. How to handle anger. I used to think anger was a bad thing. The idea of the positive uses of anger was totally new. I've been working on some things there."

## ON FINANCES

"When my mom remarried, she married somebody whom I view as a successful businessman. I don't know whether he would be middle-class or upper middle-class. We had a nice house and some horses. He commuted to New York. We could take vacations. We weren't wealthy, but comfortable. It was comfortable enough to send me off to private school and so forth. I think to the extent that I thought about money, I thought, 'Well, that's a nice lifestyle; I would like to make that much money.' I've made more money than I ever expected to. Money is great because you can do things with it. I've learned not to talk about it because being well-off is something that has a tendency to isolate you from other people because there's a jealousy, a resentment, and so forth. But it is nice to be able to not worry about money and essentially to live your life free of money worries.

"I have never been centered on having the material things; I have always been centered on having experiences. More and more, that is where my life is centered. It is easy to say the BMW and the nice houses and everything don't matter; I can do it. Sure, I like those, but that doesn't seem to be where the action is.

"For me it was luck. Just luck. I mean *luck*! I picked Marriott, the first options on the stock were $2, now the stock is at $40. I have made a lot of money on stock options. That is how you become wealthy. I became well-to-do because I am one of the top 10 people in the 10th biggest employer in the country. So it is a big successful company, and they pay competitively."

## THE PHYSICAL SIDE OF TOM CURREN

"I haven't always been physically active. Up until college, I wasn't. In college, I became a little more active. I played some intramural things. But I didn't put much energy into that and didn't imagine myself as much of an athlete. I think after working in New York four or five years, I was 29 years old, and I realized: I am not getting any exercise. If this trend continues, this isn't so good. I met a doctor at a party who said he ran. Back then, in 1971 or 1972, running was not a big thing. We lived up next to Central Park. He ran around the reservoir, which is 1.6 miles on a cinder track, and so he said 'try running'. There weren't any running shoes out then, you just went out. So for about two years, I ran this one lap, and I sure wasn't going to try a second lap, and I thought, 'Running a mile! The whole concept seems so long. What happens if I get tired and stop on the West Side? I'll be late for work!' Then, one day I just ran the second lap. 'Hey, this is no big deal!'

"When I think in terms of fitness, I have always run. I have enjoyed running, and I haven't let it get into a big competitive thing. I run maybe three times a week. I ran five miles this morning. I run four to six miles. Last winter, I thought I'd push my running times to see how fast I could run. I thought, 'If I am going to be out here, I might as well see how fast I can run.' I noticed my times were just, for me, phenomenally fast times. Running six miles at a 6.52 pace. For me, really fast. So I entered some 10Ks [10-kilometer races]. I did it more as a socialization thing, to run with a friend. I am trying not to get caught up in competitive running and running becoming something where I've got to work on my times and everything else.

"I've always been interested in the mountains. The first time I went to Switzerland, I saw the mountains, and I said, 'This is where I've got to be.' I dropped everything and found a mountain-climbing school and spent a couple of weeks in Switzerland and learned some basics of climbing, how to cut ice steps in glaciers and basic mountaineering. I really liked that.

"Clearly, in technical climbing you get in situations where, if you slip, you are dead. You don't consciously seek those situations, but you reach dicey points where you basically can only go forward rather than back. And the level of concentration and thrill of operating at that level is just ... you are alive then, and it's almost like your sense of ... your visual acuity and sensual acuity dial up tenfold, and you can see things and you are aware of things that you are not aware of in everyday life. That is the part of rock climbing that I really enjoy."

## NUTRITION

"One of the things I began doing was I started changing my health habits. In the last two years, I have started changing what I eat and drink. Two years ago, September 1986, I shifted to fruit in the morning. That's all we have in the morning is fruit and fresh orange juice. And I stopped drinking coffee.

> One of the things I began doing was I started changing my health habits. In the last two years, I have started changing what I eat and drink.

And I found the combination of those two things just made a huge difference in my energy level and general sense of aliveness and well-being. It is just amazing.

"I've realized that I can't do anything in moderation. I am all gas and no brakes. So, in terms of things like drinking, it is hard for me to drink in moderation. When I drink, I like to drink. So, when I open wine with dinner, I will drink the whole bottle of wine. If I am at a party, I'll drink martinis as fast as I am drinking 7-Up. I am not one of these people that sip on it. So what I found myself doing was constantly putting in rules that I could live by: I won't drink during the week this and that. Then I found I was always struggling with exceptions to the rules. So finally, May 10, 1988, I just stopped drinking, because it was too much of a concern. I was drinking with concern. So I stopped. I don't miss it at all. The problem is I have been a wine freak for the last 20 years, so I have this cellar of all this Bordeaux that's pretty good stuff. Maybe for a great wine I will have a sip. I would like to learn moderation and balance, and I don't do that very easily.

"Judy and I are pretty much together on our view on health. She switched over to fruit. I dropped coffee, then she dropped coffee. She still drinks; she probably has two drinks a week. You know, again, there is a technology solution. You can get those things that inject nitrogen into the wine bottles, and it will store the wine months at a time. We got one of those, so you open a bottle of wine, put this thing in it that shoots nitrogen in it. You can buy an expensive wine and just keep it, and it will last months. I found for me to try to limit the drinking — and saying what are the rules — didn't work. I have tried that. I slowly creep back into more and more, so I found that the thing I wanted to do is not drink.

"It's like smoking. I started smoking in college (and I didn't smoke in high school because I was in boarding school). By the beginning of sophomore year, I was up to three packs of *Luckys* a day. I was smoking two packs, and then during (fraternity) rush weeks, I was up to three packs. I was lighting three packs, I wasn't smoking them all. I remember I would smoke a cigarette before I got out of bed. So again, I quit, I only meant to quit for a week to be back to two packs. But after a week, I said what the heck, I'll stay off it. So, what I found is, I found myself eliminating coffee, I found myself going to fruit in the morning, I found myself cutting down drinking and then eliminating it entirely.

"I didn't intend to, in the sense of writing it down as a goal. So the goal was fitness and making choices and being 'available.' If I have a half bottle of wine on a Wednesday night and it's 9:00 pm, I am shot for the night. I am shot whether I want to work, I am shot whether I want to watch television. I wanted more

control over my life. I wanted to make the choices and found that those things limited my energy. I also found I need a lot of energy for what I want to do. I want to be resourceful. I want to not take in a lot of stuff that hinders that."

## WORKING IN THE COMMUNITY

"I have never had much of a feeling that I have to, that I want to, give anything to society at large or to community at large. I have always had a very strong belief in personal ethics and treating people that I come in contact with well. But world hunger, the bigger issues, I just never had a feeling for, although this is beginning to change somewhat. It's not because of my values as a human being and that I don't care about them. Maybe it's that I don't see that I can do anything about it, or it doesn't touch me the way it does some people. But individuals, people I can see and work with, yes, I work with them."

## COSMOLOGY

"I have always found religion in nature — in the stars, in the water, in the rock. Sunday night, I was down on the Eastern Shore, and a gale came through. I went out on our dock, and it was mind-blowing. I don't know what the wind was; it must have been 40 miles an hour; it was enough to knock over heavy furniture. It was blowing through, and the waves! It was just like the Red Sea was about to part! The lightning and the waves! I get a real sense of being in a relationship to that.

"I went out in it and put my fists up — you know, 'I'm ready to take you on!' Yeah, I really relate to that. I feel a power. If you go to Yosemite, if you go to the bottom of El Capitan. (El Capitan is the largest exposed piece of granite in the world, three thousand feet straight up.) You go up, and you put your hand on that rock. *I* can feel the power in that rock. Maybe that's why I like to climb.

"I think in a religious sense I was very influenced by Scott Peck and his book *The Road Less Traveled*. And I was particularly affected by his section on 'Grace.' In fact, I was reading and re-reading it on the plane this last January. I finished that section on grace and realized I was a Christian. Up until that time, this business of Christ and ... you know, I couldn't understand it. The Son of Man thing never made any sense to me, and I realized then 'grace,' and I realized what the human spirit is trying to be and how it relates, and all of a sudden it hit me. But I'm not a member of any organized religion."

## ON LEADERSHIP

"Having the vision, and then knowing what it takes, having the skills to enroll people in your vision or in your commitment; figuring out what needs to be done to get everyone going in the same way — that's leadership. Five years ago, I would have just said, 'It's all in my head, and I'll sort of figure it out. I'll do the technical work, and I'll figure it out.' I like figuring it out. But I have realized now I can see some things before other people see them and that's a very powerful thing: to enroll people in the vision and get them aligned so that all the arrows are going the same way."

## ON BEING ORGANIZED

"I am pretty organized, and I spend time constantly working on devices to facilitate that. I hope the intent of these systems is to free me for the other more important areas of my life. You don't want people to get hung up in correlation analysis just because they like r-squares. I don't want to get hung up with the systems that get in the way of everything else. Nevertheless, I find myself investing a lot in and constantly developing and refining systems. I found, for me, the MoreTime system — and others which I presume are comparable — was literally revolutionary. (I've since converted to Franklin Planner.) It was for me partially a calendar-management system, but what it really was was an energy-management system. The issue wasn't time; it was energy.

"The biggest drag on energy is an incomplete thought. So what you want to do is decrease the cycle time from the time you have a thought till it's dealt with. And it is dealt with either by writing it down, by setting a date to deal with it, by completing it, or by dropping it. You don't want to have anything left around uncompleted. It's like a computer with stuff in its core and it should be dumped into archive. You don't want to have anything in your mind that you are thinking about that you haven't resolved. That was the principle I got out of that.

So I took MoreTime (a time and life management seminar). (See Exhibit 1.) Affiliated with that was working through some goals and exercises in terms of incomplete things in your life, things you meant to do and haven't been doing — people you meant to talk to, things you meant to say, and ways you want to be, etc. Once you go through that, you dump that out and just handle it. Now, again, it doesn't mean that you have to be compulsive and do it all that week, but I lost 10 pounds six months after I took MoreTime and dropped two hours sleep a night. I used to think I needed seven hours sleep. It was an attitude, so that if I would wake up in the morning and only have six and a half hours of sleep, I'd say, 'I've only had six and a half hours of sleep; I must be tired.' (In this MoreTime program) you basically shift to a different attitude, so that, after the seminar, I would get only four, five, or six hours.

I would be up at 1:00 in the morning working on these principles, (of getting rid of the unnecessary) carrying old clothes out and throwing them in the dumpster, suits that I had bought and never worn. You open your closet and you say, 'I wish I hadn't bought that suit.' Get rid of it! Throw it away! So I did a lot of that, wrote a lot of letters to people saying things I wanted to say to them. I cleaned a lot of things out.

"I found a guy now that is doing some custom programming work, in effect, computerizing a MoreTime system. I'll be going on that in August. (See Exhibit 2.) So I'm always looking for devices that facilitate. (See Exhibit 3.) These (devices) are not just task-oriented. I realized that there are about 100 people in this company I need to talk to on a regular basis. Some I need to talk to, like Bill Marriott, on a two-week cycle and some on a nine-month cycle. So I have that list of people and try to schedule eight a week. I don't always make it, but I am always pushing out.

"What I do in those interviews is I let them know they are important and valued. I let them know what I am doing. I take the opportunity almost serendipitously to talk to them. It's incredible the amount of serendipity that comes up in these interviews. Both between me and them, or me getting an idea from one person and then from an interview later in the week; I am seeing somebody entirely different and get that same idea. So I found it helped from a business standpoint."

## ON BURNOUT

"I burn out all the time. I become overwhelmed and get myself in a position where the world seems like there's all this that has to be done now, and I am the only one that can do it, and I can't do it all, and I am not getting anything out of it. And you hit burnout, you hit 'overwhelm.' There are different layers and

**I burn out all the time. I become overwhelmed and get myself in a position where the world seems like there's all this that has to be done now, and I am the only one that can do it, and I can't do it all, and I am not getting anything out of it.**

approaches to managing that. There is an immediate way which gets you out of it, and then you have to do some longer-term things.

"The immediate things you do are, first, you have to go through a mental shift and move from things that must be done and ought to be done to things that you want to do. You have to shift from things that should be done yesterday to extending the time frame. Then, you say, 'I haven't done this yet, I'm not yet there.' You shift from a point where you are seeing what you haven't done to fully appreciating what you have done. You look at your schedule and reblock things. You relook at what you're delegating; you go back to your core values.

"I get overwhelmed at least once a month, but what I am able to do now, because I'm doing so much work now in the technical structure of emotions (you know, What is anger? What is loneliness? What is feeling overwhelmed?) that I put in gear neurolinguistic programming. You take the problem, you separate from it, you send it to the moon — you slingshot it. I am trying to reach the point where I can mentally make shifts.

"Now, longer term what you do is you step back and you say, 'I'm taking on too much.' One of the things I am trying to do with this Tuesday and Thursday morning thing is to protect some blocks of time. Patty (my secretary) is better at that than I am, because I schedule stuff in there. But she will protect those two mornings, and that is very important for me. So I just have some time with nothing to do."

## ON HIS WIFE

(Talking about his wife, Mr. Curren's voice wavered, his eyes misted over.) "With regard to Judy... I think that is emotional for me because it is such an important relationship to me, such an important relationship to both of us — and not always an easy one. I've found the problems in personal life are more difficult than the problems at work, because there is more emotional investment in my personal

relationships. The closer you are to somebody — and the more you get out of it, the more they can hurt you. There's a personal intensity in that relationship that's like no other relationship I have.

"One of the things I have realized is she tends to be cynical about things, and rather than that being a negative, I recently discovered how useful that is, because it is always good to have somebody to tell you what's wrong with something. Then she will come around and think of the positive. But she will always hit with the mismatch rather than the match.

"How to describe Judy? This is one of these questions where I can do all this work on intellectualizing her personality traits, and I can tell you what her Myers Briggs (a common personality test) is and this and that and about perfectionism and all the tendencies and scales. But when it comes down to it, I don't know... I'm just viscerally attracted to her. There's something about her components physically, and her personality that I am just *attracted* to."

## ON BUSINESS SCHOOL EDUCATION

"I agree with the general notion that work prior to business school makes the academic experience much more helpful. In fact, I would say work and travel experience during college is something I certainly am going to encourage my kids to do. A semester abroad, not to go right from senior year into college or not go right from college into work. To take that time off is really important — and particularly if you are committed to something. I don't care whether you are committed to being a rock musician or you're committed to the world hunger project or you're committed to washing cars, so long as you want to have the best car finish in the country. Go and pursue it and, particularly, break up that academic experience.

"If there is any science to business, don't forget to learn the science while you are in business school. In other words, don't forget to take a basic statistics course. Don't forget to do work in how to think or write clear, basic economics, or basic finance. You need a fundamental liberal arts part to the curriculum.

"In terms of looking for a job, I'd give the advice that I gave myself, which is, fundamentally, look for opportunities where you can learn. Have flexibility in as many areas of your life as you can. Drop any preconceived notions about certain industries. If you have the advantage of being willing to move and live in a lot of different countries, including lousy cities, think of what is really important — and if learning is really important, both learning from the people that you will be with and from the context that you will be with, you know, *go* for that. That's what I would go for. Forget about the money and everything else. Don't paint yourself in a box, in that you learn some specialty in a dying industry, but in your area of interest, ask how you're going to learn and what job will give you the most learning, and look at it realistically as a two- to three-year time commitment. That's the way I look at things."

## IN CONCLUSION

"I think I am a person that is interested in solving problems and developing people, and my current job is a context in which I can do that and have done that very successfully. I am a person that is struggling with spiritual issues and psychological issues and recognizing that, as Peck says, 'Life is difficult because it is fundamentally overcoming a series of problems.' And there's no life without problems. But once you have recognized that, it's no longer a problem. [Laughs.] That's what it's about, you know.

"I'll try anything that I think will help me develop. Yeah, I'll try anything. I have always done risky stuff; in college I did sky diving. I just do it for the experience..."

"I did this interview for three reasons. One, I am interested in developing people and if this is a way that some of the things I have done can be useful, match or mismatch, negative role model or positive, then good. Some of the things I have done I think could be useful to other people.

"Two, I'm interested in learning about myself, and frequently you don't learn about yourself unless you articulate it. Seeing it and getting it in play, you learn about yourself.

"Three, I've sort of got an ego. It's not a bad idea to make a movie about yourself and sort of hope, on balance, it's positive."

---

**EXHIBIT 1:**
**THE LIFE AND CAREER OF A**
**SENIOR EXECUTIVE OFFICER (TOM CURREN)**

**Excerpts from and Commentary about Tom Curren's *MoreTime* Book**

In January 1987, Tom Curren attended a *MoreTime* seminar on time and personal management. He considered it as a milestone in his life (see below). Here are some excerpts from his personal management binder that was associated with that seminar and that Mr. Curren continues to maintain.

## GOALS

### Personal Development

*Family*

1. Define and be a couple.

2. Establish a close circle of mutually supporting friends and coaches.

3. The family of man.

*Work*

1. Help people realize their potential in some impactful way.

2. Obtain and keep the flexibility and resources of financial independence.

3. Experience, challenge, fun, and excitement.

*Self*

1. Time and place to experience adventure, action, in nature, wind, and water.

2. Time and place to experience simplicity, reflection, and regeneration (drawing, poetry, and meditation).

3. Appreciate myself and richness in life and spirit.

Mr. Curren said that he reviewed these goals and their attributes and weekly expressions (past, current, and planned for next) at least once every two weeks. He also noted that he had longer-term objectives, but that they didn't have the power of the weekly goals.

## EXHIBIT 2:
## THE LIFE AND CAREER OF A
## SENIOR EXECUTIVE OFFICER (TOM CURREN)

### Project Management System

"I have a little project management system here (in his *MoreTime* book), which is a modification of a Focus program. I put into it different projects, and it automatically sorts them by priority, by date, by whose the lead responsibility is, and then up to 10 people that are involved. I print them out all different ways — by priority, by date. If I am going in to see Bill Marriott or another executive, I just print out the printout that has all the things that would involve him — an automatic little check list; it's a real fast facilitator. I give one to my direct reports so they will know where I am and what the priority is. And when they are complete, I mark them complete, and then they go into archive, and I can print them out. I can print out everything I have done in the last six months, 12 months, and look at it. So that's a tool that helps."

Conceptual Notes from Books And Other Sources.

(In this section, Tom had summary notes from the better books he'd read.)

## EXHIBIT 3:
## THE LIFE AND CAREER OF A
## SENIOR EXECUTIVE OFFICER (TOM CURREN)

### Milestones

In his *MoreTime* book, Tom Curren maintained a list of milestones, events that he thought significant in his life. This list was begun in 1986 and is shown below with excerpts from his commentary shown in parentheses.

September 1986    Read Tony Robbins, *Unlimited Power*. (Probably is the most influential single book I have ever read. Basically,

Robbins is a popular packager of a lot of these sort of self-development ideas. In one book, he hits diet, neurolinguistic programming, all these positive ways of thinking about things. I found it really tremendous.)

| | |
|---|---|
| September 1986 | Began Fit-for-Life Diet. [See "The Physical Side of Tom Curren" in text for detail.] |
| October 1986 | Stopped drinking in October 1986 and went back on again, went off again. Then, finally off completely on May 10, 1988. |
| January 1987 | Took *MoreTime* seminar. (I literally dropped two hours a night out of sleep. That was just mind-boggling!) |
| March 1987 | Judy resigned from Marriott. (She worked at Marriott for a while. She was a very successful executive, Vice President of Marketing. She took *MoreTime* and said, 'Heck this [working at Marriott] doesn't fit my goals,' so she quit, and we went to China for a month. We said, 'Let's go somewhere,' so we went to China. It was just great. We spent a month in mainland China.) |
| October 1987 | Got reading glasses. (I have contacts, and if I take my contacts out, I don't need either. But when I have my contacts in, I need them.) |
| October 1987 | Bought Oxford house. (We decided to buy a house in Oxford on the Eastern Shore, which Judy just renovated. It is a tremendous haven.) |
| November 1987 | Had a big burnout. (Regrouped and recovered from that.) |
| November 1987 | Ran six miles at a 6:52 pace. (I thought that was pretty good.) |
| January 26, 1988 | Grace. (Got the concept of 'grace,' amazing grace, and really became a Christian.) |

| March 1988 | Acupuncture. (I tried acupuncture five times. Didn't do much as far as I can tell.) |
| March 1988 | *Forum.* (I took the *Forum.* It involves 2 weekends. Sponsored by Werner Erhard, an outgrowth and improvement on his EST program. If you take Robbins' seminar, take his weekend seminar. You will walk on fire, you'll walk on hot coals. I mean, I know I can walk on hot coals! I didn't need to prove that. The *Forum* has more power than that.) |

## EXHIBIT 4:
## THE LIFE AND CAREER OF A
## SENIOR EXECUTIVE OFFICER (TOM CURREN)

### Influential Books

Here are a list of the more prominent books, programs, and tapes that Tom Curren had either read recently or kept in his office for close reference. He starred the ones he especially recommended.

### INFLUENTIAL BOOKS

*1. Anthony Robbins (1997). *Unlimited Power, the New Science of Personal Achievement,* Simon & Schuster.

*2. Hugh and Gayle Prather (2001). *A Book for Couples,* Doubleday.

*3. Scott Peck (1988). *The Road Less Traveled,* Simon & Schuster.

*4. Franklin Institute (1987). *The Franklin Time Control System,* 801-975-1776.

5. Jack Riley (1987). *Designing Quality and Balance into Your Life, Work and Play,* Wilderness Press.

6. Stephen W. Hawkins (1988). *A Brief History of Time,* Bantam.

7. McMaster and Grinder. *Precision, a New Approach to Communication,* Precision Models.

8. Leslie Cameron-Bandler (1986). *The Emotional Hostage, Rescuing Your Emotional Life,* Future Pace.

9. Joseph Campbell with Bill Moyers (1991). *The Power of Myth,* Doubleday. (Also a PBS series.)

10. Genie Z. LaBorde (2001). *Influencing with Integrity,* Sytony Publishing.

11. Tony Buzan (1991). *Use Both Sides of Your Brain,* E.P. Dutton.

12. Kepner and Tregoe (1997). *The New Rational Manager,* Princeton Research Press.

13. John Jerome (1999). *Staying Supple: The Bountiful Pleasures of Stretching,* Bantam.

14. Roger Fisher and William Ury (1992). *Getting to Yes: Negotiating Agreement Without Giving In.*

## INFLUENTIAL SOFTWARE

*1. *Max Think, Idea Processor,* Neil Larson, 415-428-0104.

*2. *Manage Your Money,* Meca Ventures, Inc. 203-222-9087.

## INFLUENTIAL TAPES

1. Erickson Institute, Berkeley, California 415-526-6846, ask for catalogue. I recommend Self-Hypnosis, Deep Self Appreciation.

---

### EXHIBIT 5:
### THE LIFE AND CAREER OF A
### SENIOR EXECUTIVE OFFICER (TOM CURREN)

Resume as of 1984

**A. Thomas Curren**

### EDUCATION

**Wharton Graduate Division**                    **University of Pennsylvania**

MBA Degree, 1967

Top 10% Directors Honor List

**Trinity College**                                **Hartford, Connecticut**

BA Degree in Economics

Honors Thesis, Deans List, President of Fraternity

### EXPERIENCE

**Allen-Curren Electronics**

President (1967–1968) *Entrepreneur*-Co-founder of small venture which designed, manufactured and marketed industrial lighting controls for night clubs, discotheques and theaters. Distributed nationally through theatrical lighting houses in NYC. Made mistakes and learned from them. Military duty forced dissolution of the company.

**U.S. NAVY, LT. Comdr. Ellis**

Officer (1968–1971) *Operations Management.* Responsible for all food service operations at Naval Station, Norfolk, VA. Managed 150 civilian and military personnel, $2.8 million budget. Introduced fast food menu, cut

---

inventories, won approval for $1.2 million in new facilities. Awarded 4.0 in all areas of performance evaluation, selected for accelerated promotion.

## COMPTON ADVERTISING, Paul Paulson

Account Executive (1971–1973)

*Marketer.* Responsible for Procter & Gamble advertising of Cascade detergent in U.S. and Canada.

## MCKINSEY & CO., NYC, Tom Wilson

Engagement Manager (1973–1977)

*Consultant.* Managed study teams of 2–4 in order to solve strategic, marketing and operational problems.

## MARRIOTT, GARY WILSON

Director Corporate Planning (57) (1977–1981)

*Strategic Planning.* Believed to have played a significant role in the following decisions: revised FSM strategy (1977), OVA establishment of In-Flite RMT, acceleration of hotel growth, development of Hotel manpower program, shift to 3 EVP, sale of Dinner House, Farrell's, World Travel, repurchase of Marriott stock, establishment of 4× coverage policy, shift to International In-Flite management contracts, Roy Rogers/Gino's eastern strategy, disposition of Rustlers, Santa Clara Land sale, improved hotel pricing SOPs, post-acquisition integration of Host, new Casa Maria prototype, development of Courtyard, pursuit of Health Care/Elderly service opportunities.

## MARRIOTT, GARY WILSON

VP-Corporate Planning (61) (1981–Present)

*Business Development.* Assumed MBO for new hotel product line on May 1980. Hired Washburn on August 1980. First five units approved by Board of Directors on May 1982. Forecast 10,000–18,000 rooms by year-end 1988.

> *Marketing Services.* Took over CMS on January 1981. Felt that department was not maximizing its potential despite wide-spread satisfaction with existing organization. Replaced 70 percent of people and shifted emphasis from technically exotic research to providing basic, ongoing information. Staffed department with people who have advancement potential within Marriott.
>
> *Hotel Feasibility.* Took over Feasibility on October 1981. Rebuilt department after departure of William, Webb, Moulton with emphasis on marketing/strategy capabilities (Isaac, Lavin, Eiseman). Created professional development programs, expanded use of computer, improved decision-making process.
>
> *Executive Development.* Curren has recruited and developed six managers at the grade 55 level (Sid Laytin, Don Washburn, Tony Isaac, Larry Murphy, Frank Camacho, Bill Eggbeer). Most of these executives have the potential to advance to substantial leadership roles in the company in the mid-1980s.

## QUESTIONS FOR REFLECTION

1. Would you say that Mr. Curren was a "success?" Why or why not?

2. What were the major incidents in Mr. Curren's life that shaped his leadership style?

3. What were the major lessons that you took away from reading Mr. Curren's story?

4. What do you think his Balance Wheel would look like?

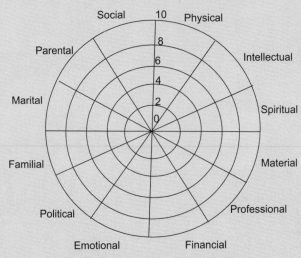

A Personal Developmental Balance Wheel.

# 13

## Judy Moore Curren: The Wife of a Senior Executive Officer

My name is Judy Moore. I was born in California and raised there. I am part of a family of four children. My father is a Lutheran minister. So, I am a "PK" as they would call it, a Preacher's Kid. I went to high school and college in southern California. I attended Pomona College, where I majored in sociology. After graduating, I married a man named Allen Moore and went into the Peace Corps in Bolivia, where we worked for two years. When I came back, he attended Stanford Business School, and I was the dutiful wife. I had two children, who are now 17 and 15. I played a pretty traditional role as a housewife and mother while they were small.

After nine years, our marriage broke up. I began to think seriously about my career. I tried several different avenues that didn't work out for me. I was a graphic designer for awhile; I worked for the government for awhile. Then I decided to get my own MBA. So I took the children and went out to Stanford. I got the MBA and then went to work at Marriott Corporation. I worked there for four years and left about a year ago because I found out that it wasn't really meeting my needs and life goals. I am currently evaluating what to do next. But in the process of (telling you about) that, I sort of skipped the part about Tom.

I met Tom a few years before I decided to go to business school. It was 1978, and we dated for a long time and saw each other seriously. He actually saw me through Stanford. We had a long-distance relationship for those two years. I came back, and we worked at Marriott in parallel for a number of years — which was not without difficulty, but it really had some positive points. So we were together for about six years until we finally felt comfortable enough to get married. That was four years ago.

We first met 10 years ago in Washington. I was not working at Marriott then; I was working as a designer, and Tom and I met on sort of a blind date. Only we weren't each other's date! We were somebody else's date. We immediately picked each other out; we were attracted to each other. So we started seeing each other then.

I really liked Tom. He was unlike a lot of the men that you meet here in Washington. I felt that he was utterly without pretense. He was just a very natural, interested person who didn't seem to be putting on airs — which is very unusual around here. I liked that immediately about him. He was very charming and without any sense of phoniness. So we began to talk about what we did. He told me that he worked at Marriott. At the time, I had very little sense of the business world. I knew that Marriott owned the Roy Rogers Fast Food chains, and I envisioned him as a unit manager. I just had no idea what he did. I thought, "Well, he's unlike the intellectual-type people that I usually know, but he seems like a nice guy." So when we began to go out, I found out more about what he actually did and became really interested in his job.

We did a lot of active things together. Tom was a rock climber at the time I first got to know him. He actually — I can't believe this — got me out there on faces of cliffs, and we'd go climbing together. Sometimes he got me out there on faces that I shouldn't have been on. I just put a lot of faith in him. Sometimes I got in over my head — it was very exciting though — it was lots of fun. We liked to do bike riding, do very active things together. So it was a lot of fun. He had just moved to Washington, and we were exploring Washington.

## ON BALANCING FAMILY AND WORK

> we both have very high standards, so we are not willing to do anything halfway. If we take something on, it has to be great, it's got to be right.

It's not always easy to balance work and family. We are both very active people, and we both tend to fill our lives with activities and things we want to do. And we both have very high standards, so we are not willing to do anything halfway. If we take something on, it has to be great, it's got to be right. And I don't know that there are a lot of brakes in this relationship. We both find ourselves frustrated in a sense, because there are too many things we want to do. That's the case even when we are having fun. I mean we go down to our place at Oxford, and we can't decide between windsurfing, tennis, bike riding, sitting by the pool and reading a book. I guess we just have to learn to deal with it. But we haven't found the great solution yet.

Sometimes (Tom will) get to the point where he feels like he's just snowed under and he can't cope. He'll kind of fall apart for a brief period. And then he'll stop, and we'll just talk about it and find out things are really manageable or how can we manage them. Sometimes I am in the role of saying, "Okay, you don't have to do that; you can cancel these appointments. We can stop this; we can just fall back." That happens.

In my first marriage, I generally had this stay-at-home role and would often get frustrated with my husband because he couldn't be home for dinner; That was a big issue between us. I would not say it led to our divorce, I don't believe things like that lead to divorces. It was just a point of friction. It was hard for me to understand, until I became a career-oriented person myself, that sometimes you just can't make it home for dinner.

I think by the time I got to know Tom, I had really assumed full responsibility for my two children. There's a certain role that a stepparent can fill. The family unit has always been important to me, and I think it is important to Tom, too. We do make an effort to have dinner together, to have meals together. That is one of our key values. But I have to say it is difficult with Tom's two children in New York. Where is the (family) unit? It's really hard to even define it. I think, for practical purposes, most of the time the unit becomes Tom and me and my two children. I think he has made a tremendous effort to become a part of this family, to build a family. It was very difficult when we were both working and both had very high-powered careers and particularly when I was traveling up to 50 percent of the time. Tom often had to step into the role of being parent when I was not home. You know, taking care of the kids. We hired a lot of household help; that is one way we got through it. I don't know, frankly, how I would have done it with small children. By the time I took this on, my kids were eight and 10, pretty much school age, and getting to be more on their own.

## ON BUSINESS SCHOOL

Business school taught me a lot of valuable skills and gave me a lot of confidence. I felt like I had been through boot camp, and if I could survive this, I could probably survive anything. So I have that brand, "Stanford MBA." But in terms of the things that really make or break you on a job, I am not even sure that that is something you can be taught at business school. I think a lot of it goes very much to common sense and "organizational savvy." I did have some good professors who tried to help us understand the term 'organizational savvy.' How you had to be alert to the signs of what was going on in the company. Keeping your ears pricked up and making sure you were listening to the signals and responding to them. That was probably as valuable as anything that I got out of my MBA. But a lot of it you have to make up on your own.

## DESCRIBING TOM CURREN

(Tom) is a very creative guy. His mind doesn't work in a typical fashion. He tends to see things very abstractly, on a high level. He is always looking at the big picture. He's very open to new ideas. Always ready to take up a new idea. Sometimes it drives me crazy, because there are too many new things being introduced. I think you only have so much time, so you have to limit yourself. Tom gets very animated about a new concept, about something new. I think he really, in a sense, becomes bored once he masters something; he becomes bored with it and wants to move on to something new. He will never stop pushing the limits of his personal development or the things he wants to do. He has a very high energy level. I think that really helps him.

In terms of his organizational life, Tom as an executive: My observation of him when we worked at Marriott was that he was different from most executives in that he didn't seem to be openly turf-conscious and seeking power, the way you can see most people doing either openly or in a disguised manner. Truly, Tom doesn't do that. He's more tuned in to conceptual purity. I don't think he has a strong sense of personal power; it's only in achieving his objectives that he (exercises power).

His objectives are really dictated by the vision he sees. I don't know what else to say about him. He loves his work; he is extremely excited about his work — I think more so than I ever was. It is clear that he has a passion for it. He likes lots of other things too. He has so many interests, again, it's hard to fit everything in. His motto would be "Never stop growing, never stop learning."

I think the area he needs to work on — and I think he is aware of it — is that he gets so wrapped up in his ideas that sometimes he loses sight of how other people may be reacting to those ideas. He needs to see the world on a practical level. I mean, Tom, he's up here. When I worked at Marriott, I was in the Hotel Division. It was more of a down-and-dirty type of place, and people at Corporate in general were seen as being a little bit suspect anyway, but one of the people that I knew described Tom as being "out in the ozone!" He referred to Tom as "Oh, that guy out in the ozone." I think in some ways it is an apt description of Tom. He tends to see things on such a high plane. So he can lose sight of the troops, what's going on, how people are really seeing things. Sometimes I think he doesn't even protect his own interests. That's true in both his career and personal life.

I think Tom is unusual. Part of the reason he can be very effective in business is that he lacks some of the power-play sense a lot of men have and take into the business world with them. It is sort of the macho, fight thing. That may have something to do with him being raised by his mother and grandmother. I mean, that would be as far as I could say. I think it makes him relate very well with women, but he also relates extremely well with other men. I just don't think people tend to be threatened very much by Tom, and that's a very positive thing.

What makes him angry is that Tom has a view of the way the world should be: it should conform to his picture of it. And when things don't go his way, he can get very frustrated and irritable.

## JENNY MOORE

I am Jenny Moore, Tom's stepdaughter, and I am 15 years old, a sophomore in high school. Playing tennis this summer, working a couple of weeks, and am going to camp next week.

I've lived with Tom for six years now, and I think he's pretty cheerful. Everybody is grumpy sometimes, a little upset, but he is usually pretty cheerful, tells jokes that aren't very funny. My brother and I think we have a more advanced sense of humor! He has a favorite joke. It's about a French restaurant and two dishes are "peche a la frog" and "frog a la peche." (Translation: Peach with frog and frog with peach.) He thought it was funny, and we didn't. And we kind of laugh at him a lot about that, just teasing. Occasionally, he dresses up and gets in a bizarre mood and starts, I don't know, stuffing towels in his pants or something. He padded himself. Just usually at home, when he and my mom are teasing each other.

The thing I like best about Tom is he's cheerful a lot and he'll usually listen to you if you want to ask him a question or just talk to him for awhile. He'll sort of try and give you advice. He'll make jokes.

The thing I like best about Tom is he's cheerful a lot and he'll usually listen to you if you want to ask him a question or just talk to him for awhile.

## JUDY COMMENTING ON THEIR MARRIAGE

Tom is really a unique person. It is really hard for me to put into words what he's like. I just think he is very special. I don't think there are many men I would be happy with. I am looking forward to growing old with him. There's never a dull moment around here. So I think we have a lot that we can learn from each other and continue learning together. I think things just keep getting better and better. Life gets better and better for us, and our relationship gets better and better. It's a tremendous amount of hard work; it's not easy. At times, it seems like a struggle. And sometimes it seems like *only* the struggle, but then there will be a wonderful payoff.

I think we need to work on communication. I mean that's what we do work on a lot. That's probably something that every married couple needs to work on. Not listening — because he's got his mind off doing a new concept and so he didn't hear when I told him when we agreed that we were going to do x, y, and z and then he went and did a, b, and c. It's very frustrating. I feel like "Where were you when we had our conversation?" That can happen.

## A TYPICAL WEEK

It seems like the weekdays just zip by. You start Monday morning and then you're at Friday and you don't know what happened in between. We take the weekends to try to start breathing and figure where we are and what we are going to do. But we tend to live by our *MoreTime* organizer. We each have lists of 20 to 30 things every day that have to get done. That is how we can organize and manage everything.

Tom leaves fairly early, between 6:30 and 7:45. Some days he will stay home and exercise if he just hasn't had a chance;, he'll get into work late. He generally gets home between 6:30 and 7:00, sometimes later.

We have dinner about 7:30 or 8:00, by the time we get together — which the kids aren't crazy about. We don't have formal meetings. We just try to cover things when we need to.

We have a new big thing in our life which is the home we have bought on the Eastern Shore. My project for the last eight months has been reconstructing and furnishing (the house), which has been a lot of fun. This summer we started using that as a retreat. We are trying to figure out how to do that effectively without making it even more of a complicating factor. It is a wonderful place. We go out there and windsurf. We will probably get a sailboat before too long. We have a pool; it is very quiet, very relaxing and nice, a great change. That's been the big (recreational) thing other than tennis. But our games aren't really that good. We love to travel; that's something we do. We do cross-country ski trips, and we spend a lot of time in California, one of our favorite places.

Rock climbing was the passion Tom had when I met him. After several years, he decided consciously to give that up. It's not something you can do on a casual basis. So, after achieving a lot of the goals that he wanted to do — climbing Yosemite and climbing this and that thing — he decided he could stop it. Windsurfing, I think, we both enjoy. There is always the skill difference. He will always be better and stronger than I am at that sport, so we won't be able to do it totally together. Sometimes, there are things he is interested in that I'm not and he goes and does them, and I do my thing. I am more interested in the arts and classical music than he is. We have tried to strike a balance and share each other's things even when they are not our favorite things. Enough so we can participate.

## THINGS WE'RE WORKING ON IN THE FUTURE

In the future, we need to work on clarity of communication. We're sort of working towards something now: how can we see the "we" in this relationship more than the "I", the "you" and the individuality. I think there's always that tension in a relationship — individuals' needs and how you merge them. I think we are working much more toward a "we" point of view that somehow has to take into account both partners' needs.

## EPILOGUE

As it turned out, Tom and Judy separated and then divorced, amiably. Tom remarried while Judy continued single until 2009. Tom became a principal in Top Team Alignment, a consulting firm focused on executive coaching and team building.

## QUESTIONS FOR REFLECTION

1. What additional insights do you get by listening to Mr. Curren's wife?

2. How does their relationship "work" for both of them?

3. What does it take to build a lasting relationship?

4. What challenges do you envision Mr. and Mrs. Curren facing in the next chapter in life?

5. Are they successful? Why or why not?

# 14

## Jackie Woods:
## The Life and
## Career of
## a Company
## President

*Jackie is like the first firecracker to be lit in a package of firecrackers... there is this constant energy, this constant edge. Once she is lit, she lights everything else around her. It becomes contagious, just like a pack of firecrackers; one right after the other, they just start to go. Once she has accomplished something, there is this huge explosion around it.*

In May 1992, Jackie Woods[a], vice president of Business Marketing for Ameritech Services, was walking down the hall in the east wing of the new Ameritech office building in Hoffman Estates, Illinois. Jackie had recently been asked to participate in a task force of 100 senior managers from throughout Ameritech which was charged with exploring significant strategic issues facing the company, including how the company should be organized to face the next century. The task force also had the responsibility of designing a structure that would allow Ameritech to reduce the layers of supervision for its 70,000-person work force. The duties of the task force were expected to span a period of at least six months. To be included in such a significant task force was a source of deep satisfaction to Jackie and signaled just how favorably she was viewed by Ameritech executives. As Jackie turned a corner, she bumped into Bob Brown, a colleague on the reorganization task force.

Bob:     So, Jackie, when are you going to tell the family?

Jackie:  Tell them what, Bob?

Bob:     You know, about the committee and the work we're going to be doing this summer. I know that you've planned a vacation to Europe with your family. I'd planned to take what we considered a once-in-a-lifetime trip to Belize this summer, but given the hectic schedule for the task force, I had to go back and cancel it. It wasn't easy. How are you going to break it to the girls?

Jackie smiled and made a pleasant comment before continuing down the hallway. She and her husband, Jack, were planning a trip to Europe with their two daughters. In fact, they had already paid for the trip before Jackie was assigned to the task force. She grimaced as she remembered the earnestness in her daughters' eyes as they anticipated the trip, and in Bob's eyes as he expressed his empathy for Jackie's dilemma.

---

[a] Please view video clips of interviews at https://store.darden.virginia.edu/business-case-study/jackie-woods-a-2565

## BACKGROUND

The major milestones in Jackie's life are shown in Exhibit 1. Jackie, born in Cleveland, Ohio, in 1947, was the only child of Jack and Gladys Dudek. She first left home to attend Muskingum College in southern Ohio. During the summer between her junior and senior years, she met Jack Woods, a student at the University of Akron. She graduated in 1969 with a double major in communications and psychology and, within a few months, she and Jack were engaged.

Two months before the big day, however, Jack was drafted into the army and sent to basic training at Fort Polk, Louisiana, interrupting both his new career at B.F. Goodrich and the couple's wedding plans. Jack and Jackie were married in December 1969 when he came home on leave. In March 1970, Jack was shipped out to Vietnam, where he spent the next two years.

This turn of events had made it necessary for Jackie to look for a job. In September 1969, she started working in the Ohio Bell business office, where she was responsible for customer ordering and billing operations in the Cleveland area:

*"All of it started right then (when Jack was drafted). Would my career ever have played out this way if Uncle Sam hadn't taken Jack away for the first three years of our marriage, or would I have worked a few months and said, "I don't think that the career life is for me?" So when people say to me, "How did you decide to have a career?" I say, "It just happened, at least a little bit, because of the war." If you would have asked me at the time whether I was going to have a 20-year career (and reach this level of success), I would have told you most likely not."*

**At that time, many employers required their female workers to submit signed statements declaring that they would not get pregnant within the first two years of their tenure at the company.**

At that time, Jackie noted, many employers required their female workers to submit signed statements declaring that they would not get pregnant within the first two years of their tenure at the company. Non-compliance was grounds for dismissal.

Jack returned from Vietnam in 1971 and went back to work for B.F. Goodrich. Jackie chose to continue working with Ohio Bell, and they continued to live and work in Cleveland. Then, in 1978, B.F. Goodrich told Jack that he would have to move in order to advance his career and assigned him to a petrochemical facility in Philadelphia, Pennsylvania. Because they had lived all their lives in Ohio and now had a six-month old daughter, Nicole, their decision was incredibly difficult. Nevertheless, they left their families and friends behind as they made the joint decision to move to Pennsylvania to pursue Jack's early career goals.

Originally, Jackie thought she would not work after the move: "I agreed to sacrifice — if that is the appropriate word — my career for my husband's at that point... and I did not intend to work. I said, 'Well, I've had a nice career here for seven or eight years, I'll tend to my family now and not do this.'"

Much appeared to be changing in Jack and Jackie's lives. Jackie's relationship with the Bell System seemed to be a source of stability in their lives, so when they got to Philadelphia, Jackie decided to pursue a job with the local telephone company: "I interviewed at Bell of Pennsylvania and decided to go ahead and pursue a career with them just to see how it would work. We moved to Philadelphia, (and I) worked in public relations, public affairs, and then moved to marketing."

Jackie's new job required her to take a step down not only in salary, but also in management responsibility. Although such a reversal can be extremely frustrating for anyone, both Jack and Jackie were confident that she would do a good job and move up quickly. Furthermore, the job allowed her some flexibility to spend more time with Nicole.

## THE WOODS RETURN TO CLEVELAND

Four years later, in 1982, Jack was transferred back to B.F. Goodrich's corporate headquarters in Cleveland. With Nicole and now Stephanie, ages four and two, Jack and Jackie gladly headed back to Ohio. Jackie went back to Ohio Bell and found a job in sales. Ironically, she was not given the same level of management responsibility that she had enjoyed before she left the company in 1978.

The transfer to sales, however, added another dimension to her professional experience. Reflecting on her move into sales, Jackie noted:

> *"My recommendation to young people starting in careers — and I would say this to men or women — is to get into highly measurable jobs. Sales is one of those. If you are in a position that is subject to someone's decisions about you and based on pretty subjective criteria, you can sit and wonder what you could have done, would have been, if there hadn't been this personality conflict or this difference in management style. If you get into a highly measurable job, the results speak for you."*

Despite the general reality that women in the telephone industry seldom went beyond first-line management, Jackie's work at Ohio Bell was punctuated by a series of promotions. While her success was driven by her management skills, her career path was certainly influenced by her multi-company experience and geographical moves.

## DIVESTITURE TRANSFORMS AN INDUSTRY AND A CAREER

In June 1982, federal Judge Greene directed American Telephone and Telegraph (AT&T) to divest itself of its local telephone operations, which comprised 22 operating companies, of which Ohio Bell was one. The reorganization of the Bell system created seven regional Bell operating companies (often referred to as RBOCs). The five Bell companies serving Michigan, Indiana, Illinois, Ohio, and Wisconsin became a part of American Information Technology Corporation (Ameritech). The divestiture also greatly enhanced the importance of the sales and marketing functions in the telephone companies nationwide. Under AT&T's service orientation, sales and marketing had been relatively quiet; they now had major responsibilities for revitalizing and building the new phone companies. The sales departments of the five Bell companies in Ameritech were consolidated into a single, unregulated organization, Ameritech Services, that was allowed to operate with little interference from its regulated telephone sibling.

In 1986, Jackie was made president of Ohio Bell Communications, the sales subsidiary of Ohio Bell. In this capacity, she oversaw a wide variety of functions

including finance, human resources, quality, vendor relationships, labor negotiations, sales, and marketing:

*"I found that customers that were going to spend a substantial amount of money, whether it be $40,000 or $1,000,000, wanted to see the president. They wanted somebody that would come out and sit there and say, "Your business is important and I'm going to make sure that this team cares about your business and delivers the service to you that we're committing to in this contract."*

## FAMILY AFFAIRS

Jackie's aging parents were living with the Woodses at this time. When Jackie's mother went into a nursing home, Jackie found herself balancing visits to daycare schools to see the two girls and to the nursing home to see her mother. This routine continued for eight months until her mother passed away. Jackie's father, Jack, continued to live with them:

*"The thing that helped (him), at least according to my dad, was that we had small children who provided a great deal of joy and entertainment. He would frequently say to us that (if it weren't for the girls) living there with my husband and me would be just terribly boring because we came home late at night if we had work to do. We weren't any fun.*

*We met with the pediatrician (about this time) and had a family conference about the role my father would play. He's a very strong kind of domineering guy, but the role he chose to play was one of unconditional love with the children. He would do no disciplining. He left that up to Jack and me."*

273

Jackie went on to explain the additional support she and Jack received in raising their children and managing the house:

*"I have always had someone that helped me with the children even if it was picking them up from daycare or working in the house, and that directly influenced how well things went. If this person worked well with us and got along well, our family life was much easier."*

## BACK TO BUSINESS

In 1988, Ed Bell, the president of Ohio Bell, told Jackie that her current position within the company would be the highest she would ever achieve if she chose to stay in Cleveland. He advised her that she needed experience at Ameritech headquarters in Chicago, Illinois. Jackie agreed to think about it and, within a matter of months, she was offered the job of chief financial officer of Ameritech Services Division. The family was now faced with a decision similar to the one it had encountered when Jack was transferred to Philadelphia. Jack had been doing quite well since his transfer back to Cleveland (see Exhibit 3), and Nicole and Stephanie, now 11 and nine, faced the possibility of separation from friends and family. The girls expressed resistance to the move. Jackie had her own misgivings:

*"At Ohio Bell Communications I was really running a microcosm of a large company like Ohio Bell. And it was a very successful operation. We enjoyed it. When the time came to leave, it was sad because the company was doing very well, and I could have easily stayed. In addition, we had a home we loved to live in. My children loved their school and their friends. My husband loved his career; he'd done very well since we had come back from Philadelphia and was moving ahead."*

Nevertheless, after considerable discussion with Jack and the girls, they agreed, now, to support Jackie's career. The family moved to Chicago in January 1989. As it turned out, Jack also took a position at Ameritech Services in the Information Technology Department managing the procurement and deployment of computers within the firm.

Jackie's new job increased her responsibility, allowed her to expand her technical and analytical skills, and gave her additional exposure at the corporate offices. She found, however, that she actually disliked the job:

*"It was an awful job, I mean a boring job. You know, they all wore navy blue suits and were wringing their hands all the time. It was just terrible! And here we were coming out of sales where you did things that mattered, where you got a lot of reinforcement from your customers when you were successful with them! And to go into something where all you heard about was if you did something wrong — and something always went wrong."*

## WRENCHING CHANGES AT HOME AND OFFICE

Soon after Jackie's arrival in Chicago, Ameritech faced some difficult market conditions and began a series of serious reorganizing efforts that included unprecedented cutbacks in the corporate work force. Many people who had supported Jackie's move to headquarters were no longer with the firm, which caused Jackie some concern:

*"We came here, and (shortly thereafter) the company changed its focus and actually fired some of our top management — people who had made commitments to me to bring me here. So, the rug was really pulled out from under us. (They) were redesigning the corporation so the kinds of jobs that I would typically look to as my next move were being done away with."*

The increasing competition and speed of technological change forced Ameritech and the other RBOCs to reexamine their basic decision-making processes. Jackie explained that, in the past:

*"We were an industry that could make decisions on substantial analytical data that was gathered over a period of time. You could go back and reassess that data before you actually had to decide. It was almost no risk to delay the decision versus making an incorrect decision by moving quickly. Well, today, in the competitive marketplace, you can't do that. So, you*

*have to make decisions on minimal amounts of data that you assess maybe once — and a lot of feeling about your customers."*

In August 1991, Jackie moved over to marketing at Ameritech Services[1] (still in Chicago) and was given the responsibility for all of Ameritech's business customers in a five-state region. Her new department, however, was not immune to the substantial reductions in force occurring throughout Ameritech. The layoffs signaled a change in culture at the company:

*"If you started with the telephone company and you did a good job, you were recognized and you were promoted and, I don't know if I'd say that you had a lifelong career, but you certainly had an extensive career. That isn't how it is today. We're really changing the design of how one succeeds in the business, so I need to go and build (my department's) morale at this point."*

As part of Ameritech's downsizing efforts, all employees were evaluated according to a variety of skills that the company believed to be crucial to its future success. Many individuals were identified as not having the necessary qualities to continue with the company. Jackie commented on the serious changes people were experiencing:

*"Now some of those people could retire, so the changes were a pretty easy move for them. Some of them, in their 30s and 40s who couldn't retire, viewed it as a betrayal on the part of the company — changing the way we deal with them, the contract, as they call it. To them, we had literally broken the contract. But instead of deserving a job or believing that it's your right to have the job, we believe you have to earn the job every day. And you earn it through customer service. As a result, we took the bottom tier of people and moved them out of the business. It was a very painful thing to do.*

*I think the real signal, though, is to people who were on the next tier. We've said to them, 'We don't know if we're ever going to have to do this again, but if we do, you're at risk and here's why.'"*

[1] Ameritech Services provided planning, development, management, and support for the Ameritech Bell Companies to help achieve common marketing and operational goals.

The upheaval caused by the downsizing prompted Ameritech officers to think carefully about how news of the restructuring was communicated to the 70,000-person work force. Jackie commented on the approach:

*"(Traditionally,) we let our employees read something in the newspaper or trade journals (about changes) that they should have understood and had explained to them before it appeared in print. Now, sometimes things just happen if there wasn't any planning, but there are other things we can do. We're working right now to figure out a decentralized communications process which says that the head of each unit would be able to (communicate the message) the way they want to. But the communication would be coordinated and prepared in documents from a centralized point of view.*

*What we have found was that if each of us explains why the corporation is downsizing we each kind of ad-lib why we think that's happening. And then we communicate that to 100 people who each kind of ad-lib to others. The message needs to be very clear. Now, whether I decide to do that over videotapes and you decide to have small group sessions and talk about it, will be your decision. These messages require conversation and interactive discussion while others are able to be communicated, maybe, in print. So, what we're trying to balance now is the centralized message and the information around it, but with a decentralized distribution system. That isn't how we've done it to date. We've had one answer for everybody. We're going to send this out in print, it'll be distributed to 70,000 employees, and you'll read about it like everyone else."*

As she examined her new job and the changes occurring in her markets, Jackie began to make what others called revolutionary changes for a telephone utility:

*"One thing I've done here is reach down and create a multi-level reporting structure so that I have some people who would come to my staff meetings who, in our hierarchy, might be several levels below someone else but they are experts in their field. Now the people feel honored because they're being recognized for their expertise and the role they're playing and are thrilled to come! What people began to realize was that the reason they were being brought in was that in this meeting we were going to*

277

*make decisions that required very specific operational information about*
*very specific projects. So, you couldn't have some (who were) represent-*
*ing it who didn't understand the project or we'd probably make the wrong*
*decision. We invite them to the meetings based on what the subject matter*
*is. So, you get to attend a meeting based on what your role is and what's*
*going to be discussed and your contribution, not because of your approved*
*"right" to attend something because of the job you hold. So, the job doesn't*
*necessarily convey the authority in power as much anymore as the indi-*
*vidual and what they are responsible for."*

The number of wrenching decisions that were being made and the daily increasing demands of marketing in a broad five-state area with stiffening competition
placed an enormous load on Jackie. Because the challenges of reorganizing her
department were only partially offset by the excitement of working with corporate
customers, Jackie was concerned about her experience at Ameritech Services. She
missed the direct responsibilities of the line jobs she had at Ohio Bell and, frankly,
missed her roots and relationships in Ohio (see Exhibits 1 and 2). Further, the
changes in management made her wonder if the kind of guidance given by those
who had talked about and coordinated her move to Chicago had disappeared.
She wondered how long and in what capacity she might stay in Chicago.

With those thoughts in mind, she and her husband began to talk about other
options. Should they look for other jobs in other firms back in Cleveland? (Jackie's
and Jack's résumés appear in Exhibits 2 and 3.) How long should they wait to see if
their decision to follow Jackie's career would prove to be a dead end? How could
they tell if the executives at Ameritech were aware of, and interested in their situation? (Comments about Jackie by some of her peers and subordinates and some of
her own views on various topics are included in Exhibit 4.) As they discussed their
thoughts, Jackie and Jack decided early in 1992 to wait another two years to see
what would happen. Then, if nothing materialized, they would begin to consider
other options:

*"Our mindset was probably (oriented toward) the beginning to middle of*
*1994. We didn't say, 'We're gonna ride this out and we'll see how it is in*
*two months.' I mean, I had invested 20 years at Ameritech! It seemed worth*
*it to invest 15 months more. We had decided that we would ride this out*

*and see — with the feeling that if it did not play out by that point, we would both reassess where we wanted to be."*

## EUROPEAN VACATION PLANS

Meanwhile, in December 1991, Jackie and Jack had decided to plan a big European family vacation for July 1992. They wanted their children to have the experience of seeing Europe firsthand, something they considered an essential part of the girls' education.

> They wanted their children to have the experience of seeing Europe firsthand, something they considered an essential part of the girls' education.

In the months following the decision to go, everyone — including Nicole, 14, and Stephanie, 11 — spent a considerable amount of time planning all aspects of the trip. They paid for all of the travel and lodging arrangements in advance. Although the package was quite expensive, the Woodses felt good about the itinerary and the experience it would be for the family. Their plans were complicated somewhat by Ameritech's restructuring announcement in May 1992 and by Jackie's subsequent assignment to the reorganization task force. Jackie viewed the assignment with mixed feelings. Although it signaled to her that she was not forgotten, it also conflicted directly with the planned family vacation:

> *"We had been working with the travel agent since January, and we very specifically picked someone here in town so on Saturday morning you could go up to town, stop at the corner store and get coffee and a doughnut and go in and sit down and chat with this lady. We laid out maps. The girls went and ate bagels over her desk, and everybody talked about where we were going and had a very vested interest. The girls got to pick places they thought would be interesting. Jack and I contributed. Everybody had read the tour books and, about June, with everything pretty well paid for and arranged, (Ameritech) said, 'Well, maybe you'd better not go.'"*

Bob Brown's comment in the hallway heightened Jackie's concern about the trip. Clearly, that summer would be a very important time in the history of the company. Decisions would be made that could shape the future of Ameritech — and of the Woods family.

## EXHIBIT 1:
## JACKIE WOODS (A)

**Milestones**

| | |
|---|---|
| Summer 1968 | Jackie Dudek meets Jack Woods. |
| September 1969 | Jackie gets job at Ohio Bell. |
| November 1969 | Jack gets drafted. |
| December 1969 | Jack and Jackie get married. |
| Mid-1978 | Jack is transferred to Philadelphia, and Jackie accepts job with Bell of Pennsylvania. |
| January 1982 | Jackie accepts sales job at Ohio Bell. |
| June 1984 | Divestiture puts Jackie in autonomous subsidiary. |
| January 1989 | President tells Jackie that she needs headquarters experience; she accepts CFO position in Chicago (family moves); Jack gets job in procurement at Ameritech. |
| August 1990 | Jackie moves back to marketing. |
| December 1991 | Jack and Jackie plan European trip for family. |

## EXHIBIT 2:
## JACKIE WOODS (A)

**Jackie's Résumé, June 1992**

**Education**

Northwestern University                                    Chicago, IL
Executive Education Program

|  | Muskingum College | Muskingum, OH |
|---|---|---|
|  | Graduated May 1968 |  |
|  | B.A. in Psychology |  |
|  | B.S. in Communications |  |

**Experience**

| 1990–Present | Ameritech Services — Business Markets<br>General Manager and Vice President | Chicago, IL |
|---|---|---|
| 1989–90 | Ameritech Services<br>Vice President of Finance and Administration | Chicago, IL |
| 1986–89 | Ohio Bell Communications<br>President and Chief Executive Officer | Cleveland, OH |
| 1982–84 | Ohio Bell Communications<br>Vice President of Marketing | Cleveland, OH |
| 1978–82 | Bell of Pennsylvania<br>Public Affairs Office<br>Marketing Department | Philadelphia, PA |
| 1970–78 | Ohio Bell Communications<br>Public Affairs District Manager<br>Public Relations Manager<br>Business Office Supervisor | Cleveland, OH |
| Outside Activities | United Way, Muskingum College Alumni Association, Chicago Junior League, Chicago Executive Club, Chicago Easter Seals | |

## EXHIBIT 3:
## JACKIE WOODS (A)

### Jack's Résumé, June 1992

**Education**

| | |
|---|---|
| University of Akron | Akron, OH |
| Graduated May 1964 | |
| B.S. in Business Administration | |

**Experience**

| | | |
|---|---|---|
| 1992–Present | Ameritech Services — Asset Management Director | Chicago, IL |
| 1990–92 | Ameritech Services — Supplies Management Director | Chicago, IL |
| 1989–90 | Ameritech Services — Procurement Director | Chicago, IL |
| 1988–89 | B.F. Goodrich — Chemical Purchasing Director | Cleveland, OH |
| 1985–87 | B.F. Goodrich — Procurement and Materials Management Director | Cleveland, OH |
| 1984 | B.F. Goodrich — Plant Purchasing General Manager | Cleveland, OH |
| 1981–83 | B.F. Goodrich — Plant Purchasing Regional Manager | Philadelphia, PA |
| Outside Activities | Shelter, Inc. — Director; American Legion; Computer Dealers/Lessors Association — Customer Advisory Council | |

## Exhibit 4:
## Jackie Woods (A)

### Comments from and about Jackie Woods

**Jackie on Networking:**

*"I also find it interesting that men have had a very strong network, so it has been easier (for them) to make decisions based on fact. You could go ask some of your buddies or your boss or the president, 'Here's what I see happening, is that how it's going to be?' Women and minorities spent a lot of time guessing because they either didn't have the network or they were afraid to ask. What we're seeing now is that these new networks are being built. There are women's groups; there are minority groups. There is a formal network within their firms so that people can get better information to understand the alternatives."*

**Jackie on Balancing Work and Family:**

*"That is the trade-off. If you are going to say, in a business environment, that you want to have so much more, that these are the jobs that I want to have, then you need to understand what it is going to take to get there. And if that's not what you are willing to do, then you have to take the responsibility for that as well."*

**A Colleague's Observation of Jackie:**

*"Jackie is probably one of the most complete managers that I have encountered throughout my career with Ameritech. She has an incredible amount of energy, an outstanding ability to retain information and absorb detail. She tends to encourage and motivate her staff effectively as well."*

**Jackie on Being Close to Employees and Customers:**

*"What I found was that if you go out and talk to people and spend your time with both your employees and your customers, it becomes easy to understand how to integrate their input into company operations. Employees need to know they have your support, and customers need to know the top executives draw from what's going on at the front line."*

## Jackie on Setting Priorities:

*"Even if there are things that are very important to the business, basic tenets that the business is built on, you really need to question them. Let me give you an example, the pricing philosophy of how we price service. Maybe my customer data tells me that (the current way) isn't the way we are going to be able to do that in the future. And my competitive data tells us that we are going to have to change. Well, pricing is something very basic to this business. Changes are going to have millions of dollars of impact. That isn't something I am going to bring up offhandedly in a meeting and expect to have resolved. I am going to evaluate the data, get more facts, and I am going to listen to people's positions on it, and I am going to, as you might say, work the issue. (Anything) that could have immediate impact to our customers is something to fight for that. So, having that sense of balance of how big this (issue) is to the corporation and customers is important to determining how quickly we need to act."*

## Jackie's Colleague on Her Consensus-Building Skills:

*"The Bell Operating Companies (in Ameritech's five-state region) do not want us here. They would prefer to continue to run their own organizations, manage their own budgets, develop their own strategies and do it in five different ways. So, we go out to the state operating companies and talk to the sales and support vice presidents about our plans, and the minute we walk into the room with the presidents and vice presidents, the guns are loaded. But by the time we leave that meeting, Jackie has really gotten a consensus on every issue that she has gone there with, and everyone feels like they have won at the end of the meeting. It's incredible how she builds the whole win-win situation."*

## Jackie on Management Fads:

*"I think that American management has to have a lot of confidence in what they do real well. We sometimes decide that someone else is good at something and all of a sudden we drop everything we do. We read this book or we heard in this country they do this, so let's drop what we are doing. American management has to develop its own style. Certainly we should utilize things from other cultures, but we should build on a framework of what we really believe in this country and on what we really want to do in managing our businesses. We can't decide quality, for example, is the program for the day! And so now all the CEOs are going to walk out and talk about quality, and all are going to have a quality advisor and in a few months we are going to decide well, quality isn't it anymore. I mean, quality has to be in the very basic way that we approach the business and every decision we make."*

## QUESTIONS FOR REFLECTION

1. How does Ms. Woods' approach to balancing her work and family life compare with that of Ms. James' presented earlier?

2. What chapter in life is Ms. Woods in?

3. What should Ms. Woods tell her boss about her participation in the reorganization meetings? How will your recommended answer affect her life and career?

4. Have you ever taken your work with you on vacation? What were the consequences of that?

5. What would Ms. Woods' Balance Wheel look like?

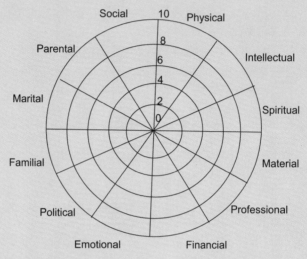

A Personal Developmental Balance Wheel.

## EPILOGUE

Ms. Woods went on the vacation with her family. She admitted to taking her phone along and making occasional teleconferences with her colleagues during the vacation. (Have you ever done that?) Her choice did not seem to affect her career negatively, as she was later appointed president of Ohio Bell, the second woman only to reach that height in the telephone industry. She believed that she could keep her commitments to her family and still be an effective executive.

# 15

## Bob Johnson: The Life and Career of a Divisional Chief Executive Officer

I'm not in a good place," said Bob Johnson. "I feel empty. Lonely. Alone. Sad." Johnson's casual, unusual cadence belied his status as an internationally respected business icon, and in this moment, seemed inconsistent with the very real malaise he was describing. "Never *been* lost," he said with a shrug. "I must figure out what to do: Make some changes!"

It was a sunny day in December 2005, and Johnson was "herding"[1] his Jaguar down an immaculate divided road in Scottsdale, Arizona. As the retiring CEO of Honeywell Aerospace division, he seemed to have everything. Yet he looked concerned. During the course of his career, Johnson had worked for, and with, industry icons Jack Welch and Larry Bossidy. He had amassed an unblemished record of 32 straight successful turnaround and managerial assignments, all of them over profit plan, under expense budget, and ahead of schedule. He'd invested wisely and capitalized on his management bonus plans to the point where he'd become independently wealthy. He'd been married for 32 years and raised three children. He'd played golf all over the world and at the best courses. He'd even been teamed with Tiger Woods and in the process finished second in a nationally recognized pro-am tournament after playing the round of his life. He'd owned the cars of his choice, including a Ferrari and a Mercedes SL500 sports car. What could be wrong with this picture?

## A "Normal" Childhood and Youth

Robert Johnson grew up in Zanesville, Ohio, where his father worked for General Electric (GE). With a German mother and Swedish father, life in the Johnson family was marked by a sense of orderliness. Both fundamentalist Christians, Johnson's parents worked hard to raise their children with discipline, clear rewards and punishments.

By his own admission, Johnson was a difficult child who seemed to naturally disobey rules. At the time, the family was unaware that Johnson had Attention Deficit Disorder (ADD), a condition characterized by the inability to maintain attention and a tendency toward impulsive behavior and blurting out, along with motor restlessness.[2] In addition, Johnson later discovered that he also had

[1] "Herding" was Johnson's term for driving while checking his Blackberry and listening to his cell phone voicemail.

[2] http://www.cdc.gov/ncbddd/adhd/ (accessed 21 March 2006).

Obsessive Compulsive Disorder (OCD), a condition in which the brain locks onto something and finds it hard to let go. Growing up, Johnson continually questioned the family rules. He seemed fixated on knowing *why* a rule was a rule. The seemingly endless repetitions of his inquiries tired his parents. His mother, for example, would say, "It's nap time," and Johnson would resist. He constantly fidgeted, jiggling his arms, knees, his whole body — he just couldn't sit still. Taking a nap was, in his words, impossible. His mother would send him to his room. Later, Johnson noted that he spent long, long, periods in his room alone struggling to figure out how to function in the world. That scenario went on until he was 15. As Johnson recalled:

*"If I objected, if I didn't go along with this form of changing my behavior or discipline, I was whipped. I spent a lot of time in that room. And while in there, I developed a very strong will to escape, to leave the room, and to have a situation where I employed a different set of principles. That's not to say my parents weren't great. But our relationship was not a holding, loving, caring relationship."*

In junior high, Johnson met Bill Stewart (now president and CEO of Stewart Glapat Corporation) in some of his classes and on the basketball court. Stewart described Johnson as everyone's friend — he was fun to be around. Johnson was able to fit well with most groups and in various settings. He made people feel good about themselves — a talent Stewart credited as being a key to Johnson's later leadership success.

When they reached high school, Stewart tried out for and made the varsity basketball team, and Johnson did not. Subsequently, Johnson organized a team of all the other players who failed to make the varsity team and entered them in the YMCA-sponsored league. They eventually won the state championship. Stewart recalled this team of what some called 'renegades':

*"I wouldn't call them renegades but they were people who didn't make the team because of discipline problems or maybe they smoked. Back then that meant something. They played a pretty rough brand of basketball. Maybe more like an NBA style — it was run and shoot — not much defense.*

*As player-coach, he took that team through the various stages of the tournament and won state champion. They just out-gunned the other teams and got a trophy for it. I never got to touch a state championship experience but Bob did — certainly in a different arena. So, Bob became legendary (in Zanesville) for having formed this state championship team."*

Johnson did make the high school golf team, however, and he and Stewart played many rounds together. Stewart described him as an "optimistic" player. Johnson apparently hit some shots that would bring most players to tears and cause them to give up. But on the very next hole, Johnson would make a great shot and be right back in the game and on top of his spirits. "He always looked for the next opportunity and didn't dwell on the past," Stewart said. "Many of us have difficulty with that since we tend to remember our mistakes and can't enjoy the moment."

After going their separate ways following high school, Johnson and Stewart remained acquaintances, meeting up occasionally at the five-year school reunions. Their mutual love for the game of golf brought them together periodically as they made plans to play various well- known courses. Their most recent excursion had been a two-week trip with six others in August 2005, playing the best courses in Ireland, Northern Ireland, Scotland, and England. Reflecting on his relationship with Johnson, Stewart noted:

*"I bet if you had asked my classmates who in our class would become a leader of industry and shake things up in the corporate world, I'd have been the one because I was going to the school that trained people (MIT).*

*I went to the Sloan School of Management, and I was a mechanical engineer. So by right and prediction, I should be the one that's being interviewed as some corporate executive. But Bob had a different quality. That was, I think, he learned very early how to get the best out of people."*

## EARNING A HIGHER EDUCATION

Johnson's innate intelligence along with the discipline imposed on him as a youth served him well in school. He got typically As in high school, and that record got him into Miami University in Oxford, Ohio, where he started out in the engineering school. After two years, he switched majors to business. Johnson graduated with an economics major in 1969. Although the then newly elected President Nixon promised peace in Vietnam, Johnson fully expected to get his draft number shortly after graduation. He attended campus recruiting hoping to find a job. "So if I did go to war," Johnson said, "I had a place to come back to."

The night before his second round of interviews with GE executives, Johnson was partying at a seniors' fraternity event. He got in late and recalled setting his alarm clock but needed his fraternity brothers' help to get him up and on his way to Cincinnati on time. The morning began with interviews with several different managers, and then the group headed to lunch. They drank "silver bullets" (very dry martinis) before Johnson returned for his afternoon interviews, first with the manager in charge of accounts payable. As he remembered:

*"I got the nods. And I was really just fighting to pay attention. As he asked questions, he was pounding a pencil on the desk (to keep me awake). I finally said, 'Look, I was studying for a test, and we celebrated afterward with this party.' I just told him the truth. 'Well, you know, the same thing happened to me when I was coming out of college,' he said, 'When can you start?'*

*It's interesting that he trusted that my value was there. (Later) I went to his retirement party and thanked him for taking a chance on me. And later on, I had some chances in my career to know somebody and observe that there was something, some event that was a little out of the norm. So, I stayed with some people (like he did with me) and it always turned out right."*

## GOING TO WORK

Johnson began his professional career at GE Aircraft Engines (GEAE) working in financial analysis and accounting (see Exhibit 1 for a timeline). He found the work, being in charge of the physical inventory for a $6 billion business, interesting and instructive. Johnson progressed the next 12 years in various finance

---

## EXHIBIT 1:
## THE LIFE AND CAREER OF A CEO: BOB JOHNSON
## AT HONEYWELL (A)

### Chronological Listing of Key Events in Bob Johnson's Life

1947   Born in Zanesville, Ohio.

1965   Graduated from Zanesville High School, having won the state championship in YMCA basketball.

1969   Graduated from Miami University of Ohio in economics.

1969   Began career at GE Aircraft Engine.

1974   Married.

1983   Moved to Singapore.

1993   Took job with AAR Corporation in Chicago.

1994   Joined AlliedSignal in Phoenix.

1999   Became CEO of Honeywell Aerospace.

2002   Underwent open heart surgery.

2005   Appointed chairman of Aerospace; retirement announced.

2006   ?

---

leadership positions. As he progressed, he came to believe the business side was easy to figure out, that the complexity of his position was managing the people and processes.

In 1972, Johnson met his future wife, Dede, while he was interviewing candidates at his alma mater. In time, she joined the company, where her father had worked for 36 years. (Johnson's father had worked for GE for 32 years.) Johnson dropped by her office occasionally to see how she was doing, and their relationship blossomed. They were married in 1974. "In a subtle way, people at GE were telling me I should be married," Johnson said. "I don't think it was a rule, but I was one of the few people in the management learning process who wasn't married." Together, the Johnsons raised two daughters and one son.

## MANAGEMENT DEVELOPMENT

General Electric had developed a management development program for vice presidents that enrolled 25 executives each year. Johnson was picked to join the program in 1992. Part of the program was held in various overseas locations including Germany. The program included various GE executives talking about their experiences. Johnson recalled one lesson in particular:

*"We had a fellow whose model had generated good results but whose behavior included killing gnats with sledgehammers come to visit us. So, Jack (Welch) sent him off to see an executive coach to change his behavior. He talked (to us) about this and how important changing his behavior was. A number of people asked him questions, and I said, 'Are you doing this because you were told to do it or because you want to do it?' In my mind, he gave the wrong answer when he said, "It doesn't matter, does it?'*

*I thought, 'Wow, how are you going to make a significant change in what is probably a deep-seated behavior if you first don't recognize that a change is what you want to make?'"*

Part of the program included team projects analyzing three business problems. There were two teams of four working on each of the three issues. Each team presented their project findings to their business leader. After getting suggestions from their business leaders, the two competing teams on each project were then suddenly told that they had to work together and condense their two separate presentations into a joint five-slide presentation to deliver to the CEO, Jack Welch, and his team.

After completing the four-week development course, Johnson was promoted to be leader of the global field service engineering team. He was given 18 months to reduce service costs by 10 percent. "And in nine months, we made it 25 percent more efficient — customers were happy," Johnson said. "I thought, wow, I know

I can make this work inside GE, but what about outside the company?" It wasn't long before he decided to give it a try.

## Singapore

In 1983, Johnson was asked to move to Singapore to rejuvenate and run the GE aircraft engine technology repair business there. Johnson found himself in a very different culture in which half the people spoke Mandarin and in charge of a very technical business he knew very little about. His predecessor had established a norm that nothing in the business moved unless it had his personal approval. Johnson described his contrasting approach:

*"Some fellows had done massive homework and analysis. They came into the meeting (a few days after I arrived) with worksheets on top of worksheets. And they walked me through their logic, which all made perfect sense. At the end of their presentation they looked at me and said, 'Bob, what do you want to do?' I said, 'What do I want to do? You did all the work, what do you think we should do?'*

*'Well, what if we're wrong?' one of them asked. So, I told them if we were wrong we would change it. We would do something else. At that point, if I had to make all the decisions, and they were the ones who knew everything, it wasn't going to work. How would they ever grow? How big and successful could we be if I was the bottleneck? So, we made a different set of rules about what they could do and what I could do. But they always came in and told me what they wanted to do. They had to start with that.*

*Through a continuous improvement process of realigning the processes, timing the processes, and getting the bottlenecks out of the way, we went from little income or losses to (profits of) almost $0.50 on the dollar. We grew that business seven times.*

*Essentially we took a business and radically changed it inside itself. This wasn't me doing this. This was a set of people who were the process owners, redesigning a business based upon the goals and needs of the customers.*

*And we could do it successfully inside its existing frame. We got all the people who had to do the work involved in implementing the changes.*

*"Those four years were a wonderful experience for me and for my family. Every moment was a learning experience. Twenty years later there are people in that plant I know and continue to visit when I'm in Singapore."*

Johnson reached the corporation's goals for the Singapore operation ahead of schedule and was then assigned to turn around an operation in central Kansas. The move from Singapore — a large, cosmopolitan city with low service-sector wage rates and extensive benefits for expatriates including housekeepers and babysitters — to Kansas, where none of that existed, was a big culture shock for the Johnsons. All of them struggled to make the change. Nevertheless, Johnson succeeded in his new assignment, once again faster and better than expected.

## AAR CORPORATION

Johnson's success at GE and the repetitive nature of his experiences — new assignment, setting high goals, working through the talents of his people, succeeding ahead of schedule — encouraged him to consider other options. In June 1993, he received and accepted an offer to join AAR Corporation, a family-owned company in Chicago, ending his 24-years career at GE. AAR was an aerospace company dealing in servicing, manufacturing, and trading. Johnson was vice president and general manager of manufacturing and services. During his 13 months at AAR, their earnings went from $0.02 a share to $0.49:

*"The process of making good decisions (at AAR) was comparable (to that at GE) but this was a small business with less resources. I was having fun but realized this company was only going to provide a limited opportunity for growth. It was a family-founded business and to be president was going to take quite a while. The phone started ringing from a headhunter who wanted me to go to Phoenix and work for some people who had left GE to go to another company, AlliedSignal. They wanted to reinvent this company."*

## AlliedSignal

Believing that he could make his established change process work in different businesses, Johnson thought it was the right time to return to a larger company. The difficult part was going to be persuading his family to move to Arizona. His two high school–age daughters had just established themselves in the Chicago school system, and the idea of moving again was not popular. Eventually, the family agreed, but for the first six months, they resented Johnson's decision:

> *"The move from Chicago to Phoenix had a lot of pluses or I wouldn't have taken the phone call. It also overcame some roadblocks that I perceived were eventually going to happen in Chicago. The negotiations were interesting because on the one hand, I would die to be in Phoenix and have all those golf courses (nearby). So, I had to emphasize areas of concern — and the company was broken. So, I had to take the risk of saying no and did so two or three times. They finally gave me the security I needed and made the commitment that my family would not have to relocate in the future."*

AlliedSignal had started out in the chemical business' producing ammonia in the early 1920s. With growth, the company introduced yarns, fabrics, tire material, oil and gas chemicals, eventually adding automotive and aerospace manufacturing. By the time Johnson joined them, AlliedSignal had, under the leadership of Larry Bossidy, another former lieutenant of Jack Welch's at GE, consolidated into three industry sectors: aerospace, engineered materials, and automotive. Johnson joined the aerospace sector, which had four businesses — engines, aircraft systems, electronics, and landing systems. Johnson formed a new business called services, which spanned all the product businesses.

Three years after Johnson's arrival, and with a flourishing service business established, Bossidy told Johnson he needed him to go to Kansas City to run a new, but faltering, part of the company. Johnson explained the "no move" clause in his contract, to which Bossidy offered an alternative: Johnson would fly to Kansas City as late as he wanted on Sunday nights and return to Phoenix early each Friday afternoon. The company would provide Johnson a condo and car in Kansas City. Bossidy gave Johnson a two-year time frame for re-establishing the business. So, in the late summer of 1997, Johnson started his shuttle management lifestyle. And in typical fashion, he completed his turnaround effort, meeting Bossidy's goals after only 16 months:

> *"For 60 straight weeks, I went back and forth. We closed some businesses, integrated others, and stopped the internal fighting. We took a business that was losing income, losing cash, and had no growth and turned it into one of the biggest cash and income generators of the company. People were now having fun there. Just a wonderful business that (later) became the basis for (analysis recommending) merging AlliedSignal and Honeywell."*

Shortly after the Kansas City success and just before his return to work in Phoenix, Bossidy told Johnson he wanted him to go Harrisburg, Pennsylvania, to run a connector business they were intending to acquire. There would be no flying back and forth on that assignment, so Johnson was expected to persuade his family to make the move. Fortunately for Johnson, the deal failed to go through, and the family stayed put in Phoenix.

By this time, in late 1998, Johnson had become president and CEO of AlliedSignal's aerospace marketing, sales, and service business. Together, Bossidy and his team had led a transformation of AlliedSignal that quintupled the market value of company shares. "The AlliedSignal opportunity gave me a bigger place to play and confirmed to me that I like to be where things aren't right," Johnson said. "And after three or four years, we were successful at fixing the business."

## HONEYWELL INTERNATIONAL

In June 1999, AlliedSignal merged with Honeywell in a stock-swap to create a *Fortune* 50 company named Honeywell International. Honeywell had started business in 1906 manufacturing furnace regulators (thermostats) and had grown to develop several famous products such as the electronic autopilot. By 1986, the Honeywell aerospace business had become one of the world's leading integrators of avionics systems.

Larry Bossidy was made chairman of the new Honeywell International, but left the company four months later. Michael Bonsignore replaced him as chairman and CEO. Robert Johnson became CEO of the combined aerospace operations with headquarters in Phoenix.

The newly merged company wrestled with many issues — as mergers often do. At one point, there was even a subsequent highly publicized effort to merge Honeywell and GE. When this effort failed, Bonsignore left the firm, and Bossidy was asked, in July of 2001, to resume managing the company. Bossidy agreed to return only long enough to help the company get out of its crisis and until a good successor could be found. Johnson was interviewed for the job, but had reservations about his complete interest in the position as corporate chairman in New Jersey. He enjoyed operational management much more than he would the lifestyle and challenges of the statesmanship role that chairmen had to play. In addition, he really liked living in Phoenix, and the new job would take him to New Jersey headquarters. A year after Bossidy returned, the company named another former GE executive, to replace him as chairman, CEO, and president.

Johnson continued as divisional CEO of the Honeywell aerospace operations, now a $10 billion business with key components on nearly every aircraft and space vehicle in the world. Then the 9/11 terrorist attacks changed the face of the industry. As the airline industry around the globe struggled to regain profitable operations, Johnson worked hard to lead the division through the difficult economic times. To cut a long story short, divisional profits grew steadily until the time of his retirement in January 2006.

Shortly thereafter, Johnson was elected chairman of the Aerospace Industry Association. In his words, their annual meetings had become "uninteresting and energy-consuming affairs" as they persisted in a time-proven format year after year. During his time leading the organization, Johnson was able to re-energize the meetings (in part, ironically, by having attendees play less golf). Executive members had asked for change and participated directly in creating it. Johnson was not surprised that the change was so easy, since all he'd done was what he'd been doing for years: asking people what they wanted to do and then letting it happen despite what had been done before. By the end of his administration at the Aerospace Industry Association (AIA), Johnson had been recognized by many as something close to an industry icon; he was even considered for Secretary of the Navy in 2005.

## THE STYLE THAT PRODUCED UNINTERRUPTED PROFESSIONAL SUCCESS

By the summer of 2005, Robert Johnson was one of the captains of the aerospace industry. He'd led numerous successful business turnarounds in a row, all of them ahead of goal and schedule. His personal goal had been consistently to meet the target ahead of schedule. "The most important principle was not *Bob*," Johnson said. "This wasn't (about) me — this was a set of people who were the process owners redesigning a business based upon the goals and needs of the customer."

Dean Flatt, President of Electronic Aerospace Systems, first met Johnson at an informal gathering while they were both at GE. Johnson, he said, seemed to live life large and bold. He apparently enjoyed telling stories and "holding court" in hotel lobbies. Flatt described Johnson as the James Joyce of business world.[3] "When I first saw him, I wasn't sure what to make of him because he's not your standard buttoned-up type of business guy," Flatt said. "He's got a very different way of talking and dealing with people."

In Flatt's opinion, Johnson did three things very well as a leader. First, he helped people who worked for him get to places where they were uncomfortable — to know and overcome their discomfort zones. Second, he did a good job of bringing disparate groups together to make sure their work was successful. Third, he demanded the organization be customer-conscious across the board.

Johnson would take something very complex, break it down into what were its most basic elements and find out what was important in the middle of those elements. He would then hammer repeatedly on the central key elements.

### In the Office

Executives in every merger struggle to learn the "other side's" way of doing things. This was also true in the Allied/Honeywell merger. Scott Starrett, vice president of military aircraft, was accustomed to the original Honeywell's "midwestern nature" and non-confrontational management style. According to Starrett, Johnson's meeting format

[3] James Joyce was an Irish novelist known for his experimental use of language.

was different, but consistent: he expected visuals and simplicity. Johnson would take something very complex, break it down into what were its most basic elements and find out what was important in the middle of those elements. He would then hammer repeatedly on the central key elements. Some managers had an apocryphal name for Johnson's methods for motivating senior executives, they called it "getting *Bobbed*." Starrett described the process:

*"If you took Bob somewhere he didn't want to go, you knew it right away. His verbal and body language changed. He's generally very intense and emotional — he doesn't buffer his feelings.[4] If you present a story or bring five people into a meeting with you when what Bob really wants to hear is the important (central) detail, he will very actively undress you in that meeting if you are off the mark. If you go off point, he'll wait awhile for you to come back. If that doesn't happen he'll turn to whoever is sitting beside him and ask, "Can I get him now? Can I get him now? Is he done?" Bob will use (that kind of) humor, but he is really being serious."*

Flatt offered an illustration of his own experience:

*"One of the first times that I worked for him, I was in the avionics business putting together an operating plan on the defense and space business. And it was tight. It was together. We knew what we were doing, and we knew where we were going. I got up there to pitch that — and it was probably one of the best pitches I've ever had in my life. But Bob kept interrupting and asking questions. Why didn't I know where our customer came from? Didn't I have any good ideas for growth? He let me know that I didn't have anything that showed I understood what was going on with customers and markets. He said I couldn't run a business very well if I didn't know the customer better. It was just a tough, tough pitch. And I finally said, 'Well, if that's the way this is going to go, I'm done, I think we're finished.' And I went and sat down.*

*Then a friend, a good friend and colleague of mine, got up to pitch, and he started talking about his business. He was a terrific product development*

---

[4] Another central characteristic of ADD.

*guy who really knew his customers cold and probably developed one of the largest-selling products that this company has known — a $2 billion product line called Enhanced Ground Proximity Warning Systems. He was presenting his annual operating report and budget. And Bob proceeded to slice and dice him. Why didn't he know anything about cost? Bob said he didn't know anything about where the inventory was, he didn't know how to manage assets, and, in fact, he didn't know how to do anything internally!*

*So, as Frank and I commiserated about the tough day we both had that night over dinner, we realized that he was hammering me on customers, on new product development, and on growth issues. I was very strong on cost and inventory. And cost and inventory was what he was hammering Frank on, and he was strong on customers, new product development, and growth. Once I got that equation, it was easy to see where Bob was trying to take people. We got the message and had great success."*

Johnson described an example of "undressing" he used to encourage someone he highly valued to do better:

*"A very experienced, highly paid executive who had a strategy assignment specific to his area came into my office, and it was clear he didn't have his head in the project. He gave me a (single) slide. I read it several times trying to find the value. All the words were spelled correctly, the grammar was proper, and I kept looking at it, and said, 'Well, it doesn't say anything.' He had spent time creating a content-free document well below his competence. And I thought I had to leave a message because this really should not happen again. So I got up, walked around the desk, dramatically threw the slide on the floor and started jumping up and down on it. While doing this I shouted, 'This is content-free, and if you ever come in here (again) with something that is content free — having spent energy creating it — then just don't come back!'*

*The next day he came back, had the message clear, and the strategy right. He probably never forgot that. He's still my friend to this day. But, I think you use tools of messaging to help people remember. Some with touch and some with 'flare.'"*

A more junior-level employee, Laura Rogers, director of global business management for the after-market services, met Johnson at the very beginning of her career. At the time, Rogers was the ISO coordinator (quality control) working on a big project. She was chatting with Johnson's assistant, Teresa Miller, about what she perceived as lack of cooperation from the leadership. Miller suggested Rogers speak to Johnson directly, so she did. He sat down with her and set her in the right direction. As Johnson described:

*"Teaching, especially around the act of communicating, is variable. This was a junior employee who was trying to get something done and had problems. She came to me and very clearly asked for specific help and a recommendation because she didn't know. So in that case, you provide guidance. I think different people have different buttons, and there's a different way to send the message (for each)."*

To help Honeywell aerospace executives improve their communication skills, especially in the area of being more precise, Johnson hired Mike Jousan, a speech and communications consultant he'd met on the golf course. Despite Johnson's sometime blustery attitude, Jousan described Johnson as "very much a people person." Many executives told Jousan that Johnson had given them a "chance." "Make it simple and get to the point because there is a window he'll look through that **few** moments[5] while you are in front of him," Jousan told Johnson's direct reports. "And he will determine what your abilities are."

## Personal Style

Robert Johnson was the kind of person who filled a room. His unusual cadence and mannerisms contradicted the stereotypical, button-down collar–popping publicly owned company CEO. He was very expressive and waved his arms about freely. Sometimes thinking out loud, he seemed to allow his thoughts to wander all over the conceptual map.[6] Starrett remembered meeting Johnson:

*"My first impression was, 'He's larger than life.' He came strolling into a meeting. He has a very strong presence as a leader and as a human being.*

---

[5] Another characteristic of ADD.
[6] Another characteristic of ADD.

*Actually, I thought he was a little bit goofy. Yet underneath it is a very sharp set of technical skills.*

*"If you are meeting him for the first time, there is definitely a fear complex for people going in. You don't just sit down and have a cup of coffee with Bob. You have to prepare, and prepare, because it's a tough job."*

Johnson's notorious multitasking[7] was part of who he was personally. He admitted his tendency to do five or six things at a time — like talking on the phone while answering e-mail, walking to a meeting, and carrying on a conversation. Some people found his multitasking irritating and disruptive and a signal he was not paying attention. Although Johnson found it "mildly frustrating," that people couldn't keep up with his rapid-fire brain, he made adaptations so that if someone was talking to him, he tried to listen more intently and sometimes resisted doing anything else at the same time.

Starrett noted that Johnson was able to cut to the heart of a matter quickly despite his propensity to multitask. "There may be 30 things to worry about and five that are important," Starrett said. "Once Bob sorted out what those five things were, then he wanted lots of data around those five." In Johnson's own words, he had learned to use his ADD and his OCD tendencies to his advantage. He would "diverge" (the ADD) and then "converge" (the OCD). First, he would range widely, exploring all the possible issues and challenges of a situation — using his natural ADD characteristics to cover lots of territory in a short amount of time. After, selecting the three to five key issues, he'd let his OCD kick in and lock onto those key issues and hammer them until they were dealt with.

People with ADD often have difficulty sleeping. Their minds are spinning so much that they struggle to fall asleep and stay asleep. Add to that OCD tendencies in which the mind locks onto an idea and can't let go, and the result is a combination that makes it difficult to rest. Johnson seemed obsessed with his work in a way that affected the executives who worked with him. Starrett recalled:

*"Bob's clock works pretty much 24 hours, and he sleeps with his Blackberry next to the bed. When he has a thought, he acts upon it. All of us who have*

[7] Another characteristic of ADD.

*worked for Bob check the Blackberry first thing in the morning. I'm an early riser. I get up at four or five a.m. and 80 percent of the time there would be things from Bob that he wanted answered before he got to the office in the morning. Many of us worked through the night lots of time because Bob would be up checking on things at two, three, four o'clock in the morning."*

Though he may not have described his behavior as ADD or OCD early on, Johnson became increasingly aware of the strengths and weaknesses of his personal approach. He developed various mental and behavioral systems for keeping himself on track and to help him channel his energy. For example, he used the Microsoft Outlook® task list and color coded items to "get some sense of satisfaction of completing these in the right order." He hired assistants to help him manage his calendar, appointments and finances. Indeed, he hired people to handle almost every aspect of his life — transportation, communications, mail — all the daily things that busy people must deal with to be productive. Johnson attributed methods like these for keeping him organized and ultimately helping him to become successful.

## JOHNSON'S THIRD OFFICE

Bob Johnson spent plenty of time in the office and board rooms. He was known to hold court in hotel lobbies during conferences and business review meetings. But where he really loved to "work" was on the golf course, a venue that also allowed him to build and renew friendships.[8] His senior executive job allowed Johnson to play with some of the game's best — like Spain's Sergio Garcia and American star Tiger Woods. In 2001, Johnson was paired with Tiger Woods in the Phoenix pro-am, and despite playing in front of close to 100,000 people, was able to play his career's best round, ensuring that the pair would finish in a tie for first in the pro-am part of the tournament. Johnson recalled fondly that employees in

---

[8] Many people with ADD actually struggle to play golf, because of the multiple things that golfers try to keep track of in their minds. People with ADD often become overwhelmed by all the various concepts to keep track of. At the same time, people with ADD often do very well when they can focus on just one consumptive thing like movies, programming, writing, quilting, and so on. Those who can turn on that singular focus more or less at will, like Payne Stewart, may become very good golfers. More commonly, people with ADD who try to play golf can be heard to say, "Oh, look at the birds!" or "See the turtle!" or "There's a ball! (six feet deep in the bush)."

the Honeywell corporate tent were yelling and screaming his name, and throwing things onto the course as he passed by while at the top of the pro-am leader board. Johnson described why he liked golfing:

*"I've played with lots of great golfers, and although they are there with you, they are really in another place. They are in a zone when they play. I'll never forget playing with Tiger and while in his back swing, he took one of his hands off the club. I asked him why he did that. He said, "If I hadn't taken my hand off the club at that time, I would have hooked the ball." Now I've never been able to know exactly where my hands were and what was going to happen during the swing. But I'm thinking about it now!"*

Johnson's interest in spectator sports, basketball in particular, continued over the years as well. He purchased season tickets to the Phoenix Suns professional basketball team's games. His tickets were on the second row right next to the Suns' bench, so he had an upfront and personal view of the players and their interactions. The tickets also came with immediate valet service, a sumptuous buffet under the grandstands, and handshaking access to the players as they emerged from the locker room.

## THE ZIPPER CLUB

When he was 56 years old, Johnson underwent heart surgery for three clogged coronary arteries. Fortunately, he had not had a heart attack; the blockages were discovered during his annual physical checkup. Following surgery, Johnson's activities were severely curtailed, and he was enrolled in a cardiac rehabilitation program. He rebuilt his strength and learned some new stress management techniques. For the first time in more than 30 years, he was unable to work — his computer was unplugged and his Blackberry idle. That forced isolation gave him a lot of time to think about his life and how he had gotten to that point:

*"This was a wakeup call. It was time to look after my health. I loved my job and didn't want to stop, so I used to work through lunch and have unlimited office hours. Now, I made new rules like never having a meeting before 8 am or after 5 pm. I hired a physical trainer and took up Pilates and yoga."*

The aftereffects of the surgery were evident when you were with Johnson. He had a large scar running from his left wrist to his shoulder where they had harvested the veins for transplant. He also had the all too widely known "cardiac zipper," a scar that ran from sternum to stomach where the thoracic surgeons had cracked his chest. But there was another "club" that Johnson was about to become a member of.

## THE BROKEN MARRIAGE CLUB

While Johnson was recuperating and re-evaluating his life, it became clear to him that he and his wife had drifted apart. Unfortunately, it was not an uncommon thing among his executive associates. The challenges of being on the road constantly, of being fully engaged in running a business 24/7, and the mental strain of dealing with a myriad of issues took their toll on both health and relationships.

In Johnson's case, he saw that he and his wife had "run our family like a business." "We had divided up all the responsibilities and were successful, Johnson said. "But when the kids were gone and my job was over, we didn't have much between the two of us." The two had developed different interests over time, and in the end, they found little, passion or otherwise, to bind them together.

## COMING UP ON RETIREMENT

The road to retirement for Johnson probably began during the search for Honeywell International's new CEO in early January of 2002, when he questioned his level of desire to be chairman and move to New Jersey. After his first interview at corporate headquarters in New Jersey, Johnson did a lot of thinking. Among the nagging issues was the very real fact that he liked living in Phoenix and the position would mean moving away. There was pressure from many who wanted Johnson in that position, and he had frequently done what company leaders asked of him. This time, though, was different. "One of the board of directors told me afterwards," Johnson said, "'When I come back in my next life, I want to be you.'" Johnson decided to retire as CEO of Honeywell Aerospace. His heart surgery in May that same year helped reinforce his decision.

In the summer of 2005, Honeywell named Johnson's successor and his retirement date: January 1, 2006. Johnson had ensured that his financial incentives were all in place and that the length of service requirements were met, so he anticipated being able to retire financially independent. Johnson spent the latter part of 2005 slowly disengaging from work and the previous 58 years of his life.

That December, at a retirement party hosted by a longtime friend, Johnson felt totally at home. There, Johnson was in his element, moving easily from group to group, making acquaintances, renewing friendships, reveling in the momentary fruits of a lengthy and very successful career. The next day, however, he felt the turbulence of the transitions he was making.

## Learning to Live as an Ordinary, Single Citizen

First, he realized that he'd forgotten much of how to function in society. Leading the busy executive's lifestyle, he had let himself become helpless in doing what many people consider routine details. It had been a long time since he had flown on a commercial airplane rather than a corporate jet, let alone buy a ticket on his own. Indeed, he didn't even know what an "e-ticket" was. Johnson was also unaware that travelers needed to remove their shoes and take their laptops out of their briefcases to go through security procedures. He laughed about his inability to mail a FedEx package. He'd stopped going grocery shopping years before, and began to discover that much had changed.

Second, he began to realize that fewer and fewer of his associates were connecting with him as their attention turned to the new CEO. Though he continued to check his Blackberry and his cell phone, the volume of business-related contacts had already begun to shrink.

Third, as Johnson continued to distance himself from his wife, he was feeling more and more disconnected. Not only was he learning new patterns of daily living, he also wrestled with the distractions inherent in the process of divorce.

Beneath it all, Johnson also wrestled with loneliness. For decades now, he'd been the center of attention, with people responding to his many requests.

Now, increasingly, he found himself alone. The employees were dwindling away, and his family was becoming more distant. And though he had accepted appointments on several boards that would keep him "in the business" he somehow felt *alone*.

Reflecting on all of that, Johnson acknowledged that looking for his own happiness was a struggle, something he'd not paid a lot of attention to:

*"If I were 30 and entering this process with the experience I have in my memory bank, I'd ask myself a couple of questions. Something I didn't ask at the time. What are the end values? Where am I really going and why? Is this about reward or security, or satisfaction? Is it about awards or fame? Is it about business success and about making people's lives better? Ask these questions at age 30, then ask them again at 35 and then at 40.*

*I spent a lot of time making everybody else happy — satisfying the people who hired me, the shareholders, the customers, the employees. And a lot of that came at my expense — my health, my stress, my family. I spent 58 years giving. You could argue that I did that for myself. And maybe I did. But I didn't actually do it at anytime for my benefit and anyone else's demise. So, I've decided to play pickup sticks here... and rearrange my priorities."*

It was just days later, as he navigated that sunny Scottsdale boulevard in his Jaguar sedan, that Johnson's thoughts and the conversation turned once more toward the balance between his professional career and his personal life. "I'm not in a good place," he said again.

## QUESTIONS FOR REFLECTION

1. How many senior business executives do you know have been divorced and remarried? What is it about executive lifestyles that often lead to divorce?

2. How many people do you know wrestle with attention deficit disorder or obsessive compulsive disorder? How do they manage their lives? Do you have any personality tendencies that might shape your ability to succeed or to balance your life?

3. How many executives do you know who have had heart surgery? What is it about executive lifestyles that often leads to health problems?

4. What chapter of life is Mr. Johnson in?

5. What do you think he should do in his next chapter in life? What challenges will he discover?

6. What do you think Mr. Johnson's balance wheel would look like?

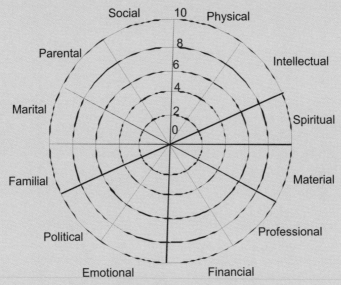

A Personal Developmental Balance Wheel.

## EPILOGUE

In August, 2006, Mr. Johnson accepted an offer to move to Dubai and lead an effort to create an aerospace industry there as the CEO. Working with a board of directors and his investors, he built a multi-billion dollar company with seven subsidiaries in a year's time. These subsidiaries included an aerospace engineering university, an aircraft service business, an airport management company, a leasing company, and a parts business. He had to keep a spreadsheet with 365 color-coded cells in it to keep track of where he was supposed to be on any given day during the year. By August 2008, conditions had changed in the emirate, and the company was being significantly downsized. As Mr. Johnson concluded his contract with Dubai Aerospace Enterprises, he began considering other options, including serving on several boards and possibly leading an American manufacturing company — again.

# 16

JAMES HAROLD
CLAWSON:
THE LIFE AND
CAREER OF A
CHIEF EXECUTIVE
OFFICER

> *"My first goal was to be a school teacher. There were very few jobs in Cache Valley, and Salt Lake City wasn't much better. Ninety percent of the people were engaged in agriculture or manual labor. If one didn't have land that meant he worked as a farmhand for somebody else. Without capital, one couldn't own land.*
>
> *There were ten children and fifteen acres in my family, so what was I to do? I had to prepare for something. The most lucrative job in those days, other than farming, was school teaching, unless one could get to the very rare jobs in a bank. The banks seldom had turnover. School teaching, while it was not lucrative, really, was a white collar job and it had something more in it than muscle work. The best job I could hope for at teaching was $65 a month."*

So began James Harold Clawson as he reflected at age 80 on his life and career as an auditor, manager, and chief executive officer of one of the United States' major private utilities. That statement was perhaps the best simple summary of the motivation that propelled Jack Clawson from a modest and isolated farm community to the paneled boardrooms of corporate America. His story is neither unique nor common; it reflects the imprints of great individual drive and of serendipitous luck. It also reflects the subtle and intricate ways in which career can become life and life become career. Mr. Clawson's family knew him as Harold; his business associates called him Jack. Yet in spite of this superficial separation of roles, whenever he was asked about his life, the dilemmas he faced, or the emotions he felt, Mr. Clawson always began by describing what was happening at the company. He was loyal yet independent; demanding yet understanding, intense yet calm. By almost any standard, he was successful.

> He was loyal yet independent; demanding yet understanding, intense yet calm. By almost any standard, he was successful.

## The Early Years

Harold Clawson was born in 1899 in Providence, near Logan in the northern, mountainous part of Utah. Automobiles were still in their infancy; airplanes were yet to fly. William McKinley was President, the Spanish American War barely ended. Harold was the second in what was to be a family of 10 children — eight boys and two girls. His father had 15 acres of land, but could not make a living out of them alone so he worked at a variety of odd jobs, working now as freighter hauling stone by wagon team from the local quarry, then as laborer, always doing his farming on the side. His mother was hardly educated at all, but worked hard and had a great love for her children.

Harold grew up farming, milking cows, and attending a small rural school. In the summer of his 12th year he contracted an unusual fever that refused to go away. He felt weak and lethargic; he could not walk more than a half mile without resting. When the Scouts went off hiking, they took a horse for Harold to ride. From that summer on, he did not feel physically strong. He did not grow so tall as his brothers and tired more quickly at physical labor. Some foods did not sit well in his stomach, and he began to have abdominal pains.

Consequently, Harold began to spend more time reading and thinking. His favorite uncle, Leo, attended Utah State University and then became a local school teacher. He brought books home from the school library for Harold to read — a new book each week.

*"I was under his influence for about five years. He got me started in seeking an education and in doing well in my studies. He was a teacher for awhile in the school to which I went, and so that he wouldn't show any favoritism, he really held me to a higher standard than the others. When I was 15, he unfortunately died from the bad effects of sickness contracted during his youth."*

In his local high school (an academy that included two years of college work), Harold did very well. He was outgoing and popular. He took up tennis, and in his junior year won an oratorical contest. His senior year, he defeated the high status and well-to-do candidate from Logan in the student-body presidential election by talking quietly to all of the students from the various small farming towns that surrounded Logan, collecting their support for a rural ticket.

Harold worked during his summer vacations as a laborer at the local sugar factory. He remembered clearly the advice of Mr. Campbell, the foreman:

*"He came up to me where I was working, sweating it out — I wasn't too strong physically — and he said, 'Harold, my boy, it's a lot easier pushing a pencil than it is pushing these shovels. It pays better, too!' That impressed and encouraged me quite deeply."*

While Harold was at the academy, the nation entered World War I. Expecting to be drafted, he enlisted voluntarily and was sent to Officer's Training School in Waco, Texas, in the fall of 1918. He took out correspondence courses at the academy to add to his credits while he was gone. The war ended a few months later, and Harold returned to school. By virtue of his earlier work and the correspondence courses, he was able to complete the six-year course for teacher certification in five years.

He no longer intended to teach, but thought it wise to have the training and credential just in case. In the meantime, his thoughts had turned to law so much that the academy yearbook predicted he would become a judge.

*"In the fall I enrolled at Utah State. There I met Parley Peterson and George B. Hendricks (professors of accounting and finance). Both of them were very strong on postgraduate work. I was in a formative stage as to what I was going to do. I didn't have any money and thought mostly of getting a job. If somebody had offered me a hundred dollars a month I probably would've postponed or given up going off to Harvard."*

Peterson and Hendricks dissuaded young Clawson from going into law ("there were too many starving lawyers") and encouraged him to think about the Harvard Business School. Harold's older brother, Charles, had gone there that year so the idea was not altogether new. He applied and was accepted. About that time, Harold also applied for a Rhodes scholarship, but did not receive the appointment.

After finishing his college program at Utah State in June 1920, Harold went to southern Idaho to work on a dry farm and to prepare for Harvard. He took with him the accounting and finance texts (acquired from his brother) written and used by Business School faculty and read them line by line, underlining as he went.

*"I spent the summer growing and harvesting wheat on a big farm. All my spare time I spent reading these first year books and some of the reports that had been written by students for the management classes. I went to HBS well prepared. I figured I had to dig because Utah State at that time was not rated too high academically."*

## THE HARVARD BUSINESS SCHOOL AND FIRST JOB

Harold Clawson went to the Harvard Business School in the fall of 1920, and having read many of the texts used at the School, he did well in his first year. He was often able to quote and argue the professor's point of view since the texts he had read the previous summer were written by the same faculty that he had as instructors. No particular professor was influential in Jack's development though he had very high respect for all of them.

Jack did not have a lot of time for extra curricular activities at the Business School. He focused his studies on finance, accounting, and auditing and was consistently at the top of his classes in these areas.

Jack financed his degree with a mixture of funds — summer jobs, part-time work at Widener Library, and borrowing from his father and other sources. The library work was ideal for him because he was able to study at work and was also able to see what books his classmates were checking out and later read them. During the summer between his first and second years, Jack lived in the campus dorms for about $6 per month. He earned his living expenses and savings by working first in a packing house and then as the editor for the Camp Devens Citizens Military Training Camp newspaper. When he finished school, Jack had about $2,000 in education debts.

Jack had a great interest in traveling so when Stone and Webster recruiters described the company's far-flung holdings and the job of a traveling auditor, Jack accepted their offer. He went home for a month and then reported to his senior traveling auditor in Houston, Texas, to begin work.

Jack and his senior companion traveled the country auditing the company's electric, gas, and street car system holdings. He learned "the ABCs" of these businesses in those early assignments, but he felt that his performance reviews were mixed:

*"One senior man I went out with said I wasn't much good, but another said I was a humdinger. So I went to the head of the department and asked which one of these men was right. He said I was doing just fine, excellent in fact. So I was okay."*

On the auditing circuit, Jack occasionally dated women in the towns where he was working. In one Midwestern city he met a banker's daughter who was eager

to get married, but their religious backgrounds were so different that Jack decided not to pursue the relationship in spite of his fondness for the lady.

After two years of heavy traveling and extremely long hours, Jack was exhausted. He told the company he was going home for the summer to regain his health. Harold spent a month in Logan chopping wood and farming. By then, he felt renewed enough to return to work on the auditing circuit. He established a regular program of exercise and health care which he followed rigorously thereafter.

> *"After a year and a half I got a call which said that our team of auditors out in Seattle needed another man, would I leave the circuit I was working on and go to Seattle? So in January 1924, I left Columbus, Georgia (where I was working), crossed the snow-covered plains and mountains and came down into Seattle where the roses were still blooming."*

## LEORA GIBBS

On his way to Seattle, Harold stopped off in Logan and had his first date with Leora Gibbs. Leora was the second of three daughters of a struggling family in Cache Valley. She was very outgoing and full of spunk — qualities which Harold liked and felt complemented his own quietness and reserved manner. Leora was teaching near Logan at the time.

Harold came to see her during his summer vacation the following year, and they were engaged. The next year, 1925, Harold was reassigned to Boston. On his way east, he stopped in Logan, married Leora, and they honeymooned across the country.

Harold spent one week in Boston, found his wife an apartment, enrolled her in a finishing school, and went to Florida and Texas on a three-month auditing trip. He had become a senior auditor himself, and his new circuits included the entire U.S., Nova Scotia, and Puerto Rico.

> *"I left her alone. I told her she was just a young girl and needed to learn more about the world and to get a little Boston culture. So she went to a finishing school. It was a choice experience and she learned a great deal, including expression, oratory, and social graces. She mixed with some very fine people.*

*Having gone to college and studied to be a teacher with the idea of help-
ing people to learn and to excel in all things, and having been through
fine colleges and a good education, I had a high sense of the responsibility
and the opportunity to help my wife to excel in those things. I got her interested in going to school in Boston, and later in Seattle I encouraged her to
take a class here at the University of Washington from an excellent professor
in child training. She took copious notes, and we both read them and studied them together. I wanted my wife to be able and capable in all things. I
wanted her to have her own personality, to do the things in life that she'd like
to do. She sometimes feels like she's been treated too independently, but I
think that the woman should have a real degree of independence. I believe
that couples can help each other and be useful to one another."*

In the fall of 1926, Jack (in Boston) was about to begin a six-month tour of
companies in the southern states. Their first child was soon to be born, and Leora
felt that six months was too long to be alone so she decided to return to Utah. They
were packed and scheduled to leave on diverging trains in the early afternoon. At
eleven o'clock, the phone rang. A man for whom Jack had worked in the south
was now in Seattle, needed help, and wanted Jack to come out. Sudden though it
was, the change in plans was more than appealing to both Jack and Leora, so they
changed his tickets, and headed west.

*"In Seattle they had an audit force of five men and needed another senior
man to work with the other senior man for about six months. So, in an hour
we were on the same train and headed in the same direction. Instead of a
sad parting it was a celebration traveling west together."*

## MOVING TO SEATTLE

Jack's first boss in Seattle left shortly thereafter and was replaced by a man
who was unfamiliar with the work. Jack was in the uncomfortable position of
having to work for a man who knew less than he. Jack was asked to stay beyond
his six-month assignment. Then in 1928, Stone and Webster put Jack in charge of
that small, but permanent auditing operation. He was responsible to the company
for all of the audits of the West Coast holdings including the principal one, Puget
Sound Power and Light Company (PSPL).

"That (auditing work) was very interesting, because it included innovative processes of suggesting improvements. It was not merely seeing if everything was in order and that all the money was accounted for. It was more finding shortcuts, things that were taking up too much time or wasting money and that sort of thing. The reports were all, 'What can be done to better performance, reduce costs and improve profits?'

When we came to Seattle I had reached a point where being away from home for long periods of time, two or three months at a time, was distasteful. I didn't intend to stay with the traveling when I got married. I had figured I would continue traveling for two or three years. Leora and I had agreed on that. I missed her terribly. It makes me almost weep to think about it, some of those long weeks away from her. (Tears.) I don't want to think about it. It wasn't easy.

It was hard on our marriage. Lorie had to take care of the boys, but she was good about it. We used to talk about it. When we came to Seattle, I traveled some, but seldom on weekends.

We recognized, looking ahead, that there were many people in the accounting department, but that there were only a few people in the auditing department of which I was head. Both roads led to the top of the company. In auditing, one had only a few competitors. Plus the work was a fine learning process. Those people in the accounting office had their daily routine work, and seldom saw the whole picture as the auditors did. I highly recommend the auditing approach for an ambitious person.

The public library was very close to my office. At five o'clock when work was over, instead of going home I would go right over to the library and stay there until ten o'clock when the library closed, then take a street car home. I'd leave the house about seven (am), and get home after 10. I did this every weekday for about two years. I went through every accounting book and auditing book in the Seattle Public Library. I also obtained the questions on every Washington State CPA examination for the previous 10 years, and without reference to the answers (which were available in other books) I worked the answers to all the questions and compared my work with the suggested answers.

*At one time, I signed up in a coaching class for CPA examinations. After listening to two lessons and the students who didn't know very much what it was all about asking simple questions about things that I knew backwards and forwards — wasting my time, I just gave up the fee I'd paid to join the class and went back to the library. By the time I sat for the examination I had it cold."*

The big depression of the 1930s caused a heavy (20 percent) reduction in staff but that was not a debilitating effect on PSPL. The Holding Company Act of 1935, however, had a much greater impact on Stone & Webster. As a result of that Act, the company had to divest itself of most of its holdings. The reduction in holdings meant the elimination of the auditing department to which Jack Clawson was attached.

In the meantime, however, the treasurer of PSPL argued successfully with his management over the course of three or four months, that they needed a senior auditor, and so Jack became an employee of Puget Sound Power and Light Company.

## OPPORTUNITIES FOR CAREER ADVANCEMENT

One year later, the treasurer of PSPL instructed his head accountant to draft a plan to centralize the accounting systems for all of its companies. The accountant spent about four months on the project, but when he brought in his report the treasurer felt that it was inadequate. Furthermore, he disagreed with its recommendations. He handed the assignment to Jack. The other man failed, Jack believed, because he did not have an overall perspective of the company. Jack knew that his Stone & Webster experience had given him that perspective. He wrote up the plan in one month including the use and assignment of various personnel and took it in to the treasurer's office. The treasurer thought the plan and proposals were "just great," and then asked Jack to go ahead and implement them. Jack, at 37, was made the assistant treasurer, in charge of the Auditing Department.

*"It was that little know-how from auditing that helped me. There's a little saying, 'An expert is a man 80 miles from his home.' When one goes out and audits companies one after another all over the country, he is keeping*

*up on all the latest procedures and practices. I saw a little benefit here, or a little better way there."*

When World War II began, Jack, an officer in the Naval Reserve, received a "critical industry" deferral from serving and continued working. In 1942 he was approached by a CPA friend on behalf of Boeing, then a fast-growing airframe manufacturer, with a proposal to become a special assistant to the president. The job held the allure of being a stepping stone to any number of positions at Boeing.

*"I was at that time third or fourth from the top at Puget and with all of the condemnation suits (by the PUDs) it looked like the company was hanging by a thread. One local newspaper had been running cartoons with the company depicted as a big corpse being hacked to pieces. It looked like I was going to be out of a job. I was invited to dinner with the president of Boeing, his financial vice president, and my CPA friend. We had a nice discussion and the president was all for employing me. Later, I talked further with my friend who was the go-between about terms. It was about double the salary I was getting, but the war was just starting and I told him, "I don't like to leave a job I've had for 20 years to work for two to three years in an industry that will decline drastically after the war." I told him I'd take it, but that I would need some assurance that I would continue with Boeing in some capacity after the war. The president of the company didn't like that and chose the other candidate. It was a big setback for me, and I could hardly live for about a week. It looked like my company was going out of business and I had insisted on something hard and sure. I should have taken my chances on my own abilities rather than ask for assurances.*

*However, it wasn't too long after that that another individual came to me and wondered if I'd be interested in taking a high financial position in Weyerhaeuser, about the largest timber company in the world. I said, 'And how!' even though it would have meant moving to another city and it was a family company. Everything was being set up and then all of a sudden I got word that the deal had died cold. I feel sure that Weyerhaeuser decided not to disturb their close relationships with Puget.*

*I had missed both jobs, and it looked like Puget was going out of business for sure. I felt very low. I didn't have much appetite for about three months. I thought I'd made a big mistake, especially in fouling up the Boeing offer.*

*Another inquiry came from Seattle-based General Insurance Company looking for a potential top executive. In this case, the president of PSPL called me in and told me that General Insurance had inquired of him about me, and he had dissuaded them from making me an offer. So I settled down to work it out with and for Puget.*

*In about a year, the man in line to succeed the treasurer of PSPL died suddenly of a heart attack and I moved into second place. Only two years later the treasurer retired because of illness. I took over as treasurer working with the president of the company.*

*The affairs of the company began to brighten. The PUDs had failed to take over and I was happy that the Boeing deal had not worked out. The war was over and Boeing was having a rough time adjusting to drastic reductions and cutbacks."*

## FINANCIAL STRATEGY

Jack had saved vigorously throughout his life. When he was traveling, he lived on an expense account and so was able to pay off his education debts within two years. He established his financial strategy early:

1. Save enough cash to cover unforeseen emergencies.

2. Carry as much life insurance as possible.

3. Protect wife and family with trusts as fast as possible.

4. Save enough to invest in income assets to cover retirement without relying on pensions.

*"I set goals for myself and made plans on which I was always working, revising and extending them from time to time, and by preparation, training and fortuitous circumstances succeeded considerably beyond my expectations. The main hope and goal in my occupation was to become the chief financial officer of a major corporation. I achieved it and went considerably*

beyond it to become the top executive of such a corporation, as well as a director in two other large corporations.

"My personal financial goal was to earn and save sufficiently that by wisely investing I could build up a personal estate to protect my family financially and to provide well for the time when I would no longer be employed. I continually studied and looked for promising investments with these essentials:

1. A basic, sound, noncyclical industry.

2. Young, capable, aggressive management.

3. Good growth prospects.

4. High earnings on investment mostly retained in the business (little or no dividends but compounding investment value).

In an unspectacular way I worked at this over my early years with a fair modicum of success. Some of my investments were good, a few were rather sorry. In fact, I almost lost my 'shirt' on three really bad ones. They could have been disastrous except for special diligence on my part.

About 1950, a close, relatively young, friend for whom I had done some favors and who had been an outstanding, successful businessman was asked to take over the management of a relatively small, struggling drug store chain. He discussed the matter with me and a couple of other friends and subsequently agreed to take over the business provided he and (we) his associates could acquire a controlling interest. The plan was to plough back all of the earnings into opening of new stores. It appeared to have all the elements for success and very much in line with my investment purposes. I liquidated all of my investments, borrowed 25 percent more than that and put it all into the business.

From the modest beginning of three small stores in the Seattle area, the company has grown to over 200 stores (in all the far western states including Alaska and Hawaii), generating over a half billion in annual sales. The original stores required an investment of around $50,000 each; present stores, which now include not only a drug division but hardware, soft goods, nurseries, sporting goods, require an investment over $500,000 *each. No dividends were paid for about the first 10 years. However, expansion became so great that it became necessary to go public and begin to pay dividends which at first were only stock dividends. The result of this compounded reinvestment of earnings plus inflation has produced a remarkable — not to say fantastic — increase in the market price of the original stock over the 30 years. The stock allowing for splits is now selling for about 75 times its original cost. Cash dividends which are a payout of only about 20 percent of earnings are annually 200 percent of the cost of the original stock; that is, an original stockholder now gets back in cash double the cost of his investment every year. Of course, there were only a few in that position but subsequent investors have done very well.*

*In 1965 when I was approaching retirement in PSPL (I remained on the board of directors for some years thereafter) I realized that I was building up a rather large estate which would be subject to very heavy state and federal inheritance taxes. I, therefore, began an orderly divestment of my holdings by liberal donations to educational, religious, civic and other organizations, and to hard-pressed relatives, but principally by gift to my three sons to permit them to establish businesses, or other investment pursuits and also educational trust funds for each of our 21 grandchildren and a few other needy and worthy young relatives, retaining sufficient to assure taking care of all of our own possible needs, including such travel (mostly to our scattered family) as we may enjoy, as well as further modest contributions to family, relatives and worthy causes."*

## FAMILY STRATEGY

When asked about his children, Jack said, "Just ask Leora what you want to know, and she'll tell you." But when pressed gently, he continued:

Jack:    I have had some rather basic principles for guiding, inspiring, and helping my children make the most of their talents and get all the education and training they possibly could. The country needed it, the church needed it, and the children needed it to have a fulfilling life. They needed knowledge and understanding and wisdom. The way to get that, of course, is to pursue a logical course of training and education and to give their best to it. However, you just don't push them into it.

Leora: And he worked with his boys on this all the way along, and I may say, very successfully.

Jack: You have to *lead* them so that they want to do it. Nothing is more sorry than pounding on the backs of children to get them to do this or that. The better way is to set before them patterns and inspiration to understand their natures so that they will grab a line of action and go with it. This was a very conscious effort on our part from the time they were small, we were determined that they would make the most of their talents and abilities.

Leora was most helpful. She did a tremendous job with those little kids. As they got older, my influence began to have a larger bearing on it, but in those early stages she was magnificent.

## REACHING THE TOP

Jack's belief had always been that he should use imagination and careful thought before he acted. This included for him a continuous attempt to do his own job well and to understand the demands and perspective of his boss' job. This was not always easy since many managers in the company were not inclined to discuss their jobs with their subordinates. Jack, however, encouraged his own employees to consider and reflect on the problems that faced the treasurer's office.

During the mid-1950s, Jack, as treasurer, was traveling with the president of PSPL making presentations to stock analysts and fighting off merger attempts. The Eisenhower administration defused the furor over the PUD takeovers so that the company no longer had to worry so much about that threat. Repeated questions about the nature of Harold's personal life and disposition during this period were always answered with descriptions of what was happening at the company. It was as if his personal life had merged with his corporate life.

While on one of the eastern trips, the president of PSPL was advised by one of the financial institutions that unless he soon made provisions for his succession, the firm would withdraw its very substantial investment. It was not apparent to the analysts who would provide the leadership of the company in the future. This was a "bolt" to both the president and to Jack. Jack had never thought of being president of the company before, and he realized for the first time that he was one of the few people in the company who was capable and familiar enough with the job to handle it. A year later he was elected chairman of the board and chief executive officer.

## CHIEF EXECUTIVE OFFICER

During his incumbency as CEO, Jack felt that his most important contribution was to change the nature of executive management in the company from one of relative secrecy and authoritarianism to one of mutual participation. He felt that the other top executives, as a result of his efforts, enjoyed their work better, were happier, and performed better.

*"The atmosphere and work became one of mutual cooperation rather than one of hard discipline and dictatorship. That was the first big job that I saw I had to do. I was not there long enough to carry out fully the long-range planning required by the physical operations of the utility business, but we set the stage for that to go on."*

When faced with difficult problems, Jack would frequently lie awake at four or five in the morning and mentally probe various alternative means of solving them. This was a very important time for him in which he could explore these potential action plans without the interruption of the office routines. The pressures of his job were demanding, but not debilitating to Jack.

*"Yes, there is a lot of stress, but there's another aspect of it. The executive who works hard and carries lots of responsibility and concerns... it isn't necessarily that which causes him to have ill health and breakdown as many do. It's more a matter of their personal nature or state of mind. It is true that 'hard work never hurt anybody.' Stress itself won't hurt you unless you let it. I don't think that the stress hurt me. I liked challenges and when I had problems that were really serious, I labored over them very hard. There were many problems where decisions had to be made. There were a lot of decisions that whichever way you went, you were partly wrong. It was as they say, 'Like being caught between a rock and a hard place.'"*

Jack's concern with his mental agility and education focused on another aspect of working as a CEO:

*"As a chief executive officer, you are waited upon. You can lose your touch with the normal activities of life. May I tell you what happened to me? When I was chief executive, I had secretaries and assistants to do practically everything. Before that I used to take care of all my own financial affairs, write my own letters, and checks, and everything. When I was CEO they did everything for me. I didn't do any arithmetic. Didn't need a computer, didn't even know how to use one. At one time, having been an accountant, I could add up a string of figures like nothing at all. By the time I retired, would you believe it, I could hardly remember a telephone number long enough to dial it! I hadn't kept accustomed to the relationship of numbers. I could feel it, and it was just enough of a warning to me. From that point on, I began to practice with figures and writing. I felt that slippage. It GOES. You get away from your skills a few years, and they leave you."*

In 1965, Jack reached retirement age and stepped down from the top job. He retained a seat on the Board of Directors for several years and took an active role in the planning and implementation of management changes over the next five years.

## RETIREMENT

Jack had few reservations about retiring.

Jack: Look at it this way. I went through some really tough years when I was working with the president of the company. I practically had no vacations. Something was always coming up. He'd call me from New York on a Saturday evening about 10 o'clock and want me to get on a plane at 11 and be back there Sunday at noon. In those days it took 14 hours by plane to get back to New York.

So, having been successful in my financial strategy, I looked forward to retirement so that I could engage in other more enjoyable activities.

I've had no problems keeping busy. The first year we took a little vacation and rest in Europe. We spent the summer over there. Then I had lunch with the president of one of the local television/radio stations here. We became good friends, and he invited me to be on the board of directors and on the management committee of the television station.

**One year, I was in New York staying in a hotel for 11 out of the 12 months. It was not easy. There were lots of early and long hours.**

One day the telephone rang while I was out in the garden, and I was asked if I would like to go to Iran. And I said, 'Fine.' The caller said, 'I am speaking for the U.S. State Department, and we have a team of experts going to Iran to study its national electric system to determine what sources of energy should be used to produce electricity.

I was invited to head up the team. They needed a name and a position to deal with the cabinet-level officials in Iran. When I got over there it was more than that. I was paid well, but it was darn hard work.

During these years, the drug store business was expanding rapidly, and it went public. The owner, my friend, had tried to keep it a family business. Since he and I were very close, he asked me to be on the board of directors so he would not have to take an outsider. So, I was on the board of directors there.

Then a local hospital asked me to be on the advisory board. I was involved in Boy Scouts, too. I was active in my church work, business, and community activities. After awhile I had to begin gradually unloading some of these responsibilities so I could have a little time for my family and myself. I began playing golf once a week. So I have been as busy as I ever was at the office.

In 1979, Jack returned to his alma mater, Utah State University, to accept an honorary doctor's degree in business management. This was a rewarding and satisfying experience for him.

As the Clawsons continued to reflect on their 50 years of marriage and career, Jack was asked how he would describe himself:

*"One thing I have, I reckon, is a pretty fair mental capacity and ability. I do not learn very rapidly. There are a lot of people who can learn faster than I, but I'm persistent and orderly in it so that in the long run I will probably come out even or on top. I may not be the first, but I am thinking about difficult problems and I can stick with it for a long time until I get an answer. A lot of others may get lost in the complexity of the problems."*

Leora:  He says he doesn't learn rapidly, and yet I've seen him take a thick book, receive it at 5:00 pm and go and give a report on it at a meeting the next morning. He doesn't learn rapidly?!

Jack:  Most executives have to be able to do that. I learned that in presenting to a superior, you have to get to the vital point at once and supply the additional data if you are asked for it. When I was chief executive, each day I'd get a stack of reports, business magazines, and papers to go through on my desk every morning. But I'd have people coming in for long conferences, discussing very serious problems all day long. Come five o'clock, the stack of papers was still there. Then I would have to bring that stack home at night to go through them. If you want understanding, you have just got to look at the reports yourself.

As a student journalist, I learned that in writing a newspaper article one has to say in the first paragraph what the whole story is about because a lot of people just read the first line or two. The first sentence of every paragraph normally is the essential point. The rest is secondary information regarding that particular idea and if you don't need it, you go to the next one and on down. That is a kind of speed reading that I've done a lot of and still do because I want to cover a lot of information.

Beyond this matter of my mental capacity, the next thing is I think I have imagination. Looking ahead and visualizing events and problems in the future, and solving them in advance or planning steps to be taken. I have solved a great many problems the first hour of the day when I wake up at 4:00 or 5:00 am. It's surprising how looking at all the angles of a particular problem at that hour would bring out things I'd never thought about.

I could always visualize myself doing things. I think I have done this all of my life — this projecting of myself. In doing so, I have visualized the problems in advance, before they happened or had to be settled. This has been a great help. Having done that early in my life — first it was to be a teacher, then it was to be a lawyer, then it was to be a businessman. At each stage I was using my imagination and saying, "What do I do so I'll be the best or at least good at it?" And then I would begin to do those things.

I had serious setbacks and times when it looked as though I were a failure and not making the grade, very off-base with serious shortcomings. I think this is a common experience, psychological ups and downs. Little things will set us back, but somehow the sun will shine, next month anyway, and better things will come up to get us going. Sacrifice comes before miracles — sometimes you have to go through the hardships in order to achieve your goals. We often learn more from our mistakes and our bad times than we do from all our successes. I have had confidence that there's always another side beyond the dark times.

I am also curious. I can't sit down where there's any kind of a book without having to pick it up and see what it is about — whether it's a women's magazine, a magazine in a dentist's office, whatever it is. I want to pick it up and read it and see what it's about. I have a lot of mental curiosity.

Leora: That all got in the way a little bit. Especially when he was so loaded with responsibilities — both company and church. I felt very neglected. I felt that I had to do something about it. I couldn't continue the way it was. There was always somebody calling him for time and attention so I had to work it out.

There's one thing that I might change in him, though I might be sorry if I did.

I'd try to have him be more aware of other people's feelings, moods, needs. He's very aware of his own, and the need to work and to do and to deliver, [pauses] but I wonder sometimes if he even *sees* my needs.

I'd try to have him be more aware of other people's feelings, moods, needs. He's very aware of his own, and the need to work and to do and to deliver, (pause) but I wonder sometimes if he even *sees* my needs.

Having finished his self-description, Harold volunteered his view of his wife:

"Among Leora's qualities, and constant endeavors, let me list a few — not necessarily in any order of importance:

- Deep concern for other people including especially her own family.
- Constantly seeking improvement.
- Outgoing friendliness and *helpfulness* to every one. Everyone who knows her, loves her.
- Generous to a fault, really!
- Indefatigable, sets highest standards of performance for herself — encourages others in same direction.
- Considerate and highly sensitive to the needs and feelings of others.
- Constantly striving to improve in cultural things and refinement, and encouraging others in that direction.
- Inveterate "student" (reader) to improve and increase in knowledge, particularly in all phases of life — health, activities, as well as cultural things.
- A competent teacher, speaker and leader — confident and winning.
- Tremendous supporter of family *and* friends.
- Constantly holding to highest standards in goals, performance, conduct *ideals*.
- Well-liked and admired wherever she goes with a multitude of friends."

During the latter part of his administration, Jack had begun having even more serious abdominal pains. He had lived with them for 55 years, excusing himself at times to go lie down and massage his stomach. Leora had made it her crusade to ease that burden and had researched diet and exercise programs constantly over the years. Jack described Leora's help in one sentence: "I could *not* have achieved what I did without the help, advice, counsel and support Leora gave me in every way, nor would I even be alive today, I am sure, without her tremendous interest and concern in everything having to do with health, and personal concern in all matters." About five years after he had retired, though, the pain was too much, so the doctors advised exploratory surgery. They found, to their surprise, that Jack's intestines had fused almost shut in several places — this the result of bovine tuberculosis contracted in Jack's 10th year. After corrective surgery, Jack regained his strength and felt better than he had for his entire working career.

## QUESTIONS FOR REFLECTION

1. What is the role of the spouse in traditional marriages?

2. What are the potential pitfalls in the traditional marriage structure?

3. While walking with my wife of 31 years recently, I was discussing possible retirement. She said, "Don't expect to come in the house and disrupt my schedule. I have my own friends and my own schedule. You plan on doing something during the day." What's your "vision" of retirement? What would happen if your spouse didn't share that vision?

4. What did you think of Leora's comment that sometimes she didn't think that Harold even saw her or heard what she'd said? How can a couple avoid that kind of problem during their marriage and career?

5. How does modern technology affect one's balance of work and family life?

# 17

## CONCLUDING
## COMMENTS

The stories you have just read present a wide array of approaches and techniques for balancing the modern day demands of one's profession, family life and personal health and growth. You've read about single people, married people, and dual career families. You've read about successful and powerful executives in business, politics and academe. You've looked behind the scenes at more than the professional side of life for both men and women, Caucasians, African Americans and Asians. And you've had glimpses of how successful executives manage their lifestyles in North America and Asia.

I wish we had been able to give you even more behind the scenes data. One of the things that has frustrated me for several decades now is the relative dearth of information about how busy executives live their lives in the whole, balancing work, family and personal agendas. One executive from a large Chicago law firm once noted that he pretty much doesn't do anything except his work and spending time with his kids. He even took his son with him on local business trips, creating "shadow time" that could be "counted" at both work and home. He noted that he didn't read books or have any hobbies, but that he loved his work and the people he worked with.

But there are surprisingly few case studies or research accounts of how executives manage beyond their professional lives. We have a lot of data on how they manage their work. Not very much on how they manage the whole of their lives. We get snippets of this in the popular press. Superficial stories about a divorce here or a visit to rehab there. Occasionally we get stories about those who have succeeded so well on all fronts that they are willing to let the press in. Richard Branson has been on the cover of Fortune magazine, for instance, with his bright, smiling face celebrating a birthday on his island in the Caribbean while working occasionally in the background on the phone.

In the celebrity world, we get perhaps more than we want with the new reality shows that give us behind the scenes, perhaps somewhat scripted or shaped, views of life with the Osbournes or the Kardashians or the Girls Next Door. But nothing similar for the Jack Welchs, the Jeff Immelts, or the Lloyd Blankfeins (CEO of Golfman Sachs) of the world.

How do they manage their health? How do they manage their relationships? How do they parent? How do they manage their emotional health? Do they go to therapy? If so, what do they talk about? What is the holistic life structure that supports a modern executive lifestyle?

Of course, you say, it will vary widely. Yes, I suppose it does. AND I'd like to know, wouldn't you, how they do it? Do they exercise at 4:00 am? Do they have someone who decides what they can eat and cannot eat? Are they loved or tolerated by their families? What are the life skills necessary to support an intense job with ever changing demands and intense pressures?

A problem I see in the world generally is the tendency for people to whitewash their stories. That is, to present only what they want others to know or only what they think others want to hear or only what they think is laudable or of "good character." Frankly, after 62 years of living, I've become very impatient with the politically correct stories. I think we'd all learn much more from the reality, from the truth about how powerful people manage their lives. This would be especially important for aspiring executives to understand.

We once had a visitor to our school who, as an African American, was disappointed with the treatment he got in his very large Fortune 500 company. He eventually quit and formed his own consulting firm and developed a theory of socio-economic status and movement. There were, he posted, seven layers in socio-economic terms, and each layer had its unique habits of eating, dressing, recreation, transportation, music, and so forth. If one wanted to move from one socio-economic stratum to the next, he said, one must learn how to behave at that next level. If you want to hang with people who enjoy golf on the weekends, proposing a trip to the bowling alley wasn't going to cut it. If you wanted to take someone to the airport, showing up in a Chevrolet wouldn't impress a person used to a Mercedes. If you liked wearing blue jeans, you'd have a difficult time impressing a person wearing khakis. Blaring rock and roll on the radio while the CEO would prefer Mozart will not likely get you invited to the next at-home reception.

We can argue whether the world should or should not be organized by these kinds of superficial, functionally irrelevant criteria, but the man had a point. People tend to hang with people with whom they can relate and feel comfortable around. To spend time with people who will become executives is likely to require the acquisition of a set of life "skills" or habits as much as it is a set of accounting or financial skills. So, we've tried to present here a variety of stories that go beyond the professional and begin to explore the personal side of life as well. Some of these stories were able to go deeper and farther than others. We didn't get

a lot about the personal lives of Robert O'Neill, for example, but his story presented such a unique set of professional challenges that we've included them here. At the other end of the spectrum, we learned a lot about Dee Dee Fisher's life issues in which professional concerns didn't play such a dominant role. In between, we had examples from all over the world.

> People tend to hang with people with whom they can relate and feel comfortable around. To spend time with people who will become executives is likely to require the acquisition of a set of life "skills" or habits as much as it is a set of accounting or financial skills.

## THREE LENSES

In our modest exploration here, we've introduced three lenses through which I've invited you to read these executive stories. First, we invited you to consider that at any point in time, we all have various -AL aspects of life: the physical, emotional, social, professional, financial, and so on. I gave you a tool we've used successfully for years to help people think about and get a visual picture of their development since birth. This Balance Wheel is a way for you to keep track of your progress, just like a corporate balance sheet does, by making reassessments annually. The Balance Wheel allows you to customize your life to your personal desires with regard to time and energy spent on personal goals and visions.

Second, I invited you to consider the research on the predictable chapters in life ranging from psychological development to professional stages. Each of the chapters in the various models presented significant challenges, personally and professionally, that we all must confront and navigate in some fashion. That chapter invited you to think about the challenges of each chapter in life and the consequences of under-attending to their resolution. Unresolved issues often come back later to haunt us. Many of these challenges can be the result of early childhood experiences as we learned from Dee Dee Fisher and Bob Johnson. While I didn't explore the nature of these processes here, I have done so elsewhere.[1] You can explore those processes more fully there if you'd like.

[1] James G. S. Clawson, *Level Three Leadership*, 4th Edition, Prentice-Hall, Upper Saddle River, New Jersey, 2008.

> **What's the balance between money, power, fame, health, family, recreation, and creativity (among other criteria) that will most satisfy you?**

Third, I invited you to consider the nature of success. What does that mean to you? What's the balance between money, power, fame, health, family, recreation, and creativity (among other criteria) that will most satisfy you? It's not that easy, perhaps, to know what you want before you get to a point where it's harder and harder to change things. Surely people's definitions of "success" change over time, yet if you go too hard in one direction, you may shortchange your ability to later on go hard in another direction. Better to be thinking about this early on so you can be moving in the general direction that you will find satisfying later on. As one Harvard Business School alumna once told me, it's not all that easy to change life management habits developed over a 10-year period and to begin placing different emphases in life. In the same way that corporations develop core capabilities, bundles of competencies, individuals do as well, and habits tend to be persistent.

## THE LIFE AND CAREER STORIES

We should be grateful that the people represented here were willing to share with us how they've lived their lives. From their stories, we can glean insights and strategies that we might not have thought of. We can compare and contrast our own backgrounds and stories with theirs and ponder the differences — and similarities. We can do a little gut checking to see if we had the same creativity, discipline, determination, vision, flexibility, shall I say, "inside-out-ness" that they demonstrated in their treks to positions of executive responsibility.

Being an executive, from these stories and in my own experience, requires enormous energy and commitment. Perhaps a main reason more of us don't find ourselves in those ranks is that we are deep down unwilling to spend the time and energy required to get there. We prefer a more "comfortable" lifestyle.

Yet we remain fascinated by those who do become our leaders. We want to know how they did it. How they manage to somehow take care of it all. Do they? Can a person be a super-being, physically fit, intellectually stimulating, well-read, powerful, influential, wealthy, happy, lovingly involved in long-term relationships, kind and compassionate parent, emotionally secure,

spiritually grounded, blessed with close friends, and societally involved in our communities? It's a tall order.

My hope is that the stories here, based on the good faith and wonderful willingness of our subjects to reveal themselves to us, will have helped you in this endeavor to find out more about who you are and how you might structure your life. Work/life balance is the single most commonly expressed issue or challenge in my seminars worldwide. My guess is you're wrestling with this as well. It's not easy. Ask any working parent or spouse. If these stories, though, have helped you to find a better way, or given you some insights about how to balance your life and work better, then great. My hope is that this volume will have helped you marginally to find yourself. That's a good thing. And better done sooner rather than later or never at all.